THE RETURN OF GERMANY

THE RETURN OF
GERMANY

*A Tale of
Two Countries*

NORBERT MUHLEN

THE BODLEY HEAD

First Published 1953

Printed in Great Britain by
BRADFORD AND DICKENS, LONDON, W.C.I.
for JOHN LANE THE BODLEY HEAD LIMITED
28 Little Russell Street, London, W.C.I.

CONTENTS

THE RETURN OF GERMANY

I

Only Yesterday

THE giant stirs again. Seven years ago, after a fight to the finish with his neighbors and enemies, he was prostrate. Some believed him dead, or at least permanently crippled. When he turned out to be neither dead nor a hopeless invalid, many became uneasy, even fearful.

The giant is Germany. The German people are more numerous than any other people of Western Europe. The German soil contains more iron and coal—the backbone of the nation's strength in peace as well as in war—than any other country in Europe. The sum total of initiative, drive, and hard work of which Germany is capable, is believed to outrival the capabilities of all the rest of the continent put together.

Only yesterday this giant set out to conquer the continent. He almost succeeded in crushing Europe and in threatening, for years to come, America's life, liberty, and pursuit of happiness. Germany then was Nazi Germany—a totalitarian giant.

Today Germany is recovering her strength. Her factories are working again, her representatives sit again as equals at international meetings, and her people seem again to be moving along the road on which they were stopped less than a decade ago in defeat and disgrace. "Again" is the key word, a word that has made Germany's return to life a not altogether cheerful event to her neighbors. For the but partly healed wounds and the painful memories of yesterday have also begun to stir again.

In the eyes of many Westerners, Germany looms up once more as the giant of yesterday, returning to the scene of action with arrogant power and undisguised threats. The outline of today's Germany merges in many minds with the memories of Hitler's Germany. Germany is still called by American newspapers "the late Third Reich" (New York *Post*), or "neo-Nazi Germany" (New York *Compass*); and the old, anxious warnings resound: "It is German militarism, German nationalism, German irredentism, German super-discipline and super-efficiency that must be feared in years to come" *(New York Times)*.

At the same time, Americans are warned, often in the same papers, that the real enemy is Soviet Russia. It is her plans for world conquest, her gigantic war machine we must fear. The totalitarian giant has moved from Berlin to Moscow. Still there are doubts among Americans. Is it wise that their government should help Germany get on her feet again, welcome her back into the community of Western nations, strengthen her defenses against the new enemy that was so recently an ally?

Most reports from Germany have done little to clear this image of Germany in American eyes. Editorials and essays in the American press discuss the questions of whether the Nazis are coming back, whether German militarism is on the march again, whether a new edition of the Third Reich is in the making. Since no responsible observer could answer these questions with a definite "no"—in the future, anything is possible—the answer given most frequently in these discussions is a cautious "maybe, quite possibly." To most readers this sounds uncomfortably close to the "yes" given by less careful or less honest observers. On the whole, these prognoses add up in American and European minds at least to a frightening "probably."

Many Americans—correspondents as well as readers—remember that they did not take Nazism very seriously when it first hit the headlines in the early 1930's. Unaware of the true import of totalitarianism, and feeling rather friendly toward the German Republic that had evolved after the First World War, they recognized only slowly the nature of their enemy. But today they are afraid of being taken unawares, of being "fooled" a second time.

They don't want to be "guilty" again of tolerating a new Nazi regime in Germany.

News from Germany has only strengthened this vague discomfort. When, as happened in 1951, 11 per cent of the vote in the German State of Lower Saxony, traditionally a Nazi stronghold, was given to the neo-Nazi *Sozialistische Reichspartei* (Socialist Reich Party), the American press headlined the portentous event. But when, in the next elections in 1952 in the Southwest State—with a population as large as that of Lower Saxony—the same neo-Nazi party polled merely 2.5 per cent of the total vote and did not gain a single seat in the assembly, the American press ignored the fact or mentioned it in an obscure line or two. When in October, 1952, a speaker at the first postwar reunion of the veterans of the armed SS divisions, former Major General Hermann Bernhard Ramcke, directed his frantically anti-American, neo-Nazi appeals to the crowd, the *New York Times* headlined the event, and reported it in seventy-five lines. But when, at the same meeting, its organizer, former General Herbert Gille, wartime commander of an armed SS division, said that he and his colleagues dissociated themselves from General Ramcke, with whose views they did not agree, it was mentioned only in twelve lines. When another former SS general, Felix Steiner, appealed to the same crowd to defend democracy and freedom, it was reported merely in five lines. At about the same time, however, the nationwide conventions of the Christian Democratic Union, the Social Democratic Party, and the German Federation of Trade Unions, as well as assemblies of university students, physicians, booksellers and book publishers, representing millions of Germans, assailed Nazism and pledged never to let it grow again. But the American press devoted less space to their numerous anti-Nazi speeches and resolutions altogether than to the one Nazi speech at one small gathering. In fact, German anti-Nazism seemed news less fit to print than German Nazism.

In November, 1952, more than 100,000 municipal, county and district representatives were elected on a local level in three

West German states. One of the one hundred thousand was a former Nazi Storm Troop leader by the name of Wilhelm Schepmann. Although he won his office by a vote which comprised less than one tenth of one per cent of the total, and although the anti-Nazi parties polled a strong majority throughout the three states, the single Nazi seemed—to judge from the headlines and space devoted to his victory in the American press —the actual winner of the elections while the tens of thousands of anti-Nazis elected to office on the same day were more or less ignored.

This was not a conspiracy of the press; it merely pointed up the fears of a number of readers who sought an answer to the troubling question: Is Nazism still capable of revival in Germany?

That the memory of the twelve years of Nazi rule in Germany is still very much alive is no matter for surprise. It was, after all, from Nazi Germany that the nature, the horrors, the evil of a totalitarian system were first revealed to the American people. It is only understandable that Americans should draw back from a "second time" in Germany.

Yet even with the best efforts of American correspondents to tell the "truth about Germany," the results are so colorless as to seem to most Americans confused, complicated, and difficult to understand. The outline of the new Germany hardly exists in their imagination at all.

Most Americans, like people everywhere, are interested primarily in news that concerns them personally. In the case of Germany, their personal concern is whether the Nazis, the fearful image of their old enemy, are likely to return. They also wonder whether the Soviets, the fearful image of their new enemy, will be resisted or helped by Germany in the present struggle for the world.

The American image of the German people, as it has grown in our minds over the years, is likely to follow only at a very slow pace the changing reality as it appears in the jigsaw puzzle of the daily news. The American image of Germany has changed too often in the last century, and was too artfully manufactured by special interests in the last decade, to be of much use in supplying an answer. As a matter of fact, old images tend to block the sight of things as they are today.

Only a hundred years ago, Americans thought that the Germans were a "peaceful, law-abiding, religious, calm, moderate, hardy, brave, kindly, quiet, domestic people," though with an unhappy lack of political intelligence:[1] "In spite of their great learning, they have not the power of self-government which a common town meeting possesses," Daniel Webster said a hundred years ago. "For the Germans in general, as painstaking scholars, amiable people, and liberal and fearless thinkers, we have great respect; but as practical men, political organizers, and reformers, asserters of ideas except in the safe categories of seven times potentialized metaphysics, no respect whatever," wrote the New York *Tribune* in 1852. The *Nation* in 1866 extolled the Germans as "the most learned, patient, industrious, civilized people on the face of the globe, which has attained the highest distinction in arts, in science, in arms, in literature, in everything, in short, but in politics."

When the war broke out between France and Prussia in 1870, the New York *Tribune* identified itself with the Prussian cause "with which is bound up so much hope, progress, and the possibility of freedom to grow," while the *New York Times* stated: "Germany embodied, to our minds, the freer ideas of the age, freedom of thought and constitutional progress."

In the century between 1852 and 1952 the American stereotypes of "the Germans"—as of most other peoples—were changed every ten or twenty years, if not completely and continuously reversed. The latest stereotype was born in the last war when Nazism ruled, and the makers of the stereotype warned it would remain valid for a long long time to come.

That the Germans could not be reformed, that they would always take to the Nazi way, that they would inevitably constitute

[1] The quotations in this and the following paragraph are from John Gerow Gazley, *American Opinion of German Unification, 1848–1871*. Studies in History, Economics and Public Law, edited by the Faculty of Political Science of Columbia University, Vol. CXXI, New York, 1926.

a danger, was implanted into the thinking of Americans while the war was still in progress. In 1944, with Germany still undefeated, America was warned, as Sigrid Schultz expressed it in the title of a book, that *Germany Will Try It Again*. Another more fanciful writer, Curt Riess, announced in 1944 yet a more sinister situation in the title of his book, *The Nazis Go Underground*. This pessimism reflected and echoed the claims of Hitler and his henchmen; according to them the Third Reich expressed the true "racial" character of the Germans and would last for the next thousand years. Immediately after Germany's surrender American opinion makers alarmed the country with the revelation that Germany was planning a third world war. Only if the Morgenthau Plan to keep Germany permanently emasculated after the war was faithfully executed, according to the *New York Times* Book Review, would America "be able to prevent that third world war for which we know preparations have already begun." Radio commentators attacked emergency food supplies for starving German children as the first step to the third world war. The entire German people were equated with their Nazi government, and every German was denounced as a Nazi. The totalitarian catastrophe, which had been brought about by a unique meeting of many unhappy events, was explained to Americans as "typically German," and every German held guilty of totalitarianism.

In reply to the unscientific racism of the Nazis, scholars and amateurs indulged in a seemingly more scientific racism acceptable to Americans by using odds and ends of history, anthropology, and psychology, rather than biology, for their claim that "the Germans" were an inferior people and by their very nature Nazis. Dilettantes, lawyers (like Paul Nizer), writers of murder mysteries (like Rex Stout) and of historical fiction (like Emil Ludwig), psychiatrists (like Dr. Richard Brickner), all published their explanations as to why the Germans were "that way" and "what to do with Germany." Their dicta were taken as seriously as if there really was a racial character common to all "the Germans." No one any longer seemed to remember that one of the most American of all writers, the late Sinclair Lewis, had warned his countrymen when Hitler took power in Germany: *It Can Happen Here*. Now those who had once hearkened to that warning let themselves believe those who declaimed: "It could happen only in Germany, the nature of the Germans being what it is."

The campaign of hatred against "the Germans" was bound to quiet down when the war was over and Nazism smashed. Understandably, some Americans, who had suffered a lasting trauma from their personal experiences of Nazism, kept fearing and hating "the Germans." Yet neither their fears nor the misgivings of many other Americans could have interfered with a better understanding of the changing German realities in our day if the Soviet propaganda machine—often using these fears and misgivings—had not deliberately and artfully kept alive the specter of a new Nazi Germany in American eyes. To succeed in this was actually an essential objective in the Soviet plan to subdue America and to rule the world.

As far back as the 1920's and 1930's, according to the authoritative Soviet historian, A. Berezkin (writing in 1951), "the United States started to build up Germany for an eventual attack against Russia." As recorded in Soviet history, "the United States supported Hitler, helped his expansion, and joined with Britain and France in making Munich possible so that Hitler might be 'the strangler' of the Soviet Union." Furthermore, "the United States rejoiced when Hitler attacked the Soviet Union in 1941." (Actually, of course, from 1941 on, the United States, far from rejoicing when Hitler attacked the Soviet Union, helped and supported Stalin so that *he* might be "the strangler" of the Third Reich.)

The power and the threat of the U.S.S.R., the Soviet apologists in America claimed, was merely a "bogey" deliberately conjured up to distract Americans from the real threat of Germany and to blind Americans to the necessity of destroying Germany forever. "There have never been advanced any reasonable grounds for supposing that America is really menaced by Russia or the spread of Communism," Henry Morgenthau, Jr., Secretary of the Treasury in President Roosevelt's administration, wrote in 1945. Opponents of his plan to destroy Germany by starvation were, according to Mr. Morgenthau, primarily "red-baiters," who wanted to use Germany as a bulwark against Communism. "It is unreasonable to suppose that the United States is in danger from Russia or Communism," he said. "The nomination of Germany as the watchdog to guard us against peril attains fantastic heights of madness." Subsequently, it became common knowledge that Mr. Morgenthau's history-making plan was ghostwritten by secret agents of the Communist conspiracy, particularly the economist Harry Dexter White who, like Alger Hiss in the U. S. State Department, had risen to high influence in the U. S. Treasury Department. According to Morgenthau's Communist ghost writers of 1945, only a half-dead Germany could be a good Germany; those who opposed this view were acting merely from hatred of Communism. But regardless of Communism, America had to learn in the postwar years that the recovery of all Europe, if not the rehabilitation of the war-ravaged world, depended to a not inconsiderable degree on a revival of Germany.

Since 1945, again according to the Soviet historian A. Berezkin and his American echoes, America has been building up a new Nazi Germany for the single purpose of attacking and destroying Soviet Russia. In fact, it has seemed—in marked contrast to the opinion of Mr. Morgenthau's ghost writers—since 1945 increasingly less "unreasonable to suppose that the United States is in danger from Russia or Communism." Doubts began to disappear when Soviet Russia openly displayed her expansive world-wide aggressiveness. The cold war was forced upon America. Reluctantly, the United States had to invite Germany to participate in the Western defense; Germany was even more reluctant to accept the invitation. Given Germany's position as the buffer between the Eastern plains and Western Europe, as well as her potential of manpower and material power, her participation in the resistance to Russia seemed essential if all Europe was not to be Bolshevized.

With the signing in June, 1952, of the contractual agreement that served as a peace treaty between Germany and the West, and accepted a recovering Germany in the community of free nations, the last hopes which Moscow had set on the Morgenthau Plan were finally frustrated. It could no longer rely on an impoverished Germany and Europe while it assaulted America. (The same applied to Japan, for which Communist-inspired Far East experts in the U. S. Department of State, ably assisted by Owen Lattimore, had also worked out a Morgenthau Plan, although they did not succeed in having it adopted even for the short period for which it was adopted in Germany.) Soviet Russia had failed in separating Germany from the West by persuading the West to cripple Germany permanently. It had to find a new line to alienate Germany, and Europe, from America.

Stalin himself—in his opening statement to the nineteenth congress of the Communist Party of the Soviet Union in October, 1952—revealed the new line to be followed: a breakup of the new relationship between America and Germany was the new great hope of world Communism on its way to world-wide victory. "These countries," he said about Germany (and Japan), "are eking out a pitiful existence under the heel of American imperialism. Their industry and agriculture, their foreign and internal policy, their entire existence is shackled by the American occupation rule. . . . Is it believing in miracles to think that these countries will not try again to rise to their feet, to break the American rule, and to strike out on the path of independent development?" Thus, the Western, "capitalist" countries would mutually weaken and destroy themselves until the Soviets could take over all of them. With a turn of the theoretical party line, which only a short while before had denounced the threat against the Soviet Union presented by Hitler's Germany as America's agent, Stalin now recalled meaningfully that Germany under the Weimar Republic had been enslaved by the Western powers until, under Hitler, Germany "broke out of slavery." The specter of a new Nazi Germany was Stalin's dream. It would again "break out of Western slavery"—that is, the Western alliance, and lead to a war between the Western nations.

If this specter did not actually exist, it was to be conjured up at least before American eyes as a living phantom. In this regard, the Soviet interest in scaring America with the specter of a Germany forever Nazi had not changed at all since the time of the Morgenthau Plan. If, as Communist propagandists said at the time, the alternative was between a peaceful Soviet Russia and an aggressive Nazi Germany, the American choice—in favor of Russia and the Morgenthau Plan—was easy to make. If the Communists in the subsequent years convinced America that, though Soviet Russia was perhaps less peaceful and harmless than had been assumed, post-Hitler Germany was at any rate merely a whistle-stop station on the way from "the late Third Reich" to the coming "neo-Nazi Germany," then the choice was hardly more difficult. Americans would not proceed on the slippery road of helping one evil against another evil; they would, rather, cease helping West Germany and perhaps cease resisting the Soviets altogether, retreating to non-Communist neutralism and new isolationism. This would help the Soviets as much toward their goal of weakening and finally conquering America as the first way.

The hate-the-Germans propaganda was as efficient a secret weapon of the Communists in America as the hate-America propaganda has become an efficient secret weapon of the Communists in Germany and many other countries today.

Since 1952, when the Soviets hoped for the breakdown of relations between a recovered, strong Germany and America, the specter of a new Nazi Germany in American eyes has seemed greatly to promote their hope. Using as their spokesmen non-Communists (who have sometimes naïvely been misled by, and sometimes consciously been following, the hidden Communists), the Soviet machine of shaping American opinion has conjured up the neo-Nazi specter so often, so loudly, and with so much conviction that many people in America have begun to fear it is real. After all, Americans know that the Third Reich was no phantom, that the Nazis of yesterday could not be ignored as a product of Communist propaganda; they were real enough. The Communists have made clever use of the human tendency to face all new experiences in the light of past experiences and to expect their repetition rather than alteration. After being released from prison, the convict is feared by many fellow citizens as sure to commit new crimes, however much he may have reformed; unfortunately, it is exactly this reaction of the citizenry which often forces him back to a life of crime.

The real Germany of today—with many discomforting and unhappy features as well as some brighter, perhaps promising facets—can not be discerned through the dust of old clichés. We need an open mind to see the new facts, and to understand their new meaning.

It would seem that the majority of Americans are rather optimistic as well as realistic, for neither in the hate-mongering atmosphere of war, nor in the flush of victory have many of them ceased to believe that the Germans—like all people—might be different from the repulsive appearance they presented in their years of war and totalitarian tyranny.[2] With information on German realities often deficient, and not infrequently biassed, the American majority in their opinion on Germany have seemed to confirm the remark of the late columnist Raymond Clapper: "Never overestimate the information of the people, never underestimate their intelligence." The American people seem wiser than their spokesmen; Americans feel that the course of human events is no repetitive mechanism, that history rarely plagiarizes itself, that no people is innately, "racially" good or evil—in short, they have kept their minds open.

This book attempts to tell—with an equally open mind—what Germans felt, thought and set out to do in that period of the cold war which has not yet ended in the year 1953. This is a report on Germany—on West Germany and on East Germany, that is—a tale of two countries.

---

[2] This was shown by my analysis of American public opinion polls with regard to Germany. See my article, "Americans are Poor Haters," *America,* September 25, 1948.

II

Ruins, Reminders, and Rip Van Winkle

THE ninth of November, a memorable day in German history, was spent by most Germans like any other day. Early in the morning, workmen in West Germany began to hammer away at the scaffolds of new buildings. In West Berlin teenage boys in worn-out U. S. Army jackets and frayed Wehrmacht pants sorted bricks from rubble. They were assisted by women in torn sweaters under men's greatcoats, whose straw-blonde hair, large breasts, and deeply-lined faces marked them as refugees from East Germany. At the University of Göttingen, studious youngsters wrote diligently in their notebooks what their professors recounted on the history of medieval painting, the new philosophy of Existentialism, the theory of nuclear fission. Some students were distracted; they hadn't had a smoke for quite a few days and hankered after the cigarettes they could not afford to buy. Other students sported colored ribbons and caps as they went forth to watch a new member of their fraternity fight his first fencing duel, as new members had done for centuries. In Ruhrort, two well-dressed gentlemen lifted their Scotch-and-sodas and said *unisono,* "Okayee," for they had just concluded a big secret sale of several tons of iron.

In a village near Ansbach, a woman was killed because the curlers she used happened to be sensitive high-explosive igniters; she had picked them up in a field where they had lain since the last battle of the last war. A live shell of similar origin was used by a peasant near Würzburg as a weight on his barn door. When the rope from which the shell was suspended broke, he and his wife were killed.

Throughout West Germany on the ninth of November, as if it were any other day, housewives went to the market, the grocery store, and the vegetable stand to buy their provisions for the next day. A seamstress sent her daughter to the delicatessen. "Sorry, no Braunschweiger sausage left today," said the salesgirl to the pig-tailed child, "but I can give you peasant's liverwurst for five pfennigs more." The little shopper said, "I have to ask Mamma," and the salesgirl asked the next customer: "With what may I serve you, sir?" He winked and said: "With a little kiss, little fraulein." The owner, his fat wife, and the salesgirl herself laughed, and the jesting customer bought his supplies for dinner that night, breakfast and luncheon the next day: a quarter pound of liverwurst, three slices of rye bread, two cigarettes.

That same day in Leipzig—a big city of East Germany—a little girl entered the state-run delicatessen with a shopping list from her mother for a quarter pound of liverwurst and a cake of soap. "Doesn't your mother read the paper?" the salesgirl grumbled. "There hasn't been any liverwurst for sale for the last three weeks. And the soap was sold out this morning, five minutes after the shop opened." As a second salesgirl approached, she quickly stopped talking; the little girl left the shop with a frightened look.

At the University of Jena, studious youngsters faithfully took down what their professors said about the drive of American capitalism to subdue the world, the history of revolutionary movements in England, and the new philology based on the dicta and discoveries of the greatest of all thinkers, Joseph Vissarionovich Stalin. The minds of some students were distracted because they were hungry; others wondered whether their neighbor was watching them and whether they were perhaps under suspicion of subversive thoughts. In Werder, five high school boys aged sixteen and seventeen were arrested and accused of having thrown a stink bomb into the recent meeting of the Society for the Study of Social Sciences. Actually, they merely refused to reveal the names of their two classmates who had thrown the bomb.

When evening came, most people in West Germany stayed home as usual. Father read his illustrated weekly paper. Mother did the supper dishes, the children plugged away at their homework until nine o'clock when their mother announced: "Now you go to bed, but pronto—otherwise Father will give you a good beating." Obediently they kissed their parents good night.

Elsewhere young men kissed their best girls good night after a walk in the park or through country lanes. Or, if they had the money, perhaps they went to the movies to see the latest picture from France (a prostitute killing herself in the end), or an old Western from Hollywood (a cowboy shooting it out with sheriff and Indians). Older men who could afford it dropped in at the tavern, drank two glasses of beer, played a few hands of cards with their friends. The two gentlemen from Ruhrort went celebrating to a night club in Düsseldorf, where the show, all foreign visitors said, was naughtier and more naked than the most celebrated night clubs of Paris before the war.

In East Germany a few people went to the movies to see the latest picture from Soviet Hungary (a peasant girl bringing in the harvest quicker than before), or from Soviet Russia (a working girl making more steel quicker than before), but most people stayed home. They pulled their shades down, made sure the children were sound asleep (they mustn't hear and blab at school next day), and turned on their radios to learn what RIAS, the American-sponsored station in West Berlin, was telling them about their life. A boy of eighteen came home and made the sign of the cross, after distributing almost fifty leaflets in mailboxes without being caught by the secret police. He had printed the leaflets himself; they bore the headline: "We want freedom."

In many cities of West Germany a few old men and women met to celebrate on this historic day the memory of November 9,

1918, when the Kaiser had been overthrown and the first demo-cratic republic of Germany proclaimed. No firecrackers, no danc-ing, no oratory with happy truths shining beneath time-worn clichés marked the occasion. Tired men and women remembered a tired past, and quietly went home to bed.

A few younger men and women met in the back rooms of West German "Bierstuben" to celebrate on this historic day the memory of November 9, 1923, when Adolf Hitler had first attempted to take power in Germany, and the swastika flag had first waved for a few hectic hours over Munich. They sang their old songs; a speaker recalled that the first failure of their revolution had been followed ultimately by victory—remember and hold out, you old fighters. And so to bed.

A few people met before the monuments erected after Hitler's fall in Hitler's concentration camps to commemorate Hitler's vic-tims. Their persecution had started in earnest on the historic day of November 9, 1938, when Hitler's mobs marched at the Führ-er's orders through the cities of Germany, burning synagogues, looting Jewish shops, arresting Jews.

The newspapers of West Germany dutifully reported all these commemorations of the historical date in a few lines on their in-ner pages. The papers of East Germany were still carrying long accounts of a very different celebration—that of the glorious Bol-shevik Revolution of November 7, 1917, which had been grandly commemorated in Moscow and throughout the U.S.S.R., the Peo-ple's Democracies, and the Eastern zone of Germany.

November 9 was a day on which, as on other weekdays, most Germans went about their business as usual amid the memories and reminders of a past that lay around them in ruins. The mem-ories were dead like the politics that had created them. But few Germans were much concerned with politics, past or present, on a historical or any other day.

Germany was no more. There were now two Germanies. A line arbitrarily drawn by the foreign victors had turned into a deep trench, separating the East Germans in their "German Democratic Republic" with 27 per cent of the former population of Germany and 31 per cent of its area, from the West Germans in their "Federal Republic of Germany." Their separateness and their differences grew as time and the cold war went on; they retained in common only the reminders of the last war—the ruins in their midst.

According to the best estimates 54 to 60 per cent of Germany's buildings were in ruins at the end of the Second World War. In the first years after the war, Germans and foreigners alike used to say that in Germany "life went on amidst ruins"; in the early 1950's it was equally evident, though not so generally admitted by Germans and foreigners, that the ruins stayed on amidst life.

From all appearances the Germans seemed by 1952 to have become adjusted to the ruins. They went about their daily business, with little more attention to the ruins than New Yorkers give to the skyscrapers towering above them. But just as foreign visitors in America for the first time are most impressed by New York's skyscrapers, so foreigners visiting postwar Germany for the first time saw everywhere a landscape of ruins. Words like rubble, ravage, or destruction are inadequate to convey the reality of the mass ruins, for they were beyond the previous experience of modern man, beyond his imagination and even his nightmares. They bore no resemblance to, say, the remnants of medieval castles, or ancient Greek temples, or even so large-scale a best-seller of the sight-seeing business as Pompeii.

But if the Germans no longer saw the ruins, they were nevertheless aware of them on a deeper level of their minds. And on that level the ruins were a constant reminder of the good old times (before they became ruins) and of death. It did not matter any more whether they had been created by a direct bomb hit, an incendiary bomb, an explosive bomb, a ravaging fire, artillery barrages from Allied invaders or Nazi defenders, whether what was left was heaps of rubble, a façade with all the structure behind it burned away, a gaping hole or a heap of twisted, broken, useless steel, stones, bricks, cement. The peculiar uniqueness of individual life can still be perceived in the obituaries; in the morgue there is only the sameness of death. Seven years after the obituaries of their cities, churches, and homes had been written, read, and forgotten, the Germans still lived among the corpses. In the year 1952, more than one third of Germany was still in ruins, in spite of the efforts of removal and the success of reconstruction.

Almost immediately after the war Germany undertook to clear away her 11,000,000,000 cubic feet of rubble. From the rubble mountains, men, women, and children, working with their bare hands, selected, cleaned, and piled in neat rows seventeen billion bricks. Enterprising people scavenged the ruins to find and sell materials that were still usable, from scrap iron and steel girders to nails. Homeless families found a corner among the ruins and moved in, with a flower-pot or two on the windowsill that soon blossomed in gay refutation of the great claim of destruction. Smart speculators bought "real estate with ruins," a cheap commodity to be sold later at enormous profits. The West Berliners even "erected" rather lovely mountains out of some of the rubble (the first mountains in Berlin), planted grass and flowers on them, laid out paths, put up benches, and named them Monte Klamotte (Mount Rubbish).

While removal of the ruins went on with undiminished energy, the emphasis shifted after 1949 to reconstruction. In 1950 West Germany set a European all-time and all-nations record by erecting seven and a half dwelling units per thousand heads, while at the same time in France, for instance, less than two, and in England, less than four units were built.

How the Germans would rise above their ruins, what they would build in their place, was the clearest indication of the way Germany would go in the future. Would they rebuild the destroyed cities in their old image? Or would they, from the rubble-strewn *tabula rasa*, reconstruct cities that were new in form and in spirit? Would the new effort lead back to the old, or forward to something new? Or would, perhaps, a middle way be found between "restoration" of the old and experiments with the new?

In Frankfurt-am-Main, a city of over 500,000 people, 55 per cent of the buildings had been destroyed. Of its 177,000 dwelling units, only 44,000 were intact. In 1952, its famous Old Town, which had survived almost without change since the Middle Ages, was still a vast valley of ruins, only barely covered but not hidden by a sickly growth of bush and underbrush. Thousands of man-sized holes, dug originally as entrances to bombed houses or torn into the earth by explosives, served now as secret doors to a secret underground where vice and crime flourished in the city's former subterranean waterways and drains and sewers. According to expert estimate, in 1951 "many thousands" were still living in these hidden bordellos, in caves to which criminals retreated after their nightly exploits, in ruined catacombs under the ruined city that were home to ruined people.

In the ruins above ground, clinging to honest life, an old woman sold pretzels, a student his books (*The Collected Works of Hegel,* Spengler's *The Decline of the West*). An open-air theater gave its performances in the Carmelite Cloister, of which only the fine outer walls were preserved, forming a beautiful backdrop and side scenes. The tower of the cathedral pointed toward heaven above the rubble that had once been the nave. In a corner of the burned-out holy house, the faithful had built a chapel large enough to hold a small altar with its cross testifying to salvation and survival.

Amid the ruins of Frankfurt, the house in which Johann Wolfgang von Goethe was born in 1749 stood as though untouched. Destroyed as thoroughly as its neighbors, the home of Germany's most famous man had been rebuilt with faithful exactitude, down to the smallest detail. It had been quite difficult, the custodian told me, to find the stonemasons and the roof-tilers who could master the craft as practiced in the eighteenth century when the house had been built. After a long search a retired artisan was discovered who knew the old ways. He trained the apprentices to work on the restoration of Goethe's house. Even the steps in the staircase, which, according to the scholars, had already been worn from decades of use when young Goethe trod them, were artificially worn again. Only the wallpaper was made to look—after long discussions by the historical, artistic, and literary experts—not as slightly darkened as it had become by 1944, but bright and new, for "that's exactly as it was in Goethe's day," the custodian said.

Also reconstructed in its old shape was St. Paul's Church, where in 1848 the first parliament of a united German republic—soon to pass again into oblivion—met after Germany's first revolution. To pay for the expense of the restoration, the city of Frankfurt rented out the shrine for educational, artistic, and community meetings. (In 1951, for instance, in this historic church Gayelord Hauser addressed the Germans on the subject "Look younger, live longer.") In process of restoration was the Römer, a proud building in which, from the sixteenth century, the kings of Germany had been elected and its emperors crowned.

A five-minute walk from these lonely monuments of a glorious past, and you were in a different and altogether new world: bustling streets of banks and insurance companies, department stores and amusement places, new buildings going up with large posters on their scaffolds: "Built with the help of the Marshall Plan." While the Germans called these buildings "Americanistic," to Americans they appeared rather dull and uninspired, a sort of cross between barracks and a giant cigar box. With their façades of clean, white stucco, these new monuments of business recovery looked like strong forts put up to protect their prosperous garrison against the armies of misery encamped in the ruins.

Of its 133,000 completely destroyed or partly damaged housing units, Frankfurt had at the beginning of 1952 rebuilt approximately 20,000—one out of six and a half. The rate of reconstruction is indicated in the following figures: 4,148 housing units were constructed in 1948, 5,970 in 1949, 6,413 in 1950, and 4,000 in 1951.

Altogether, from 1945 to 1952, West Germany constructed

1,500,000 new dwelling units—a great performance and even a great success compared with the destruction and paralysis of the first postwar years. Yet 4,200,000 additional new dwellings were still needed in 1952 to satisfy the demand of the people for decent housing; there were still three to four West Germans to one room. Five to ten families were often living in dwellings that had formerly housed one family. Great as recovery was, the greater effort lay still ahead.

Most of the new houses and apartments were closely identical in style to those built ten or twenty years ago, particularly the more conservative ones of that time. The architects of the Dessau Bauhaus, who had revolutionized architecture after the First World War by their discoveries of new building ideas and materials, criticized severely the old-fashioned, staid style of new German construction after the Second World War. Martin Wagner, once a leading city planner in Germany, asked his former colleagues, from his exile in Cambridge, Massachusetts, whether they were building their houses for modern living or as decorations for a historical costume party. When, in 1951, the Marshall Plan administration held a competition in fifteen German cities for new blueprints and ideas and less costly methods in housing architecture, only three hundred out of the thousand entries submitted contained new ideas, and none touched the matter of reduced costs. The public rejected the prize-winning entry, as it likewise rejected all other new experiments in building, such as the Simplex houses of Hamburg, the Mannheim apartments and the Hanover Constructa houses (both consisting of one combined living-room—kitchen and two bedrooms), or the Lübeck apartments with their "balcony-in-the apartment." Despite their low rents—from forty to sixty marks, that is, little more than ten dollars a month—the people were not receptive to any of these ideas that would change their traditional way of life as it had been in the good old times before the war.

Not only were houses and buildings reconstructed in the spirit and shape of the past—the cities themselves emerging from the ruins were reconstructions of yesterday's memories. Their new look was the remembered old look. A few city planners and enterprising builders thought they could now build their cities in new forms and ways responding to the changing needs of the new times. They argued that the Germans ought to accept the fact that they had to build from scratch as a great opportunity rather than a misfortune; they could now build modern cities. They argued that motorization, for instance, exploded the old, narrow, criss-crossing streets like a load of dynamite and made modern living a continuous death hazard, with more cars than ever before running through cities built for pedestrians and horses. The new German cities should be planned for modern mass life rather than to restore the past. But these innovators were a small minority, and their blueprints soon disappeared in the wastebaskets of other city planners, architects, and experts who clung to restoration and strengthened their arguments with fine points from history, poetry, and metaphysics. While some revolutionary blueprints of city planning were published, an Association of the Victims of Planning was formed, and the people went on restoring their houses, streets, and cities in the old pattern, in melancholy search of the lost yesterday, in deep distrust of innovation.

Homesick for the past, the survivors filled the empty shell of former life with memories to conjure up again the good old times before the nightmare. Their post cards and their Christmas cards presented the pictures of former landmarks as if they still existed, although they were now part of the ruins.

Simultaneously, and almost paradoxically, the ruins that made Germans turn their thoughts backwards broke off their living relations to the past, their sense of tradition, and the tangible continuity of their history. Before the destruction their past had been alive, preserved in an eternal present, sure to continue into the future. When the old churches, houses, streets disappeared around them, this sense of the living past was replaced by a sense of futility and insecurity. Like their houses, some people had survived while their neighbors had been killed. Unaccountably, they had escaped the mass catastrophe to be left as lonely, single, atomized individuals, no longer members of a society in whose ruins they now lived. If they were to survive they must rely only on themselves, their good luck, their toughness, their skill or foresight—at any rate, their superiority as individuals, not as members of their community. Seeing the blatant, unexplainable injustice of one house still standing untouched next to other houses in ruins, many Germans lost all faith in the community and trusted only their own, personal strength.

The longer these ruins remained in the center of German life, the deeper became their impact on the Germans, and the less did the Germans talk or think of them. Instead, they tried to build a new world as similar as possible to their old world, a fool's paradise of restoration.

A German Rip Van Winkle who stretched out for a nap many years ago and awoke in 1952 might have been as confused as his American predecessor. If sleep had overcome him twenty-five years before, at a table of one of the open-air cafés on the main boulevards of Hamburg or Düsseldorf, he might think he had slept just a night rather than a quarter of a century. Just as in 1927, contented, well-dressed strollers passed by on the streets, the shop windows were filled with fine, beautiful wares from all over the world, and Germany was accepted by the other democracies of the Western world as a prosperous, healthy, strong republic. The other customers sitting at the tables around him and sipping their drinks with enjoyment still chatted about the same topics—seemingly far removed from the world and its great events, living in their private kingdoms where politics got at most an unfriendly remark or two—"What can you do about it? . . . Prosit, Mister Neighbor. . . ." Rising from the table and walking along the streets, our Rip might still see the same buildings that had been there in 1927, or even, for that matter, in 1852. How could he know they were merely copies of the past?

Yet if he walked farther, just five minutes off Düsseldorf's elegant Koenigsallee with its splendid show of wealth, he would come upon a new world of empty lots where ragged children fled at sight of him like frightened mice into a hole in the ground. If he had fallen asleep in Hamburg, a brief walk from the city's center of solid department stores and office buildings would bring him to a street lined on either side by the charred front walls of houses that had been burned away. It would be the same in Freiburg, Munich, everywhere.

The great country fair of Erding near Munich in the summer of 1952 was as gay as ever to our Rip—with its beer tents, yodeler bands, merry-go-rounds, Wild West shows. He hardly noticed the new, yet already decrepit barracks at the edge of the fair grounds, from which cheerless faces gazed out at the riotry. "They are only German expellees from the East, Herr Winkle." Whereupon Rip returned to his stein of beer as the band struck up an old song: "Prosit to Gemütlichkeit."

In the lovely Bavarian lake resort of Schliersee, a poster would direct Rip to the beach he had often visited; there he would find hundreds of old people in strange clothing, a rigid look of despair on their faces, living in bathing cabins. "Why, they are refugees, Herr Winkle."

The words would fade from his mind as he walked quickly back to the village of Schliersee, where nothing had changed in the last twenty-five years. For Herr Van Winkle had decided to ignore the changes, not to see the new world of ruins—to look back rather to the times when he had fallen asleep, and try to transform the present as much as possible into the past.

If, like Rip, most of his contemporaries preferred to look backward, nevertheless the present, driven from the conscious layers of the mind to a half-buried subconscious—as it was from the cleared-up empty lots of the ruins to the weird subterranean life below the cities—asserted itself on occasion and nearly led to panic. In quiet Bonn as well as in cosmopolitan West Berlin, people were caught by terror in the summer of 1951 when rumors spread that from the underground catacombs crime and death were reaching up to the good burghers above ground. Excited people expected to see their daughters snatched away into the ruins of Berlin, their children disappear into the catacombs of Bonn. But when the police undertook to find the young girls who had been abducted, to smoke out the kidnapers of little children, they discovered neither. Herr Van Winkle and his contemporaries read the police communiqué with contentment, and settled back into the old life.

In East Germany, it was not so easy to ignore the ruins. Many of them, indeed, were more recent even than the war itself. For in East Germany, no sooner had the dust settled on the ruins of the war than destruction began anew. There were, for instance, Berlin's great architectural masterpieces and monuments, occupying in all a few city blocks. These castles, built in the eighteenth and nineteenth centuries by the rulers of Prussia, had been only slightly harmed by wartime bombings; they could easily be restored. But when, in October, 1949, the Soviets made a movie, "The End of Berlin," designed to glorify the victory of the Soviet armies on the spot of the fighting, the production was so realistic that many of the elaborate doorways and other sculptural works were destroyed. In 1950 the cultural organizations of the Eastern city, the trade unions, and the scientists decided to repair the castles and other buildings of the neighborhood; but orders came from Moscow—through the German Communist leaders—that "here was to be erected now a great square of demonstrations where the will of our people to reconstruct and to fight can be expressed forever."

A wide square between the castles—the Lustgarten (Pleasure Garden)—had been a friendly gardened spot before Hitler had it paved to serve as the swastika-decorated parade ground for great Nazi festivals in Berlin. With all the buildings around it removed, the square would be an even bigger, more impressive parade ground for the Communists. Some East Berliners protested—but in vain. A party historian was commissioned to prove that the castle and the other buildings were nothing but memories of the feudalist Prussian past—as if the fact that the Kremlin in Moscow was a memory of the feudalist Russian past had prevented the new Soviet rulers from keeping it and using it for their own aims and glory. On November 4, 1950, workers began to blow up the buildings; in the next three days, the work was finished with the help of 13,000 kilograms of explosives and voluntary "construction" brigades of the Communist Youth. By the end of the year, the paving of the new square—appropriately renamed the Marx-Engels Square—was triumphantly finished. If there was to be no German Kremlin, there was at least to be a German Red Square—Moscow's satellite needed marching natives, not native leaders. The Embassy of the Soviet Union was the only new building erected on East Berlin's ruined main avenue, Unter den Linden. Opened with pomp and pride in 1951, it towered over the city in skyscraper proportions, designed like a pie-maker's dream of a Greek temple, decorated with ornaments and sculptures of all ages, its centerpiece a gigantic red star brightly lit at night in the dark city.

While most of Soviet-occupied Prussia's old castles and churches were destroyed, building by building, by "activist brigades" on orders from their rulers, "the main task," the government pronounced, "is the reconstruction of our cities, especially of the all-German capital of Berlin." Yet in 1952, East Berlin and East Germany were still covered by ruins exactly as they had been after the war—"victims of capitalist American bombing barbarism," as the new rulers proclaimed. On New Year's Day, 1952, the people were ordered to remove the ruins "in voluntary shifts," with everybody bringing his tools and devoting three nights a week to this community work. But the people sabotaged the order and the great campaign against the ruins had to be postponed. Of the 800,000,000 cubic feet of rubble covering Soviet Berlin in the year 1945, there remained in 1952 still 600,000,000. (In West Berlin, almost half of the rubble, 550,000,000 cubic feet of the original 1,200,000,000, had been removed by that time.) Of East Berlin's 36 bridges destroyed in the war, only 4 were rebuilt, while in West Berlin 42 of the 48 destroyed bridges were rebuilt. No streets were repaved in Soviet Berlin, while West Berlin in the same period repaved 20 miles of its streets and avenues.

What was built in East Berlin were large barracks and training grounds, in addition to 5,000 apartments reserved for party dignitaries and pompous buildings for the party itself. Unlike West Germans, East Germans did not even discuss the style and spirit of their reconstruction, blueprinted and decreed from Moscow in accordance with the architectural party line. That line, ironically, was based on a distorted imitation of the very style which the great builders of the Prussian past, Schlüter and Schinkel, had developed to such cool, serene perfection in the Berlin castles the Soviets destroyed. "Socialist realism," it was called, and prevailed in Moscow, Warsaw, and Bucharest as well as in East Berlin.

In contrast to America's "constructivism, functionalism, and counter-revolutionary formalism" (which is Soviet jargon for the fact that American modern buildings are designed with primary emphasis on the comfort of the people who live and work in them) the Soviet houses were distinguished by their façades—heavy statics, weighty socles and pedestals, high Greek columns and numerous sculptured figures of muscular young workers and bosomy peasant girls. The apartment houses might have only a single staircase to serve the eight apartments on each floor, but their façades were cluttered with Corinthian columns, Renaissance leaves, and tiny towers copied from Venetian palaces.

These apartments had only paper-thin walls, in keeping with specifications of the Five-Year Plan, "since in the new society there is no need for the previously preferred privacy of every household"; for the same reason, the kitchens were such tiny cubicles that housewives had to do their washing in the community laundry, where, as intended, they could spy on each other and "penetrate mutually their ideological education." In short, East Germany's new citizens were guaranteed against privacy and thrust into the collective mass.

"The cities of the new Germany," said Kurt Liebknecht, President of East Berlin's Academy of Architecture, "are to be so beautiful and monumental that they express in their architecture the greatness of the new era and the greatness of the German people. The houses we are building have a perspective spanning many centuries to come." In short, as in the Nazi past, the Eastern perspective was toward the Thousand-Year Reich for which, the Soviet builders explained, glass, that popular modern American building material, would not be sufficiently stable.

Aside from these exterior changes, nothing was essentially different from the Nazi past to our East German Rip Van Winkle, who, in 1937, had gone off for a day's respite from the drumbeat monotone of Nazi boots, and stretched out for a nap along the Harz Mountains, on a Havel lake near Berlin, on the beach of the Baltic Sea, or anywhere else in eastern Germany. Awaking in 1952, he went down to his native village, town, or city, and learned from his neighbors what great events had transpired in the meantime. Hitler's Third Reich, which was to last for a thousand years, had gone down in defeat and disgrace. Rip's own town had been occupied by the Soviet army and ruled by the Soviet Military Administration. Now, after liberation and peace, there was a great "German Democratic Republic" presiding over the new, democratic era of peace, progress, and plenty. This the newspapers, the countless posters on the walls, the radio, the glossy new history books told him. Yet what did his eyes see? Under the thin disguise of new words and uniforms, the scene was, amazingly, what it had been fifteen years before.

Hailing a neighbor with a friendly "What's the news?" Herr Van Winkle was greeted with that strange motion invented during the Third Reich and dubbed "The German Glance" *(Der deutsche Blick)* as a counterpart to the Nazi "German salute"; it consisted of a quick look-around to see whether any informers were loitering in the vicinity. Walking along the street, he saw everywhere the same cold-faced, black-booted, black-uniformed young men of the SS, Adolf Hitler's dread élite corps; the only changes were in the color of their neckties, now red, and the name of their organization, now the "People's Police." There were the same cocky boys in abbreviated shorts and open sport shirts, the original brown showing through the blue in patches, and now calling themselves the "Free German Youth." The Gestapo had ceased to exist, but, he learned, its employees had now joined a new fraternity called the *Staatssicherheitsdient* (State Security Service). He learned further that if any member of this fraternity denounced him as an enemy of the people, he would be arrested, probably beaten, perhaps tortured, until he admitted a crime, then sentenced by a "People's Court" to prison, or maybe transported to the wide, not-at-all open spaces of Siberia and thereabouts.

At the inn he found himself seated for a *Gemeinschaftsempfang,* the compulsory group listening to a radio broadcast, just as in the old days. And the same programs still seemed to come from the loud-speaker—first the military marches hammered out by drums and fanfares, then old folk songs with new political texts sung by a choir of youngsters, finally the same speech bellowed by the same voices eulogizing "the greatest friend of the people," "the greatest thinker of all times," "the creator of all new life, liberty and people's happiness"—now called Joseph Stalin. The same radio voices were still denouncing and—as they still described it—"unmasking" the enemy, the reactionaries, the American imperialists and exploiters, the international gang of money-mad warmongers. And they still promised a better life to all as soon as these foreign criminals and their hidden accomplices here at home were liquidated by the people and eradicated from the face of the earth. Long lists of names were read of those who, in words too high-falutin' for Herr Van Winkle to understand, pledged their enthusiastic, eternal support of the government and all its goals. The names ranged from university professors to housewives to high school boys to undertakers.

True, the vocabulary of 1937 seemed slightly altered. Bad things were now almost always American rather than Jewish. Good things were "progressive" rather than Aryan. The mustache of the man whose portrait hung over the bar was larger and greyer than in 1937, and a big five-pointed red star occupied the corner in the inn which the swastika had once decorated. But a good-humored, quiet man like our Rip would not apply himself to the subtleties of political semantics; he cared little about the differences of wall decorations. Nor did he give heed to all the other differences between the old Third Reich in which he had fallen asleep, and the new Red Reich in which he had awakened. Rather he noticed first the much more conspicuous, much more important likenesses. Why should he bother? He knew the old game and how to play it, even with a newly colored deck.

However, when he visited the shrines of the Nazi era to which for twelve hectic years Germans had made pious pilgrimages, Herr Van Winkle discovered that something had changed. As a matter of fact, the visit taught him to take with a grain of salt the claims of the totalitarian Reichs, whatever their slogans and appeals, that they would last a thousand years.

The Reich Chancellery and the bunker in which Der Führer died, situated in the Eastern sector of Berlin, was destroyed, blown to pieces by artillery shells, the ruined fragments dynamited by the Red Army, their square stones, cement, and iron pieces strewn over the ground. The swastika-holding eagles on the portals of the Nazi State Bank and Göring's Air Ministry in East Berlin had been replaced by Soviet emblems.

Elsewhere in Berlin the charming, birch-flanked villas of Hjalmar Schacht and other ministers of the Third Reich had been turned into living and working quarters for American officers. The never completed, great *Parteitagsgelände* of Nürnberg, designed by Hitler himself, where the annual Nazi conventions had taken place with marches, torch-parades, and speeches that frightened the world, was now a camp for war orphans of all nations.

To Hitler's mountain hideout on Obersalzberg a stream of tourists had come immediately after the war, although most of the buildings had been destroyed by Allied bombs, Nazi-instigated arson, and looters. Visiting GI's bought the tiles from Hitler's bathroom—red tiles for a dollar, green tiles for two dollars. So many of them were sold that a smart local businessman manufactured thousands of new tiles for sale to tourists. According to

local police statistics, 136,560 people visited Obersalzberg between July 13 and October 20, 1951; almost 110,000 of them,
or 80 per cent, were foreigners. When a German reporter discovered that the guide, one Zyschke, Hermann Göring's former
house superintendent, was reverently pointing to the holy spots
where "our beloved Führer himself has stood," the Bavarian government decided to demolish the remnants of the ruins and to
plant in their stead a forest. The local authorities protested violently against this plan (which was carried out in 1952). They
considered the ruined buildings worth many thousands of dollars
in tourist trade. Whether people came in melancholy adoration
of the Nazi past, or—like many foreigners—in fascinated horror
and to enjoy their triumph, was of no importance to them. The
charming village of Berchtesgaden had always lived by its tourist
trade, and its Nazi past seemed an even stronger drawing card
for visitors than its beautiful Alpine landscape.

The former Dachau concentration camp, first of the infernos
in which, from 1933 to 1945, 230,000 men of all creeds and nations had been tortured and killed, still, in 1952, attracted tourists with its barbed wire, barracks for inmates and guards, villas
for little führers and two camouflaged crematoriums. The tourists
here were often former inmates who had survived; most other
people avoided the place.

Less distinguished was the Austrian birthplace of Germany's
first Führer, now sleepy, almost deserted. The pig-tailed little girl
of ten whom we met on entering the town, did not know where
Hitler's birthplace was: "I believe the gentleman has moved,"
she said, and walked off. We next asked the elderly man who was
standing on the corner. "To hell with that ne'er-do-well," he
mumbled. It turned out that he meant a drinking companion who
had been thrown out of the local inn. But in the small coffee-
house, the waiter was as quick to give proper directions as would
any waiter living near a minor sight-seeing point.

The *Führerhaus,* a rather ugly big building among the charming houses of the neighborhood, showed no outward signs of its

claim to glory. Above and on its big-hinged front door two shingles bearing the United States Army coat-of-arms proclaimed that the Army Counter Intelligence Corps had its headquarters on the second floor. A third larger shingle announced the location on the first floor of the Braunau Municipal Library, the *Volksbücherei Braunau.* Its reserve books were stored in the room in which Hitler was born. The library itself did not own a single book on Hitler, Nazism, or the Third Reich. In its department on History and Politics, there were only three books on Soviet Russia. When the librarian asked me what book I was looking for I apologetically admitted I was just browsing around. "Seems that's what everybody's doing here," she mumbled.

Across from the *Führerhaus,* on the opposite side of the street, the headquarters of the Communist Party of Upper Austria displayed the usual number of pamphlets and posters. From the inn next door you could watch the few silent and secret sight-seers pass the *Führerhaus* with nondescript looks. The guest book of the local museum, whose pages for the years 1933 to 1945 were crowded with countless inscriptions by visitors signing their names with a *Heil Hitler,* contained scarcely an entry since 1945. In the stationery shop, picture post cards were sold—one showing the likeness of the town's celebrity, a beer brewer who lived in the sixteenth century and whose mustache was so long that the emperor in appreciation elevated him and his family to a baronetcy. Another post card bore a picture of Braunau's only monument, a memorial statue of the German printer and bookdealer, Johann Philipp Palm, shot in Braunau on Napoleon's orders in the year 1806 because he had published a pamphlet against the foreign dictator and conqueror under the title: "Germany in Her Deepest Humiliation." A third post card showed the Braunau Municipal Library—a building not distinguished but for the fact that Hitler was born there. Nowhere in Germany were there picture post cards showing the Berlin shelter where he killed himself fifty-six years later, amid the German ruins which are his true memorial.

III

Hitler's Post-Mortem

O N THE badly bombed campus of the University of Freiburg-im-Breisgau, the American Friends' Foreign Service Committee built, shortly after the war, a primitive, log cabin-like barracks where students could read foreign magazines, take home English or German books from the circulating library, listen to free lectures—or just talk. Cynics suspected that the cookies and hot chocolate served to every visitor by a congenial, idealistic student from Wisconsin were the real attraction. But then, the cookies and chocolates probably did more to "re-educate" the youngsters than books, speeches, and professional publicity of amateurish foreign "re-educators"; the students sensed an atmosphere of unquestioning helpfulness to which, after initial distrust, they responded warmly.

Most of the young Germans whom I met in Freiburg's Quaker barracks were under twenty-five years of age. When they asked me about America, I talked at some length about life, liberty, happiness, unhappiness, and hope in this country. In the discussion that followed, they assured me with detached politeness that of course democracy was a very fine way of life, perhaps the best. But, they added, it had little chance of succeeding in postwar West Germany. Immediately after the war the conversion of their country to democracy might have been accomplished, when everybody was fed up with Nazism—"the rule of mentally retarded drill sergeants," as a serious-looking girl called it. But now, the basis for democracy had been shaken, and perhaps destroyed, for a long time to come. This, they said, was mainly the fault of the foreign occupation and Germany's political leaders. They reported incidents of pettiness, rowdiness, and revengeful arrogance on the part of occupation personnel, attacked Allied policies and administrative actions, criticized their own leaders and spokesmen.

Granted all this, why did it stop them, I asked, from creating themselves a free and decent society—call it democracy or some other name? Was it not to their own interest to want a better government in which they could participate, no matter how foreign conquerors might have misbehaved and how many weaknesses their parties and leaders might have? Was it not their own honor as Germans to build for themselves a political community of which they could be proud? To this a student answered that theirs was probably the old story of the little boy who, having been refused by his father a new pair of gloves, went out into a snowstorm barehanded, saying: "It will serve my father right if my hands are frostbitten."

The other students laughed, agreed, and, considering this part of the discussion finished, quickly went on to questions nearer their hearts: What were the chances of emigrating to America? What examinations did a German graduate have to pass in the States before he could start working? How much money could he earn in this or that field?

On my way back to my hotel, I was joined by one of these students, who said he wanted to talk to me. He had not spoken up before because he had not wanted to be shouted down by the others—the "model democrats," as he called them scornfully. "I never talk in public," he explained. "Neither do my friends. Most people think us indifferent, but we are only silent. And when we speak, we have nothing to say; we ask for answers that are never given."

He kept looking at me as if to make sure I was listening, and as if to decide whether he could trust me; he seemed to find it hard to speak. He was twenty-five years old; the son of a Prussian officers' family, he had joined the Nazi boys' organization at ten and later had become a minor leader in the Hitler Youth, which at that time, though Hitler ruled already, was still a voluntary organization. His years in the Hitler Youth, he said, were the only happy ones in his life; there he had found *Kameradschaftsgeist,* a spirit of community among comrades.

When shortly before the war all German boys were compelled to join the Hitler Youth, he had planned to resign in protest, since he felt that true comradeship could not flourish among forced members. But soon he was old enough for the army. When he returned from the war—wounded, promoted, and decorated— his world was a shambles. He worked for two years in the coal mines of the Ruhr; now he was a freshman student of philosophy supporting himself by odd jobs.

After his return from the war, he told me, he began to feel that "much was rotten in the Third Reich, and quite a lot was wrong with National Socialism." But he resented the tendency of many Germans and foreigners to call all Nazis, and sometimes even all Germans, criminals. He had been a Nazi but not a criminal; he repeated this as if driven by an obsession, although no one had accused him of being a criminal. He was, he said, a former Boy Scout and a former soldier, whose country had happened to lose the war. Though in both capacities he had been a faithful Nazi, neither had made him do anything criminal. Therefore he could never embrace a new philosophy such as democracy; it would look as if under fire he had deserted his old ideals, sold out to the victors of the day, admitted that he was a repentant criminal. What had made Nazism so bad, he said, was that the leaders were liars and the whole system based on lies. Yet the *Kameradschaftsgeist* among the Nazi youth was a thing he would always cherish. "There aren't many other values in the world, are there?"

He did not believe in God, he said, in reply to my question. Nor did he believe in personal freedom: "It leads to chaos, which in turn leads to another dictator." What did he think of the doc-

trine of superior races, and of Hitler's extermination of the Jews?
He had no strong opinions about it; he had never met a Jew except for two occupation officers after the war, one a mean fellow,
the other quite decent. "Hitler probably lied about the Jews, as
he lied about almost everything." Did he believe in the sanctity
of human life? "No," he answered very decidedly, "no idea, no
community is worth anything unless you are willing to give your
life for it." Other men's lives, too? That wouldn't be necessary
in a decent world, he said after some reflection; and then he suddenly and shyly declared: "I wish I could do something for a new,
decent world." After a moment of silence, he lighted a cigarette,
and almost hissed: "But I don't suppose I can." He walked away
to disappear in the ruins.

"Belief, like any other moving body, follows the path of least
resistance," as Samuel Butler observed. Like this boy, most young
Germans who had followed the path of least resistance and believed in Nazism while Hitler ruled, found after his fall the
shambles of their Nazi belief blocking their way and resisting
their progress toward any new belief. No new path of least resistance seemed to remain for them.

When the Third Reich went down in defeat, it "debunked"
itself in the eyes of the young who had been taught by the Nazis
themselves to judge political ideas in terms of power and success
alone. "Being suddenly hurled away from all the ideas on which
I stood, it took a long time for me to get my feet on the ground
again. Then I discovered how much we had been deceived. I did
not find a new faith in the hatred of those who pulled everything
into the gutter that before, rightly or wrongly, had been appre-
ciated," said Gerhard H., age 18.[1]

"In vain did I even in the last weeks of the war try to gain
new strength by reading Adolf Hitler's *Mein Kampf* in order to
keep believing in the idea according to which I had lived for

[1] This and the following quotations from autobiographical statements given
by young Germans at their application for graduation from high school are collected in *Jugend unterm Schicksal, Lebensberichte Junger Deutscher,* edited by
Kurt Hass, introduction by Albert Goes, Hamburg, 1950.

twelve years. Nevertheless, I had to see my ideals sink into the gutter. This blow of fate struck against our people hit me so hard that I almost lost my faith in God and the world," said Arnold P., age 20.

"With the end of the war there came to me a gradual dis-illusionment and the realization that the views in which we had been educated, and for which we had unconditionally fought, were a large-scale swindle and fraud that had to lead us to defeat. I was seized with a deep disappointment about men, and I re-proached myself very much. I could not understand any more how I could have accepted such an erroneous doctrine," said Kurt M., age 19.

Whenever young Germans disclosed their life-stories, they were dominated by the trauma of 1945 when sudden catastrophe had blasted their faith and their world view, their *Weltanschauung*. If Nazism had made uniform their thinking, their disenchantment about Nazism was also more or less uniform. One after the other of them told the same story.

"It is certain that the military and political events of 1945 forced me to revise my world view. Like most of my comrades I had believed that Nazism was a great thing. . . . Only its complete defeat totally shattered the structure of that illusion," said Johann St., age 21, maimed in the war for the rest of his life.

"When the collapse came,[2] my inner self looked empty," wrote Rolf J., age 18, who had joined the Hitler Youth enthusiastically when he was ten. "Now everything that had been right in our eyes for eight years, was supposed to be wrong. When I thought about it, there collapsed more inside myself than merely my faith in the Nazi movement. In whom could one still have faith? Had not all we had been taught sounded authentic and correct? And now all the words for which we had walked through fire seemed to be merely swindle and fraud. I stood at an abyss. Could one still trust any man after such an experience? My faith in all hu-

---

[2] Characteristically, most Germans prefer speaking of "the collapse" rather than defeat or surrender, *Zusammenbruch,* rather than *Niederlage* or *Uebergabe.*

mans began to tumble. This inner rift can heal only slowly. Let's hope that this inner uncertainty can soon be overcome."

These moods and sentiments were shared by practically all young Germans after 1945. Among them, only extremely few conscious, and still fewer fanatical, believers in Nazism as a dogma, a political world view, were left.

But a "passion can be overcome only by a new passion." After the passion of Nazism had been eradicated, little in the way of political passion came to replace it in the hearts and minds of Germany's once-Nazi youth. It took more time and was more difficult to remove the ruins of ideals than the ruins of cities. The great ruination which the "collapse" of 1945 produced among young Germans was to be removed only by eventual development of their spiritual insight into, and moral hatred of, the evil of totalitarianism—by an intellectual, moral, and spiritual divorce from their past. Without the soul-searching that alone could direct them to new intentions for new purposes, the young Germans who ceased being Nazis became non-Nazis rather than anti-Nazis. More precisely, they did not become anti-totalitarians, but merely non-totalitarians. Their political trauma led them to the attitude which had been held before, and still dominated, most older Germans, who themselves had never been Nazis, or anti-Nazis either, but *unpolitische*—"non-political." The disenchanted young Germans joined with the rest in their *unpolitische* view of the Nazi past.

Their attitude toward the Third Reich—present as well as past —was less determined by Nazism itself than by the relation of the German *unpolitische* individual toward his political community, an attitude which preceded and survived Nazism, and which could not be changed by the Nazis, hard as they tried.

Only by understanding this "non-political" attitude can one understand why many Germans remembered the Third Reich as an historical episode for which they felt as little responsible as for any other episode in their history. In their view, the government originates and exists in a sphere outside their influence and control; they felt that the course of public events was not of their making. The state was in their eyes a superior entity high above its individual citizens. While they disliked its course, grumbled about it in public and, when this was *verboten,* in secret, they nevertheless accepted it, as a *force majeure.*

Public life in the eyes of the *unpolitische* was very much like the weather. While they talked about both politics and weather a great deal, they did nothing about it because they thought they could not change its course. Both were shaped beyond their control, somewhere between the earth and the high skies. Politics were made by the *Obrigkeiten,* as the authorities are called in German; translated literally, it would be the "upperdoms," a vague and submissive word. Like the weather, politics and public life made by the *Obrigkeiten* appeared to non-political minds as ever-changing, unpredictable, eternal sequences of better and worse days. Let the cops, the mailmen, the other public servants who were paid for it brave the weather and take the risks, and let the kids have their harmless fun. Adult citizens kept aloof and safe from weather and politics—an attitude which was not changed even in Nazism's totalitarian climate.

Shortly after the war, Germans spoke about Nazism as if it were an extinct monster of the past, which they had dimly seen from afar while it roamed. After 1950, this outlook changed. The Nazi era became in their minds a period of German history like any other, a bit more spectacular than most, yet not basically different. Nazism had, in this view, its bad and its good sides; and their balance appeared in the popular "non-political" German image of the Third Reich.

Among the bad sides, there were the "excesses," as the planned cruelty and mass terror against Jews, foreigners, and German anti-Nazis came to be termed in German usage—a term which shows that the "non-political ones" did not gain an insight into the essentially terroristic nature of Nazism (and every other genuine form of totalitarianism). As they had disliked and shaken their heads about these "excesses" during the period of the Third

Reich, they continued carrying them on the negative side of its ledger.

A second bad side was, as they also had learned by experience in the Third Reich, the totalitarian claim that the Nazi rulers made on every German. It conflicted with his longing of a *Privatmann*[3] to be left alone in his privacy. He thought that—contrary to the demands of the Nazis—his evenings belonged to him rather than to some party auxiliary; what he did in his apartment was his business rather than that of the Nazi party *blockwart,* the bloc captain; what he said to his wife, however critical it might be of the state, should not be reported by and to anybody.

But in addition to this, he did not want to participate actively or passively in any public affairs as the totalitarians wanted him to do, if they did not enforce his participation. He did not want to be responsible for the course of his community, whatever its goal.

A third bad side of Nazism which the "non-political" German resented in the Third Reich, and remembered after its fall, was that the Nazi leaders often were inept newcomers to authority whom he could not respect. Many Nazi mayors, youth leaders, economic führers and other leaders in the middle and lower echelons, and the dictatorial power vested in them, did not harmonize with the *unpolitische* German's sense of genuine authority vested in the state and its representatives. To some extent, this applied even to the highest levels of führers. Göring's clever clowning or Goebbels' intellectual hysterics, and the luxury, immorality, adultery, alcoholism, personal thievery and larceny in which, as many Germans learned from gossip, quite a few of the highest führers indulged, offended their traditional image of the *Obrigkeiten* which embody the state. Because of his incompetence brought about by his lowly origins, his poor education and his extravagant bohemian style of living, Hitler himself did not fully satisfy the

[3] The *Privatmann,* literally "the private man," as opposed to the citizen concerned with public life and responsibilities, is what the *unpolitische* likes to call himself.

4

image of his citizens as their supreme *Obrigkeit*. The people's main charge against him in the postwar years was that he had tried to lead the army though he was only a corporal, and that he had wanted to lead Germany although he had never graduated from a high school, not to mention a university.

From the late 1940's on, an avalanche of publications in West Germany publicized the secret lives and loves of the Nazi leaders; the public was eager for that literature of valets in whose eyes there are no heroes. The more than two dozen illustrated weeklies which became the main media of information and entertainment in Western Germany abounded with indiscreet gossip of the cooks, mistresses, butlers, astrologists, podiatrists, psychiatrists, soothsayers, and servants of Hitler and his satraps. The "non-political" Germans craved this intimate look from below at their past *Obrigkeiten* which under Nazism had been denied them. Their belated delving into the iconography of the former führers neither betrayed Nazi sentiments on their part, as some observers suspected, nor did their interest in the foibles and personal secrets of their past rulers reveal anti-Nazi feelings. The *Privatmann's* curiosity about gossip surrounding the *Obrigkeiten* was simply at long last satisfied.

The second wave of books in which active participants of the Nazi era remembered and revealed the past, and which began in 1949 to gain momentum, was of a different character. These books were concerned primarily with apologies. But instead of apologizing for the Nazi era altogether, they apologized only for Germany's defeat in the Nazi war. Their authors were generals rather than valets. Their intention was to prove that the defeat had been the fault of Hitler in particular, and of the Nazi system in general, rather than the fault of the officers and soldiers. All these books, from the best-seller by General Franz Halder, chief of staff of the German army from 1938 to September, 1942, when he was dismissed for not carrying out Hitler's orders in Russia, to the memoirs of General Hans Speidel, General Siegfried Westphal, General Adolph Heussinger, and other high-ranking officers, defended the professional honor of the military leaders—rather convincingly—from the blame for the defeat, and criticized and censured the Nazis as political intruders into a specialized non-political field. The great mass of other "non-political" *Privatmänner,* who were themselves experts at their jobs and willing to do them well for any *Obrigkeit* but resented it when the *Obrigkeit* intruded and ordered them around, felt deeply sympathetic with these apologies of the *unpolitische* generals. This was in their eyes another of the "bad sides" of the Nazi era.

Only a minority of Germans saw that the war itself was another "bad side" inherent in Nazism. To most Germans, the war was a catastrophe (as wars always are in German as well as in non-German eyes), a *force majeure,* brought about by all the governments of the world. When the inquiring photographer of a Frankfurt newspaper in 1951 asked whether present times were better or worse than Nazi times, five out of six who replied that Nazi times had been better referred in their answers to the years from 1933 to 1939, before the war began. Only one man replied that "the Germans had to pay the Nazi debt with the years when war ravaged Germany." In the German mind, images and memories of the Nazi past and of the last war remained apart and almost disconnected from each other. Not the Nazis, but the war had led to the ruins.

The first six years of peace under the Nazi regime were—except for the small groups of active, voluntary anti-Nazis, and the Jews—actually a rather normal, peaceful, prosperous time for most ordinary Germans. The growing totalitarian regime brought to most of them none of the elementary experiences which would have made these years appear strikingly different from other normal years, whereas the war, with widespread death and destruction, brought such an experience to everybody. Non-political people did not tend to look for cause and effect between war and government. The first six years of peace under Nazi rule were followed by the six years of war, during which the Nazis still happened to rule—a fact that seemed to "non-political" Germans of rather secondary importance. In addition, the war—as the enemy proclaimed, as he proved by his actions, and as every German learned when his house was bombed and his life attacked without regard to his political opinions—actually turned into a war against Germany and all Germans, rather than against the Third Reich and the Nazis.

In the 1950's, the non-political Germans began to recollect the good sides of the 1930's, the last peacetime years, which had also been the first Nazi years, in an ever more friendly light, while the bad sides faded into oblivion. This seems a usual reaction of the human mind, which prefers to suppress unpleasant recollections. Even when former concentration camp inmates met after a few years, they barely mentioned the hard times they had shared except in a smiling, jocular mood reminiscent of old classmates swapping memories. It was the same with most veterans at their later peacetime meetings.

Nazism had different good sides to different Germans. There were the peasants, Hitler's favorite group, whose incomes he protected by generous price fixing, and whose property holdings he guaranteed by special laws. Many of them had been better off and more secure during the Nazi time than before or after. The same held true of some groups of workers, industrialists, businessmen, and students.

Large groups of young people in general had enjoyed in the past Nazi time a sense of security and solidarity which they had been missing since. In most Hitler Youth groups, membership in which was compulsory, the boys as well as the girls were considerably more occupied with non-Nazi activities, such as hiking, group-singing, folk-dances, than with Nazi activities. In the years after the end of the war many young people often felt homesick for their past community, which had seemed to give a deeper meaning to their individual lives.

"This *Kameradschaft,* that was the thing for which I loved the Hitler youth," one of these boys told me in 1950. "When I entered at ten the ranks of the *Jungvolk,* I was enthusiastic, as any boy would be when such high ideals as *Kameradschaft*, Loyalty, and Honor are introduced to him. I still remember how deeply moved I was when we learned the oath of the sword: 'Jungvolk boys are hard, silent, faithful; Jungvolk boys are comrades; the highest value of a Jungvolk boy is Honor.' These words seemed holy to me. And then the outings! Is there anything more beautiful than to enjoy the beauties of the homeland among comrades?"

A third good side of Nazism seemed to many Germans its fight against Soviet Russia, the threat of which their former leaders, they felt, discerned considerably sooner than did their former enemies. Unless they were deep political thinkers or genuine all-out anti-Nazis, they could not be expected to see much difference between the "anti-Communism" of the Nazis and that of the Western powers, worlds apart though they were. Even the term of the "Iron Curtain" had been coined in the Nazi mint before Winston Churchill put it into general currency with his Fulton, Missouri speech on March 5, 1946: "From Stettin in the Baltic to Trieste in the Adriatic an iron curtain has descended across the continent. . . ." This was an almost verbal translation of the words of Count Lutz Schwerin von Krosigk, the German Foreign Minister in the short-lived government preceding unconditional surrender, who in a radio address on May 2, 1945, offered a separate peace to the Western powers: "In the east an iron curtain is incessantly advancing, keeping the world from seeing the work of destruction going on behind it." And Count Schwerin himself was probably but remembering an editorial of February, 1945, in *Das Reich,* the weekly paper edited by the Third Reich's Propaganda Ministry: "If the German people lay down their arms, the whole of Eastern and Southeastern Europe, together with the Reich, would come under Russian occupation. Behind an iron curtain mass butcheries of peoples would begin. . . ." Many Germans have remarked since the cold war that "the Nazis were right in their foreign politics; except for their mistake to start a war on two fronts which can never be won, and except for their excesses at home, they only knew and did prematurely what today all their former enemies in the West are also knowing and doing."

When almost half of the West German population in postwar opinion polls answered in the affirmative the question whether "Nazism was a good idea badly carried out," they meant that its general program of promises was good, but in reality, the bad sides outweighed the good ones. If the number of those who felt "Nazism was a good idea badly carried out" slightly increased over the years, it expressed rather the discontent of many Germans with the present and their melancholy for the good old times than any special hankering for the totalitarian Nazism they had experienced.

The *unpolitische* attitude of many Germans toward the Third Reich was demonstrated by their attitude toward anti-Nazis of the past—those Germans who actively and responsibly resisted the Third Reich, tried to overthrow it, and failed. Of the organized and spontaneous acts of German resistance against the Nazi tyrants, the plot which became famous as "July 20, 1944" stands out as the greatest. Frustrated by the Nazi police, about 7,000 German participants in this conspiracy for freedom were arrested, and more than 4,980 shot, hanged, or tortured to death. Among the conspirators who wanted to substitute a constitutional "decent" government for the Nazi dictatorship, after killing the dictator as *sine qua non,* were army officers, trade union officials, high civil servants, lawyers, priests, businessmen and professors, former Nazis and old-time anti-Nazis, conservatives, liberals, Socialists, Catholics, Protestants, agnostics. The deadly experience of dictatorship transformed these Germans from *unpolitische* or politically naïve experts obedient to the state into responsible citizens, willing to pay with their lives for their past mistakes, illusions, or omissions. They felt duty-bound to revolt against the Nazis and to save the religious, social, patriotic values in which they deeply believed.

But the men of July 20 failed to become heroes in the eyes of their own people, even after the fall of Nazism. Of the posthumous writings of the dead conspirators—some being works of true greatness—of the memoirs of surviving conspirators, of the recollections of friends and relatives of the murdered men which were published after 1945, of all these proud classics of human and German bondage in its fight for freedom, none became a "best-seller." The public paid them almost no attention. Ricarda Huch, a great German writer, died before she could write, as she planned, a history of "the figures of the German Resistance." No history of the conspiracy was written by historians inside Germany. (However, a drama fictionally using elements of the conspiracy, *The Devil's General* by Carl Zuckmayer, became Germany's most successful play, totaling 2,069 performances in the season of 1948–1949.) The names, life-stories, writings of such men as Count Klaus Schenk von Stauffenberg, Johannes Popitz, Reverend Alois Delp, S.J., Adam von Trott zu Solz, Wilhelm Leuschner, and other great Germans who perished for their country and their conscience, were unknown to most Germans eight years after the sacrifice of their lives. With the exception of a few cities that honored the memory of a native son, the avenues and squares of post-Hitler Germany were not named in honor of these heroes in the fight for freedom.

"It must be said that basically only few [soldiers] had to concern themselves inwardly with the problems of July 20. And the masses [of soldiers] were present at these events of July 20 merely as spectators," Major General Erich Dethleffsen, formerly in the General Staff and one of its most progressive younger members, wrote in 1951.[4] They remained "spectators," innocent "non-political" bystanders who avoided taking sides, though some belatedly turned into judges of the men whom they had been too "non-political" to join, and—exculpating perhaps their own consciences—half-heartedly censured them. In 1951 a public controversy raged openly, after being carried on for some time underground, on whether the men of July 20 who tried to save the

[4] Adelbert Weinstein, *Armee ohne Pathos,* Bonn, 1951.

honor of Germany were honorable men. Some Germans discovered that their former comrades in the army or bureaucracy who had plotted against Hitler were guilty of perjury: they had taken their oath to Führer and fatherland; whatever evil the Führer might have done, however pure their motives had been, they had no right to violate their oath to the state. Allegedly in the name of 200,000 former soldiers organized in the Association of German Soldiers *(Verband Deutscher Soldaten, VDS)* Colonel General Friessner, who in the Third Reich had directed the educational services of the Wehrmacht, declared in September, 1951, that he "rejected political murder in general, as a soldier and as a Christian. For if the supreme commander could be murdered behind its back, no army could ever fight."

It seems that many non-Nazi soldiers—representing the temper and opinion of "non-political" non-Nazi Germans at large—felt that, as was often to be heard, "no army, and no state, for that matter, could exist if everybody had the right to decide for himself whether he approved of what the *Obrigkeiten* did, and if he disapproved of it, disobeyed them." There was little sympathy for the rebels, because rebellion is taboo in the behavior code of a "non-political" German. In the fall of 1951 August Haussleiter, a director of the very Rightist "National Community" group *(Deutsche Gemeinschaft)* said: "Honor is due to the successful rebel, but the failing rebel ought to remain silent." The successful rebel, it might be added, becomes a government, a ruler, an *Obrigkeit*. While the men of July 20 were slandered as traitors by a minority of hard-core Nazis and glorified as heroes by a minority of free citizens, the majority uneasily ignored them.

Despite the declarations of Catholic and Protestant theologians that it was permissible according to natural and human law to kill a tyrant who forced his subjects to murder the innocent and who drove his people into death and destruction, and despite the scrupulously moral motivation of the plotters, most of whom had themselves faithfully served state and tyranny for a long time, many Germans did not deviate from their code according to which the individual must obey the rulers. German public opinion seemed more sympathetic to the German Jews who had been victimized by the Nazis—they had mostly been *unpolitische* Germans themselves, and had not rebelled against the state; they were merely innocent victims of the state. German public opinion also seemed more sympathetic to the claims of civil servants who were removed from office after the war because they had been Nazi Party members, and who claimed their right to full pension payments. These so-called *131ers* (from the paragraph of the law pertaining to their problem) were in 1951 adjudged entitled to full pensions; Nazis or not, they were first and foremost servants of the state, and as such their claims were above "politics."

If many non-political Germans kept toward defeated Nazism the same apathy and passive tolerance they had shown toward ruling Nazism, they were quite sincere when they denied the charge of their "responsibility," a word they confused with "guilt." As a matter of fact, the victors themselves, who wanted to introduce democracy to Germany, fell into this primordial and undemocratic trap of confusing the two things. By accusing the "non-political" Germans of a guilt of which they were innocent, rather than reminding them of their civic responsibilities of which they were ignorant, the victors provoked a German reaction to remain "non-political," for to change would indicate an admission of guilt. It took courage for Germans to accept the responsibility for the past without seeming to grovel before the foreign victors who had become the new *Obrigkeiten*. As one mistake often provokes another mistake in the opposite direction, the foolish, hypocritical, often evil charge of "collective guilt" leveled at the Germans by the victors after 1945 gave way in the early 1950's to a German claim to collective innocence, which was equally foolish, hypocritical, and often evil. The guilt and responsibility which many "non-political" Germans as well as Nazis bore in individually varying degrees was denied with a moral sloppiness that was of no help to them in overcoming the past and cleansing the air of their community.

If after the death of Nazism no serious autopsy of the German body politic was undertaken by the Germans, there were many reasons to explain, and to excuse, this failure; but it was also a symptom that the body politic of the new Germany had not yet recovered its health. "You must obliterate all parts of the past which are not useful to the future," Winston Churchill once wisely admonished his countrymen. But there are also parts of the past which it is dangerous for the future of a people to obliterate without first having discerned them and rejected them. The totalitarian disease was such a part of the German past. The obliteration of the facts, the causes and the consequences of past failure might prepare the grounds for a future similar failure.

Early in 1952, a representative cross section of West Germans was questioned: "If a new party similar to the Nazi party should try to come to power in the Federal Republic, what would be your attitude toward it?" Only 3 per cent of the total said they would welcome it and do everything possible to support it; on the other hand, 20 per cent of the total said they would do their utmost to prevent it. Thus, activist Nazis and anti-Nazis made up less than one third of the whole people, with the decided anti-Nazis outnumbering the decided Nazis by a ratio of almost 7 to 1. Together, however, they were but a small minority. Ten per cent said they would like to see a party similar to the Nazi Party try to come to power, but would not do anything for its struggle and success. The most numerous group, 30 per cent, replied they "would not like to see a new Nazi Party try to come to power again, but would not do anything to prevent it." The passive anti-Nazis outnumbered the passive pro-Nazis by a ratio of 3 to 1. Together, the passive group was more than twice as numerous as the active.

Actively or passively, 13 per cent were favorable to the Nazis; 50 per cent, unfavorable to the Nazis. In addition, 23 per cent answered: "I don't care, one way or the other." And 14 per cent had no opinion.

Whether or not some people in 1952 were still hiding their

true inclination toward Nazism and thus concealed somewhat the real number of the pro-Nazi activists (although these figures closely correspond to the figures the Nazis polled in secret general popular elections, as shall be shown), a bloc of passive people came out as the majority. Besides the small hard core of Nazis, and the larger hard core of anti-Nazis, there were the 77 per cent who would not do anything about the issue one way or the other. That the passive "non-political" men who looked at the Nazis with dislike outnumbered, at a ratio of 3 to 1, those who looked at them with favor was characteristic of the nature of the non-political man as well as of the climate of German postwar opinion. The majority of Germans neither opposed nor supported Nazism actively, and would not do so now, although most do not want Nazism to return.

The figures of distribution of German attitudes toward a future Nazism, as shown in the poll of 1952, tallied closely with the figures of distribution of German behavior in the past Third Reich.

When, immediately after the war, the American Military Government, after carefully checking the self-admitted records of individual Germans in the Nazi years, classified them according to whether they could be given public office and other positions of public influence, it was found that 18 per cent of the sample (out of more than a million cases) had been genuine Nazis, 1 per cent, active and tested anti-Nazis, and 31 per cent, vaguely wavering toward Nazism or anti-Nazism; but the majority had been simply non-Nazis—50 per cent "showed no evidence of Nazi activity." They were the distinct "non-political" ones. Whether these figures were quite correct or not, they tended to indicate how the majority of Germans under the Nazis had acted. The group of Germans who in 1952, seven years later, either didn't care or wouldn't do anything for or against a Nazi revival that most of them didn't want, was still more or less of the same number. Whether the group somewhat increased or decreased these last seven years—and there would be reasons for both—did not

matter as much as the fact that the great passive human foundation on which alone a Nazi dictatorship could be erected had kept
the strength that came from its weakness. Some former non-
Nazis, who learned about the "bad sides" of Nazism only after
the war, had become anti-Nazis; some former anti-Nazis, who
were deeply disappointed by conditions and events after the overthrow of the Third Reich, which they had desired, who felt slighted by the accusations of the "collective guilt" and the ensuing
policies of the postwar years, who grew weary under strain and
stress, definitely became "non-Nazis"; they still opposed in their
hearts the ideas and realities of the Nazis, but were no longer
willing actively to fight them again.

Whether the large middle group of passive non-Nazis decreased or increased somewhat, they still formed the largest group
of German society. They will no doubt remain passive; they will
tolerate democracy as well as Nazism or any other form of totalitarian government. Since the totalitarian order threatens their
sacred privacy, the *unpolitische* majority does not view with favor
the return of Nazism. Yet while they dislike totalitarianism, they
are, nevertheless, the ground on which the totalitarian minority
can grow and strive and rule. The Communists in Russia as well
as the Nazis in Germany came to power and ruled on the foundation of a non-political majority.

Yet the non-political majority is merely one of the many fac-
tors requisite to a totalitarian revival, and only in passive ways
can it contribute to such a revival. It does not kindle or promote
it. For totalitarianism to revive and to come to power, there is
necessary a totalitarian party led by shrewd professional revolutionaries, and by fanatics obsessed by the lust for power. It must
have an equally fanatical activist rank-and-file following. And it
must have symbols, slogans, battle cries, and promises which appeal to some extent at least to the passive people. To make this
possible, the domestic and foreign relations of the existing non-
totalitarian order must seem so devoid of hope as to make many
people agree with the totalitarian catch-phrase that "everything

must change," and that the majority cannot lose much, but win a great deal by such a change—as many Germans felt in 1933 with a background of three years of economic crisis and mass unemployment. Finally, the active anti-totalitarian forces must be considerably weaker than the active totalitarian forces—as was the case in Germany in 1933 when the continuous onslaught of the combined Nazi and Communist forces finally had disheartened and emasculated the conservative, liberal, and Socialist anti-totalitarians.

The year 1953, then, was quite different from the year 1933.

IV

Old Nazis and Neo-Nazis

FRITZ ROESLER was a simple schoolteacher in his native Saxony in 1930 when he joined the Nazi Party. The Nazis came to power three years later. As an "Old Fighter" he quit his teaching job to work in Dr. Paul Joseph Goebbels' Propaganda Ministry, and was soon promoted to the post of a deputy gauleiter. When Roesler was killed in the war, a comrade of his who had been with him in his last hours brought the news to his widow, soon thereafter married her himself, and adopted his two children.

His name was Franz Richter, Ph.D., born of German parents in Smyrna (Ifmir), Asia Minor, a city, incidentally, without birth records, since a great fire had destroyed them in 1920. Like his dead comrade, Dr. Richter had taught school in the Sudeten part of Czechoslovakia before the war. After the war, when the Czechs expelled the German-speaking people of the Sudeten regions, he fled to West Germany. A self-appointed spokesman for his fellow-expellees, he was elected to the Bundestag. He presented himself as a non-Nazi, but was considered one of the four representatives of the neo-Nazi movement in the West German parliament.

When I asked him what he thought of the Third Reich, he stroked his thin mustache nervously.

"I never gave much thought to it at all," he said sarcastically, "I am more concerned with the criminals who today rule Washington, London, Bonn. All the blood which has been spilled in the world since 1939 is on the heads of your Presidents, and of Mr. Churchill, and of the Pope at Rome. Ask me what I think of them rather than of the so-called Third Reich."

What did he think of the Soviets? "They are realists," he said, "and they do not think they are godlike, as you Americans think you are. They are true National Socialists."

A short while after our talk—in March, 1952—Dr. Franz Richter was arrested. It was discovered that he himself was Fritz Roesler, whose death he had faked to escape internment. He had built for himself the new identity in order to be able to continue his old life and to agitate for his old ideas.

A man in his early fifties, Roesler-Richter was a typical higher Nazi Party official—not so high and outstanding as to have the Allies hunt him down after the war, yet too deeply imbued with the Nazi spirit to forego it after the collapse. A large number of people with a past like his were interned by the Allies in 1945, and only several years later did some of them cautiously emerge again and more or less openly join each other.

Beginning in 1950, various Nazi veteran groups openly paraded their past. Among them was the former Parachutists' Auxiliary League led by ex-General Ramcke, who stubbornly declared the solidarity of his group with the "brave comrades from the SD," the Nazi secret police army outfits. The leader of the former members of Hitler's Body Guard division, ex-SS Obersturmbann-Führer Bechel, demanded "unqualified identification with the idea of the 'Führer Adolf Hitler.'" The Free Corps Germany, led by two ex-subaltern officers of the SS, asked for "remilitarization under officers who still feel bound by their oath to the Führer." But these groups of diehard Nazi veterans appealed only to a small minority of Germany's former soldiers. The majority kept as clear of the Nazi group after the war as, during the war, they had avoided, with a mixture of fear and contempt, the Nazi military outfits. A few other old and still convinced Nazis tried to infiltrate the existing political parties, since they could not obtain an Allied license to have their own party. They succeeded in gaining some influence—though never a dominating one—in smaller parties, especially the BHE—the League of the Expellees and Outlawed, appealing equally to refugees and to ex-Nazis.

But in 1949, with Allied restrictions gradually being lifted, a new party was founded, which by 1951 emerged with a new Nazi claim for nationwide influence and power. This party, the Socialist Reich Party (*Sozialistische Reichpartei*, SRP), was an offspring of the German Right Party (*Deutsche Rechtspartei*, DRP), a splinter group officially organized only in 1946 by a combination of several insignificant right-wing rural groups, yet with a history dating back to the nineteenth century. The DRP had polled 1.5 per cent of the total vote of West Germany at the first Federal elections in 1949. Its successor, the SRP, participated in three more limited elections between its foundation in 1949 and its dissolution in 1952. In May, 1951, when the SRP ran candidates for the first time in the predominantly Protestant, predominantly rural, refugee-flooded state of Lower Saxony, it won 11 per cent of the total vote. In October, 1951, it ran again, in Bremen, the smallest German state, also a mainly Protestant area but with a greater proportion of industrial workers, and won only 7 per cent of the total vote. In March, 1952, there were elections in the newly-founded Southwest State, predominantly Catholic and rural; the neo-Nazi party received 2.5 per cent of the votes cast.

Many foreign observers were alarmed by the victory of the neo-Nazis in Lower Saxony. Pamphlets and a flood of editorials in America warned against the "recent growth of neo-Nazism" in West Germany. The next two election returns, with their decreasing neo-Nazi vote, were almost ignored, and the neo-Nazi defeat in Bremen and the Southwest State was not even reported by many American newspapers that had been so shocked by the Lower Saxony neo-Nazi victory.

What was more significant, however, than the small number of active party members, was their manifest lack of aggressiveness and self-assertion, especially when contrasted with the last years of the Weimar Republic, when the Nazis fought their cold civil war so fanatically that, though a minority, they dominated a large and ever-increasing section of the German population. At the time, they had succeeded in making themselves seen, heard, talked-about, and feared always and everywhere. Between 1930 and 1933, continuous incidents instigated by ubiquitous Nazis became a routine matter in Germany, acquainting the people at large with the Nazi claim to power, as well as with the weakness of the government which appeared unable to hold down the Nazis. Between 1950 and 1953, however, West Germany witnessed practically no such public disturbances instigated by Nazis. Neither did the neo-Nazis produce the "werewolves" who would put up a terroristic underground resistance against the occupation powers, as Goebbels in his last days had hoped. Evidently, the neo-Nazi movement was too weak and insecure to be able to engage in that propaganda by action without which no totalitarian movement can make headway.

Only in some parts of West Germany were the neo-Nazis able to gain a noteworthy foothold at all—mainly in Lower Saxony, Schleswig-Holstein, and Franconian Bavaria. In the more predominantly Catholic parts of Bavaria, in the Rhineland and the industrial Ruhr district, in Württemberg and Baden, they did not succeed in winning a following. Those who followed it were usually middle-aged people, men and women who had been convinced Nazis and had not changed their convictions. The absence from neo-Nazi gatherings of young and very young people presented a striking contrast to the old Nazi assemblies. Also missing from the new Nazi rank and file were the disgruntled and bitter intellectuals who had played such a decisive part in the old Nazi Party.

The will to resist a postwar rebirth of Nazism was considerably stronger, more widespread, and more alert among the anti-Nazis than the vigor of the neo-Nazis. Although active anti-Nazis were only a minority like the active neo-Nazis, they were a more numer-

5

ous minority. The trade unions, business groups, universities, and particularly the Church, chastened by their past experiences with Nazism in power, were firmly opposed to any toleration of a new Nazi movement and its rise through terror and slander. The Federal Government, as well as the governments of such important states as Bavaria and North-Rhine-Westphalia, were prepared to outlaw all totalitarian parties, including the neo-Nazi and the Communist parties.

Even more significant to the failure of the neo-Nazi movement was the fact that, although founded on the "leader" principle, it was unable to produce the powerful, if not charismatic, leader who would have been essential to its success.

Widely though erroneously regarded as the boss of the SRP was Otto Ernst Remer, its leading figure, chief vote-getter, a symbol indeed of no more than the aims of the party, its frustrations and hopes. A colorless, stupid man with a sinister past, he was a genuine spokesman of genuine Nazis. His past was closely tied to the plot of July 20 when he happened to command the Berlin Guard Battalion. His superior, the Berlin commander, Lieutenant General Paul von Hase who participated in the plot, ordered Major Remer to occupy the Reich Chancellery and to arrest the SS officers. Although it was known that Remer was himself a Nazi, it was believed that he would blindly obey the orders of his superiors.

But Remer doubted the authenticity of these orders and discussed them with his lieutenants. The political commissar informed Goebbels, who ordered Remer to come to his office and connected him by phone with Hitler. Orders were bellowed over the wire from the supreme commander to the little major: "Shoot as many rebels as you like." Major Remer executed the order. As a reward Hitler promoted Remer to Major General commanding the so-called Führer Escort Brigade. This irregular promotion for "political" rather than military merits or seniority made Remer forever unpopular with the army officers. In the only major military engagement of his brigade in which he himself took part, he was badly defeated by American troops near Bastogne in the Battle of the Bulge.

After the war, when denazification banned him from other jobs, Remer made his living for a short while as a stonemason's helper. He entered politics in 1948. Though a dull speaker, he appealed to Nazis as a symbol of their past glory as well as of their more recent hardships. In his first speeches he apologized for his hangman's job of July 20, which, he said, he performed merely as a soldier's duty, but from about 1949, he boasted more and more that he saved German honor by purging the traitors and would do it again. In 1951, in a pamphlet, "July 20, 1944," he attacked the victims as "a disgraceful clique." Subsequently he was jailed for four months for insulting the Federal Government in an election speech. Released from jail, he received from the Brunswick Court a second sentence of three months for calling the plotters of July 20 "mainly traitors paid from abroad."

A relic from the past rather than a forward-looking political leader, Remer's position resembled very much that of General Erich Ludendorff at the beginning of the old Nazi movement after the First World War. Most foreign observers at that time saw in Ludendorff the leader of Nazism, and in Nazism itself a "neo-monarchical" party trying to restore the past with the Kaiser and the army, for whose glory and disgrace Ludendorff stood. The Nazi Party, they thought, would pick up where the old nationalists had left off. Hitler seemed to them only an agent and a "drummer"—used by the leaders, but never himself to be a leader of the new movement.

Similarly, after the Second World War, Remer represented merely the link of the "neo-Nazis" to the Nazi past, from which they have actually already moved away. The moving spirit and the actual Führer of these new trends in the SRP was its "first president" and spokesman in parliament, Fritz Dorls, a haggard man with drawn features and burning eyes that reveal his frustrated, fanatical intellect as well as his addiction to pervitin, a habit-forming drug like benzedrine, which he consumed publicly in great amounts. Born in 1911, he was forty-one years old in 1952, the same age as Hitler two years before his rise to power. An apostate from the Catholic faith, in which he was born and which (like Hitler) he hated, he took a doctorate in history during the time of the Third Reich and served Nazism as a faithful follower of minor rank, and as a sergeant in the army during the war. Under the influence of pervitin and alcohol he admitted at private gatherings that he had dodged the dangerous service in the Russian campaigns and done a great deal of black-marketing in Italy while there as an occupation soldier; publicly he boasted of his battle record as an officer. His wardrobe in 1952 consisted of numerous civilian suits carefully tailored to look like the dyed old officer's tunics which many poor ex-officers still were wearing. "Morals have nothing to do with politics," he boasted when I talked to him. "Good and evil are in God's realm; what I believe in is power, and three years from now, we shall be in power." "We," of course, was the SRP led by Dorls.

The program of the SRP on the domestic scene, as elaborated by Fritz Dorls, comprised careful selections from "the good sides of Nazism" as they appeared in the minds and memories of Germans homesick for old times. "We shall not abolish political parties, but they will be servants of the government as they were under King Frederick the Great of Prussia," Dorls explained to me. This Führer Prinzip carefully catered to monarchists as well as to ex-Nazis who had lost their faith in Hitler, and avoided any reminder of the "excesses" of the Nazi dictatorship. "There shall be no dictatorship, the state will enforce the supremacy of the commonweal over individual interests"—this ambiguous phrase, which had already been a stock-in-trade of the old Nazi propaganda in its struggle for power, was an appeal to all the frustrated and discontented. The SRP was for "folk socialism," the nondescript slogan invented by Otto Strasser (expelled from the Nazi Party in 1930 by Hitler, who called him a "parlor Bolshevik"); this meant little except an appeal to all those who suffered from free competition. The party should not persecute or discriminate against Jews, should not suppress dissenting newspapers, the Church and religion; in short, no "excesses," no "bad sides" in this new Nazism. To those who believed that "Nazism was a good idea badly carried out," the neo-Nazis offered the expurgated program of the good idea to be well carried out.

None of these slogans caught hold of the popular imagination, as similar slogans of the Nazis did before 1933. People in Germany had become wary of glittering generalities promising a grand change. The Frederician "Führer principle" as well as "folk socialism" were merely the red lamps by which the SRP hoped to attract the politically homeless and somewhat impotent former Nazis still mindful of their exciting past.

The original Nazis had in a similar vein appealed after the First World War to many militant monarchists homesick for their recently-destroyed past. That Nazism was actually an anti-monarchist movement was revealed to many followers only after Hitler finally came to power. Behind the cloak of pure monarchic restoration, Nazi totalitarianism in the 1920's developed slowly as a new political movement; similarly, behind the cloak of pure Nazi restoration, a new form of totalitarianism—unknown to many followers, yet systematically followed by the leaders—developed in the neo-Nazi movement after the Second World War.

This change was centered in foreign politics, which, as Hitler had proclaimed and as the SRP leaders repeated, must have "top priority over domestic politics." Hitler's Nazism hated the Bolsheviks and the Slavonic East as much as the democracies and the French-dominated West—both, in Nazi eyes, different extensions of world Jewry. In its new form, Nazism à la Dorls still hated the democracies of the American-dominated West and, in the first place, America itself, which, as the SRP speakers were quick to explain, wanted to subjugate the whole world, to enslave all free peoples, to exploit them for the profit of its ruling classes.

What was new in neo-Nazi thinking was that Soviet Russia appeared as a healthy, good country, where true National Socialism reigned. The Soviets did not want to conquer or rule anybody outside their sphere, the neo-Nazi propagandists protested.

"When Hitler and Stalin concluded their pact in 1939," Dorls said to me, "the two national socialisms of our time joined each other forever in the logical line of history; for both had basically the same ideals and the same goals. America was aware of the fact that this alliance meant death to its capitalist aspirations and its lust for power. Therefore, Wall Street dispatched its secret agents to Hitler and to Stalin, and these American devils actually succeeded in breaking up the pact and the friendship of the two great men, and in driving the two great systems against each other. Truman explained the background of this Wall Street maneuver when he said that Nazi Germany and Soviet Russia should destroy each other so America alone would be left after their struggle. That's the American technique—to divide, to let others bleed themselves to death, and then to rule. The breaking of the Nazi-Soviet Pact was the greatest catastrophe of the century. We must never let it happen again; Nazi Germany and Soviet Russia must stand together."

Despite the anti-Communist mood prevailing in West Germany, the SRP had little use for the Nazis' propagandistic "anti-Bolshevik" line, and in more or less veiled words, according to their audience, propagandized the need for Soviet-Nazi friendship in the common struggle against America and democracy. To achieve this aim, Dorls and his neo-Nazis pleaded for Germany to remain neutral in the global struggle. Despite their fervent public admiration for "the German soldier" and the values of Prussian militarism, they fought against the plan of a West German army, or of arming the West Germans in any form.

"If war comes, we must greet the Russians with open arms, and let them pass through our country," Dorls told me. "If we participated, the *Amis* and the Russians would throw their atom bombs on our poor country and destroy us forever. A new National Socialist Germany leading Western Europe will, as a third force between East and West, ally herself with the Soviet bloc, which it recognizes as Eastern National Socialism. As its ally rather than its satellite, new Nazi Germany would share the world with Soviet Russia."

It may be perhaps that behind this grandiose vista lurked a secret hope that Germany might outsmart her Soviet allies in the end. At any rate, their immediate goal was a renewed Hitler-Stalin Pact which would not be broken up by Wall Street agents and which would, as a matter of fact, break up "Wall Street rule"—that is, America's power and the forces of anti-totalitarianism.

That more than merely ideological ties bound the neo-Nazis to the Soviets seemed at least likely. When I asked Dorls about it in the bar where I met him, he said: "The Russians put their money on the right horse while the Americans don't. In China the Americans supported Chiang Kai-shek with all their money while the Russians with little money, but with the right political instinct, supported the winning side and thus won the race. In Germany, it's the same. The Americans support the democrats, and don't see that they are again putting their money on the wrong horse. The Russians know better—they know that I am the man who shall be able to rally the Germans." When I asked him how much money the Russians had put on him, and how it was paid, Dorls was either too drunk or not yet drunk enough, to answer. He just smiled slyly.

Former party members who had broken with the SRP produced some evidence to show that the neo-Nazis in West Germany were receiving financial support from the Soviets in the East. Eberhardt Stern, the former chairman of the Berlin branch of the SRP, stated under oath that the third chairman of the party, Count Westarp, had received the sum of 32,000 marks (almost $8,000) from the Communist party office in East Berlin. Another underling of the SRP, Heinrich Keseberg, a man with a long criminal record, who split from the SRP to found a new "SRP German Group" in Rhineland-Westphalia in 1951, published the copy of a telegram in which Dorls asked the Polish Soviet agent in Lodz, Colonel Stanislav Dombrovski, for further support.

While conclusive evidence is rarely available in secret financial transactions of that kind, the record proved that the neo-Nazis had teamed up in their struggle with their Eastern fellow-totalitarians. After the SRP was outlawed in West Berlin, it was substituted by, or disguised in, almost thirty new small, semi-independent groups. By the end of 1951, five of these groups were "neutral" between East and West, as hostile to Western Europe and America and democracy as to Russia and Communism, while more than twenty openly professed their leanings toward, and sympathies with, the East.

Most of the minor neo-Nazi groups formed of unregenerate old Nazis followed the new, pro-Communist line. In commemoration of the first Nazi putsch, on November 9, 1951, the president of the small Racist Liberty Party *(Voelkische Freiheitspartei)*, Alfred Formann, a former official Nazi party speaker of the Propaganda Ministry, proclaiming that "we old Nazis must remember our mission," explained that this mission was an alliance with Soviet Russia—the great country of freedom and National Socialism. At the end of the meeting, to which only former Nazi officials were admitted, the participants sang the *Horst Wessel Lied,* the old Nazi party hymn, and a song, "Do you see the dawn in the East?"

At a meeting of the Racist Action Group *(Voelkische Aktionsgruppe)* in 1951 to celebrate the same occasion, the president and speaker, Erhard Scholten, stated to the assembly of Hitler Youth leaders: "Our aim is a new and unified Reich allied with Russia, that traditional partner of the German people." The assembly applauded.

In the Malmö Manifesto (issued jointly with other neo-Nazi groups of Europe) the SRP proclaimed "the aim of convincing hesitant pro-Communist elements to align themselves with the national socialist movement," which was an invitation to the fellow-traveling fringe to find a home in its ranks.

In the fall of 1952, the Federal Court of West Germany indicted the SRP as a subversive organization and forbade it to engage in public activities. The party, in anticipation of this ruling and in preparation of its underground existence, had dissolved itself voluntarily—with the strange explanation that its membership lists had fallen into Communist hands, apparently a move to cover its future tracks. Count Westarp publicly divorced himself from the SRP leader Fritz Dorls, whom he charged with close and dishonorable ties to Communist authorities, and with preparations to move the secret headquarters of the SRP after its dissolution to Communist East Germany. Although the truth of these charges was never effectively denied by the SRP leaders, they expelled Count Westarp from their party.

After the dissolution of the SRP, a number of small camouflaged successor organizations tried actually to continue the neo-Nazi tradition in some parts of West Germany, but Federal, state, and local authorities quickly uncovered and cracked down on them. In Lower Saxony, whose rural parts were the main bastion of neo-Nazism (although the elections showed that it remained a small minority even in this bastion), sixty-one illegal successor organizations of the SRP appeared, named candidates for local elections, but were barred from the ballots and their headquarters raided by the police. According to Richard Borowski, Social Democratic Minister of the Interior of the state of Lower Saxony, documents were seized which proved that the leaders of these groups were in contact with the Communist Party.

After the dissolution of the SRP, the Communists offered the functionaries of the neo-Nazi party corresponding posts in their own party provided they would first voluntarily undergo a three-months' training course in Soviet Russia. Many accepted.

"Communism and Bolshevism have effectively emerged as the most intransigent, anti-Roman, anti-European fanaticism. The moment several hundred millions of Russian fanatics are joined by eighty million German fanatics, the old order will fall apart like a house of cards built by childish hands. The East will give birth to a mighty Germanic-Slavic world empire. But this only with the help of Prussian discipline, Prussian self-sacrifice, Prussian order, Prussian combativeness. . . ." This was written more

than twenty years ago, in a book called *Decision;*[1] its author was
Ernst Niekisch, a former German Social Democrat who became
one of the leaders of "intellectual fascism," which, to stress its
difference from National Socialism in its position towards the
East, he called "National Bolshevism." Jailed by Hitler against
whom he conspired, he was liberated after the war, and became a
leading Communist German spokesman, professor of history at
East Berlin's Communist University, and one of the party's foremost traveling propagandists in West Germany. In another book,
Ernst Niekisch had written:[2] "Germany's decision in behalf of
Russia is a decision in behalf of Asia; it places its hope in Asia's
revenge against imperialist Europe. . . . Outside of national Bolshevism, there are only two paths: either Asia or Africa—either
Tartar Russia or Negroid France. National Bolshevism would
give Germany the leadership of Europe, but to arrive at this goal,
Germany must necessarily travel long distances on the side of
Russia."

In December, 1949, Ernst Niekisch (in the paper of the
German Communist Party's "mass auxiliary," the Society for German-Soviet Friendship, a semi-official organization of East Germany) discussed "Revolutionary Realism" and found Stalin to
be its greatest representative, since he never in his past had allowed himself to be trapped by "illusions" or "sentiments," or
to be led astray by the pathos of "great words or ideals." Exactly
this absence of "illusions" and "sentiments," this freedom from
"great words and ideals," was, after 1950, again and again proclaimed by the führers of neo-Nazism as their political line of
action. According to them, Hitler blundered only because he was
sometimes led astray by such "great words and ideals"; Stalin,
on the other hand, with his realism, succeeded in "carrying out
well the great idea" of National Socialist totalitarianism.

If Niekisch's premature neo-Nazism—outlawed by the Third
Reich—was becoming the new doctrine and world-view of the
new Nazis, the Communists had made premature attempts on

[1] Ernst Niekisch, *Entscheidung,* Berlin, 1930.
[2] Ernst Niekisch, *Gedanken über deutsche Politik,* Dresden, 1929.

their side to ally themselves with, and to use, the Nazis in their fight against the West, and to reach through them those Germans over whom they could not otherwise gain control.

As far back as 1922 and 1923, the German Communist Party, egged on by the Kremlin, had begun its open overtures to the German Nazis. *Die Rote Fahne,* the Communist daily newspaper of Berlin, invited Nazi leaders to write in its columns. Radek, then a leading Russian Bolshevik, celebrated the memory of Albert Leo Schlageter, a bomb-throwing terrorist and Nazi hero who had been sentenced to death by a French Military Occupation Court: "Against whom do the German people wish to fight: against the Entente capitalists, or against the Russian people? With whom do they wish to ally themselves: with the Russian workers and peasants in order to throw off the yoke of Entente capital or for the enslavement of the German and Russian peoples?" And he went on to plead with the Nazis that Germans had to fight for "national independence" in alliance with the Communists, in mutual hatred of the West. The German Communists took up this new party line, which they called the "Schlageter line": their press and assemblies resounded with offers to the Nazis. Under the leadership of Ruth Fischer, at that time a leader of German Communism, the Communists glorified the Nazi "heroes who are willing to lay down their lives for nation and freedom on the altar of the fatherland." A little later, Hitler made his putsch in Munich (to protect Germany from the "bolsheviks"), and the Communists made their putsch in Hamburg and Saxony (to protect Germany from the "fascists"). Both attempts being frustrated by the resistance of the German majority (which ranged from the Socialist trade unions to the officers of the German army), the first short-lived alliance of the two totalitarian parties was shattered.

In 1939, when the pact between Stalin and Hitler had been concluded, a leading German Communist, Walter Ulbricht, then living as an exile in Moscow, declared: "When the former Socialist and Catholic leaders direct their war propaganda against the German-Soviet Pact, the reason is that the British plans are being frustrated by the growing friendship between the German people and the Soviet people. Who works against the friendship of the German and the Soviet peoples is an enemy of the German people and has to be branded as a helper of Western imperialism." This was shortly before the pact was broken by Hitler—under the influence of Wall Street agents, as the new Nazis later explained.

It took the Second World War, the strange alliance between America and the Soviets, the defeat of the Nazis, to make the natural alliance between Soviets and Nazis become finally a reality.[3]

After 1945 the old Nazis found themselves in the unhappy role of the *ci-devants* of every revolution. Time had passed judgment on them. Either they would cling to their orthodox past doctrines, and isolate themselves from reality—even most people with a vague homesickness for the good old Nazi times did not seriously want their revival—or they would change the direction of their movement and adjust it to the new reality. This could mean only teaming up with the Soviets, whose program and methods were indeed not very dissimilar from their own and who represented the only thing Nazis really admire and strive after—power unbridled by law and justice, the struggle against the Judeo-Christian values of the West, and the will to subdue the world.

This covert alliance, sensed by many Germans even if it was not openly proclaimed, constituted the most powerful barrier on the neo-Nazis' road to new power. Nazi movements always fed on the threat of a strong domestic Communist movement, which in turn grew stronger by the "fascist" threat. In postwar Germany, the domestic Communist threat was missing; Communism represented merely a strong foreign threat. Since the neo-Nazis allied themselves with this threat, they had to remain (in addition to the other reasons already discussed) a negligible minority in German politics.

[3] Strangely, the American press, which gave so much attention to the neo-Nazi movement, failed to notice this newest and most revolutionary of its traits.

But even that small West German neo-Nazi movement, as little of a "threat" as it was, sufficed for world Communism to profit greatly from its existence. Much more than for creating occasional minor domestic disturbances in West Germany, it was used to keep foreign suspicion and antagonism against Germany alive, to slow up her acceptance in the Western defense community, and to weaken an effective anti-Soviet alliance. Therefore, the Soviets hoped for a future strengthening of the neo-Nazi movement, as Stalin explained at the nineteenth congress of his party in October, 1952. "Is it believing in miracles," he oratorically asked, that Germany (which, he meaningfully asserted, "was yesterday still a great imperialist power") "will not try again to rise to her feet, to break the American rule and strike out on the path of independent development?"

To separate Germany from the West had been the amazingly consistent line of the Soviet Union since its inception—it was so consistent because it was imposed by geopolitical rather than theoretical or ideological reasons. But the Soviets had failed when they tried to produce a Communist Germany as an ally against the West. They had also failed when they tried to ally themselves against the West first with the German Nazis, later with a Nazi Germany. To some degree, they had failed even in their postwar stratagem to turn Germany—by means of the Morgenthau Plan, whose basic tenets were never realized or soon abandoned—into a great slum, too weak and resentful ever to be able to ally herself with the West. For the third time now, they attempted their alliance with the German Nazis. For the first time, they themselves had to encourage the rebirth of German neo-Nazism as their ally in West Germany, as a bridgehead in the country which their own party could not win. The neo-Nazis became a secret German battalion of the Soviet power, a disguised fellow-traveling auxiliary of world Communism. As of 1953, the latest Soviet stratagem of separating the West from Germany by means of a neo-Nazi movement seemed destined to failure, like the neo-Nazi movement itself.

V

East Germany's Red Reich

"TODAY former members of the Nazi Party and former professional soldiers and officers occupy responsible positions in all branches of [East German] economic, political, and cultural life. They are men of good will fighting for a democratic united Germany," reported Vincenz Mueller on March 26, 1952, in the Berlin *Tägliche Rundschau,* the official daily newspaper of the Soviet Control Commission in the Soviet-occupied "German Democratic Republic." Vincenz Mueller had been a Lieutenant General commanding the 12th German Army, and was now a high-ranking functionary of East Germany's "National Front," as well as a full General in the Communist "People's Police."

These Nazis had been invited to engage in the public life of Communist East Germany at its very inception. "For the enlistment of Nazis in our National Front, there is no other condition than their sincere will to fight for the unity and independence of Germany," Wilhelm Pieck, the President of the East German satellite state, declared in 1949, when it was founded.

As a matter of fact, many unreformed former Nazis found in East Germany a refuge and an opportunity to continue without change at their old jobs. In 1950, a delegation of the former Hitler Youth leaders requested an interview with the President of the West German Republic, who proudly refused to see them: "I do not know," he said, "about what I could talk with these gentlemen." Three days later, they received an invitation to visit the leaders of the East German Republic. A special bus was sent for them, and after crossing the frontier to East Germany, they were given the treatment reserved for Very Important Persons. They were shown the sights by party functionaries; they were received by the highest ranking leaders of the state and the party, who told them exactly what, in 1923, the Communist Paul Froehlich had told the Nazi leader Count Ernst von Reventlow: "You are most welcome to be our fellow-marchers toward the common goal."

By 1952 the "fellow-marchers" in East Germany had merged into a single unit to which West Germany's Nazis gravitated. The middle and lower levels of the new East German state bureaucracy, especially the army, secret police, youth, propaganda and intelligence units, abounded with men from the higher, middle, and lower Nazi levels.

From the first occupation years the former Nazis had been encouraged to form their own political organization, the National Democratic Party, in which the thinking of Hitler was blended with the politics of Stalin. Scores of former Nazi officers, captured and indoctrinated by the Russians during the war, held important posts in this party.

From the summer of 1952, when the "People's Police" began to take the open and official shape of a full-fledged "People's Army," the Communist appeal to the Nazis became more intense. In June, 1952, all former Nazi officers were invited by an open letter to join the new military organization of East Germany. In October, 1952—when the Red Reich celebrated the third anniversary of its foundation—a law was enacted which restored full citizenship to former Nazis, thereby making it possible for them to hold government posts and serve in the army. (All this time, Communist propaganda throughout the world echoed the denunciation against the "renazification" of West Germany, where Nazis were said to be infiltrating defense and foreign politics, presumably on American orders.) To seal its final reconciliation and merger with the Nazis, the East German Government released 1,590 Nazis imprisoned for war crimes in their zone, and "considerably" reduced the sentences of the remaining 1,022 prisoners.

The Nazis in Communist army and government posts wrote chain letters to their former comrades in West Germany: "Why continue a hopeless struggle over there? Why emigrate to Egypt, Argentina, the Middle East as some of us have done? Come here; you'll find the old comrades, the old spirit, and the old ideals."

By 1950 the Soviet-occupied zone of East Germany was a complete totalitarian dictatorship. All power was vested in a few men, who were thereby in a position to control the bodies, minds, and souls of their fellow-citizens.

The establishment of this new totalitarian dictatorship over a people which, with the defeat of 1945, had been liberated from totalitarian dictatorship, was not achieved by any mere change-over of labels and leaders. It took a hard struggle of almost five years, with great sacrifices of human life, tremendous foreign pressure, and the continuous threat of a foreign army against the disarmed people to achieve the transition from the Third Reich to the Red Reich of East Germany.

After the debacle of the Führer state, the overwhelming majority of Germans were distrustful of totalitarian methods and dictatorial promises. Indeed, the foremost German Communist leaders, most of whom had been living as exiles in Moscow during the Hitler years and had returned as graduates of the Kremlin with Soviet passports in their pockets, took cognizance of this new, non-totalitarian temper when they published, after Hitler's fall in 1945, their first "program of action." It pledged the Communists to "absolutely unhampered development of free trade and free private initiative in an economy based on free private property; re-establishment of all democratic rights and civil liberties for all people; a truly democratic, free, and liberal education; absolute freedom of scientific research and of artistic creation. . . ." This program, drafted in Moscow and written by Anton Ackermann, a member of the Politbureau of the East German party, was signed by Wilhelm Pieck and Walter Ulbricht. Pieck was then chairman of the German Communist Party; in 1952 he became President of the German Democratic Republic, as the East German satellite was called. Walter Ulbricht was Secretary General of the Communist Party and became, in addition, the all-powerful deputy premier of the new state.

Designed to appeal to all Germans, the 1945 party platform stressed that "it would be erroneous to enforce the Soviet system upon Germany." Instead, the Communists advocated a "parliamentarian republic with democratic rights and civil liberties for all the people." What, then, was called by the party theoreticians "the party's German way" was actually the party's German trap carefully contrived by its leaders. In essence the trap consisted (as it had in Hitler's and Mussolini's first years of power as well as in various of the now completely sovietized East European countries) of a coalition government, a united front in power, in which the non-Communist parties—that is, the majority of the people—would be held in a firm grip until devoured.

The first elections under this coalition in what was then the Soviet zone of occupation in Germany were held in 1946. The Communists were sure to win. The democratic disguise would lead them over the steppingstone of the coalition to Soviet victory. Four political parties had been licensed in 1945 by the four Allied occupation authorities in their zones of occupation: the Social Democratic Party, identified with the moderate majority of the German working class; the Communist Party; the Christian Democratic Union, which believed in social justice and political democracy; and the economically liberal and socially upper-class-minded Free Democratic Party.

Since the Communists were aware that their party could not win a majority in such a four-sided race, they eliminated "democratically," by shrewd maneuvers and by use of force, the Social Democratic Party, the strongest vote-getter and with a long record of opposition to the Communists. The elimination was to take place by a voluntary merger of the two "workers" parties, whose "proletarian unity" had long been a hope of the German Left. While Soviet occupation officers and advisers requested such a merger, and backed up their request with threats, a number of East German Socialist leaders opposed what they called the "shot-gun marriage between the two parties," the gun being held by the Soviet army. Equally opposed to the merger were the Berlin and West German Socialists, who were outside the reach of the Soviet guns. Promulgated by their new party chairman, Kurt Schumacher, their opposition actually had the effect of persuading some East German Socialists to submit to the shot-gun marriage; they feared—in a tragic error, no doubt—that Schumacher's personal ambition to dictate the course of his party without outside interference, which the merger would have frustrated, was the primary motive of his opposition.

Leading the Socialists toward proletarian unity with the Communists was Otto Grotewohl. Unlike Schumacher, he was of proletarian background, and popular among the Socialist rank and file as "one of the boys." A man in his fifties and a typographer by trade, he had held office in the Socialist Party in the pre-Hitler administration of Prussia, and been a deputy of his party in the Reichstag for eight years. In the Third Reich he was involved in anti-Nazi activities, arrested several times, imprisoned for seven months, and had lived underground during the last year of the Nazi regime. After Hitler's fall, he was appointed editor in chief of the leading Social Democratic daily paper, the Berlin *Vorwaerts*. He succeeded in persuading his East German fellow-Socialists to join with the Communists in the new "Socialist Unity Party" (SED) of which he and the Communist leader Wilhelm Pieck were named co-presidents. With Socialists formally in the majority, all the key posts of the new party were given to the Communists.

With the strongest opposition party eliminated, numerous candidates of the two "bourgeois parties" stricken from the ticket by orders of the occupation power, various Communist-controlled "independent" organizations ("women's committees" and "peas-

ants' groups") on the ticket, and the Soviet army strongly supporting the SED and hindering the two other parties, victory
seemed certain. Yet it was not won. In two of the five states of the
zone—in Brandenburg and Sachsen-Anhalt—the Communists
polled no majority at all; in three others—Saxony, Thuringia,
and Mecklenburg—the majority was so small that it could not
govern.

One year later, in 1947, another election was held. After the
first failure, the Communists licensed two new political parties—
the National Democratic Party, which was to appeal to former
Nazis, and the Peasants' Party, both completely controlled by
Communists in key posts. In addition, five new "non-political"
organizations appeared on the ticket, representing the peasants,
the women, the trade unions, the youth, the co-operatives, and
the intellectuals of the Eastern zone. Their candidates were actually all Communists, but it was hoped that many voters would
vote for these fronts, split the non-Communist parties, and establish a final Communist majority. Of the non-Communist parties,
only candidates endorsed by the Communists were admitted;
others, whose independence from the Communists was branded
as "neo-fascist" by the occupation authorities, were arrested, and
votes cast for them declared "invalid," since they were cast to
advocate "a revival of fascism." The non-Communist press of
East Germany was throttled if it campaigned against the Communists, and the whole state machinery was brought to bear on the
side of the SED. Despite these elaborate precautions, the second
elections of 1947 ended with a Communist failure worse than
that of the previous year. In East Berlin, the SED polled less than
30 per cent of the total vote.

Two years later, in May, 1949, the Communists tried again.
This time, the "People's Congress," as the parliament was then
called, was to be elected by a new and completely sure-fire method. The Communists declared in advance a "unity ticket," on
which there appeared side by side the hand-picked candidates of
the various competing parties, and those of the "independent"

organizations. The government allotted the number of seats that the different parties would have in parliament, regardless of the vote. The voters had simply to fill in their "Yes" or "No." That this ingenious mixture of democratic trimmings and totalitarian substance would lead to a genuinely totalitarian majority of "Yes" votes, and thus to a final Communist victory, seemed certain. But only 48 per cent of the voters gave their "Yes"; the majority either said "No," or purposely invalidated their ticket.

In October, 1950, the bulky trap was finally sprung. The single-ticket method was used again for elections to the first "People's Parliament"—one year after the West German democratic parliament met for the first time. Although the Soviet Military Administration, which up to then had ruled the Soviet zone as a Military Government, was withdrawn, and "sovereignty" formally given back to the country, the Soviet army remained in East Germany in full strength, and its officers, donning civilian attire, "advised" the German Communists. The "National Front," as the mixture of Communists and Communist puppets allegedly representing the different political parties and "independent organizations" was called, did not have seriously to electioneer. It merely had to spread rumors that any "No" vote or abstention from voting would be detected and treated as treason. Everybody knew what this meant.

For the first time in five energetic years, the Communist scheme succeeded. Breaking the previous election records of Hitler, who in 1936 had received 98.81 per cent of the total vote, the Communists announced that this time 99.71 per cent of the East German electors had registered their "Yes." Oddly enough, the Communist-controlled National Democratic Party, composed of unreconstructed Nazis, was allotted 7.5 per cent of the unity vote, while the Communist-controlled Association of the Victims of Nazism received a mere 3.79 per cent.

Notwithstanding the comfortable notion widespread in the West that a vote under such conditions was "just a farce that cannot deceive anybody," and that it merely expressed a hypocritical concession made by totalitarian vice to democratic virtue, these rigged elections had a serious and important function in the totalitarian dictatorship, and their "success" proved to be a genuine victory. It was to test how well the dictatorship was organized; its result served as proof that it worked to perfection. The elections of October, 1950, demonstrated that the Communist dictators, after five years of rule and after five years of resistance from their subjects, had attained their goal of Communist government. Open protest was now suppressed; the full submission of the people was palpably established, whatever their secret thoughts. This was the triumph of the totalitarian dictators.

The new dictatorship over the people of East Germany was placed in the hands of men whose life-stories lacked the exciting colors and the perverted political greatness of a Hitler or a Lenin, a Mussolini or a Stalin, a Mao or a Tito. In contrast to these dictators of our time, whose rise to power was of their own making, the dictators of East Germany were merely chosen and made for their job by the Kremlin. Their performance was only to follow the twists and turns of Moscow's party line and to obey it with unquestioning vigor. Their life-stories were the Comintern's shortened shadow in German history.

As deputy minister president of the German Democratic Republic and secretary general of the Socialist Unity Party (SED), Walter Ulbricht was in fact the most powerful man of the East German dictatorship, which in turn depended on the dictates of Moscow. Nobody recalled ever seeing him smile since he emerged in 1923—at the age of thirty—from the Communist rank and file as a local party organizer in his native Saxony. At the time, himself a worker, he helped lead an armed revolt in his industrial homeland. Under orders of a colonel in the Red Army, he gave orders to the Communist intellectuals, workers, and Nazi officers organized in a "committee of uprising" against the Weimar Republic. The revolt was defeated, and Ulbricht at once denounced his German party superiors in Moscow for their guilt in the failure. Moscow removed them from office, and gave Ulbricht the task of "bolshevizing the German party," that is, turning it into a more obedient tool of the Moscow masters, building up a more efficient secret underground machine, and subordinating the German supreme party leadership, of which he had become a member, to the Soviet secret police. From 1923 to 1933, he worked diligently at this job; only a few close students of the Communist Party then knew as much as his name. In 1933, when Hitler came to power, Ulbricht emigrated to Moscow. As the leading functionary at the German desk of the Comintern, he was sent to the Spanish Civil War as a political commissar. Left-wingers of Socialist, Trotskyist, or anarchist convictions who had volunteered to fight without accepting the Communist party line were arrested on his orders, tortured, shot, or burned to death. When a Communist physician serving in the International Brigade reproached him for these cruelties, Ulbricht replied coolly: "What interests me is only the elimination of potential disturbances; what happens to these people in the process of elimination doesn't concern me."

After Spain he returned to Moscow. In 1943, he set up the two committees in which captured German officers, many of them Nazi party members, were persuaded, bribed, and blackmailed to join the Communist ranks, and to be prepared to take over a Germany liberated from Hitler in the service of Stalin. He returned to Germany in a Russian army plane with the first Soviet troops and took over the leadership of the Communist Party in Germany, interrupted only by visits to Moscow. With his goatee and his cold, clever eyes, he managed to look like a blurred carbon copy of Lenin himself. Only his Saxonian accent—which sounds quite hilarious to German ears—betrayed his origin.

Above the unpopular, dreaded Ulbricht in the official hierarchy of the Republic, yet actually little more than a figure head, was the President of the Republic, Wilhelm Pieck, a German "Old Bolshevik." In 1951 the celebration of his seventy-fifth birthday was declared an official East German holiday. A revolutionary since his early youth, he was one of the founders and first functionaries of the German Communist Party. Along with its leaders, Karl Liebknecht and Rosa Luxemburg, he was arrested by counter-revolutionary troops during the party's first attempt to seize power in 1919. He saved his life only by divulging to his captors all the party and personal secrets they demanded of him. His co-leaders were shot; he was released. After that, he managed always to side with the winners in the countless party intrigues. From 1924 on, he received secret funds from the Soviet Embassy to be channeled to the German party. After his return from Moscow to Germany in 1945, as a fat, elderly gentleman, he was regarded in the popular mind as a sort of Communist successor to Hermann Göring. His love of luxury, his castles donated by the grateful people of Germany (after being taken from their owners), and his love-life with a quick succession of young secretaries were a never-ending source of under-the-counter jokes, which in a totalitarian state serve as a substitute for active protest.

The other holders of high office in the Red Reich—Otto Grotewohl, the premier, or Otto Nuschke, the deputy premier, leaders of the former non-Communist parties in the Soviet zone before they surrendered, functioned merely as well-fed, well-publicized decorations symbolizing the idea of the coalition government before the streamlined totalitarian façade. They were destined to be removed in time like those other non-Communist experts in economics and international affairs who try to straddle the fence and end up as handy scapegoats for all the failures of the regime they helped to power.

Behind these officials were the almost faceless men wielding real power and hardly ever confronting the people. Among Communism's professional revolutionaries of German origin, well-trained in the international business of civil war, conspiracy, party rule, the most outstanding in the powerful under-hierarchy of the new state was Wilhelm Zaisser, chief of "internal security." He had previously served the Kremlin as confidential liaison man to King Ibn Saud, as the Comintern delegate to the Red Chinese high command, and, under the name of "General Gomez," as a commander of the International Brigade in the Spanish Civil War —with frequent sojourns in Moscow in between. As the personal representative of Moscow's MVD chief Beria, Zaisser was regarded in higher circles as the personal enemy and closest rival of Ulbricht himself. Almost unknown, yet holding the Red Reich's steering wheel in their hands, were old Communist professional revolutionaries, such as Franz Dahlen and Anton Ackermann, both active Comintern leaders in Moscow from 1933 to 1945, and younger men who got their training in Moscow and on the Communist side in the Chinese Civil War: Herman Axen, Robert Korb, Georg Hansen—the leading public relations men of East Germany (Gerhart Eisler was better known, but served actually as their subaltern front); Heinz Hoffman and Erwin Porada—the political commissars of the "People's Police," as the new army of remilitarized East Germany was called.

These unpublicized leaders were protected from any criticism or dissent of the people by the monopoly of power in their hands. This monopoly was sustained by enforced political collectivization of the whole people, by universal indoctrination, by control over every means of communication, and, most of all, by terror and physical violence. Gerhart Eisler called this system "a democracy of higher rank." (These were the exact words, incidentally, with which Goebbels, in 1933, explained away the Nazi order to the League of Nations.) It might more appropriately be called the democracy of the dungeon, for its jails, threatening every citizen with equality before the totalitarian law of fear and force, were the essential basis of the community.

In a totalitarian state everybody must have a political class status. In Communist Germany there were three main classes, so firmly established that only a successful revolution could change the structure. Between the upper, the middle, and the lower classes of this totalitarian society, there were sharper contrasts than ever existed in any capitalist society. What sociologists call "vertical mobility," the chance for members of one class easily to move into another, was highly developed. But whereas in a

capitalist society this works both ways, with people moving upwards as well as downwards, the totalitarian Communist society
knows only the downward movement—nobody banned to the
lowest class can move to the top, whereas many close to the top
are demoted to the bottom. As a matter of fact, everybody in the
Red Reich continually feared that he might be moved downward,
without advance notice and without a chance to save himself.

The lowest class was made up of those whom the dictatorship
had branded as "enemies of the people." A vastly heterogeneous
group, it included the so-called economic criminals, capitalists,
exploiters, saboteurs of reconstruction—that is, industrialists,
small tradesmen, or artisans, who had to be removed in the interest of the rulers' monopoly of economic ownership, production, and distribution. It included also the so-called neo-fascists,
militarists, American agents, spies in the service of Wall Street,
rowdies and hooligans, diversionists, Social Democrats, clerico-
reactionaries, servants of foreign intelligence, terrorists—in short,
those actively or passively critical of the regime for political reasons. However, the Red Reich abolished the term "political of-
fenders," since it recalled too strongly the Nazi past when the
Communists had campaigned for the glorification of "political
prisoners," and, also, since the existence of a political opposition
was to be denied. By a Circular Order (Docket 4300-II-1365,
1951) the Red Minister of Justice decreed: "He who attacks our
anti-fascist and democratic order, or disturbs the construction of
our peaceful economy, commits a punishable act and is punished
for his criminal deeds. The convicts of that kind are therefore no
political prisoners, but criminal felons. Therefore, it is *verboten*
from now on to use the name of 'political prisoners' for these
malefactors."

By the end of 1951, close to 160,000 "enemies of the people"
and 185,000 "war criminals" had been arrested and imprisoned
or killed in East Germany. This figure was at least as high as the
number of political prisoners of the peacetime period of the Third
Reich, when the victims were drawn from a population almost

three times as large as that of East Germany as now constituted. Of the new convict population, almost 10,000 were "economic criminals"; the others were held guilty of political opposition.

The new dictatorship took over from the Nazis the concentration camps of Buchenwald near Weimar, Sachsenhausen near Oranienburg, and Neu-Brandenburg. In addition, it established nine new concentration camps of its own. By 1950, according to the most conservative accounts, the number of prisoners sent to these camps exceeded 200,000. Of these, 96,000 died in the camps; 41,000 were deported to the slave-labor camps of the Soviet Union. The same year the government announced that all camps had been dissolved. What it did not reveal, but what was soon reliably established, was that only 37,500 prisoners, or somewhat more than 10 per cent, were released; of these, 71 per cent were very sick people; the others were Nazis needed to bolster the new Communist-controlled National Democratic Party. The majority of the prisoners were transferred to prisons which were not called concentration camps—to the old state prison of Waldheim, to new forced-labor camps in East Germany, or to Siberia.

In October, 1950, to celebrate its first anniversary, the East German Reich announced a second amnesty for its prisoners. Twenty thousand were to be released in a demonstration of political security and forgiveness. As it turned out, however, these were not political prisoners, but only common criminals.

In contrast to the old Nazi concentration camps, prisoners in the East German concentration camps were rarely tortured or worked to death. The method of exterminating them was what in scientific Soviet language is called dystrophy, the slow and certain wasting away of a prisoner's life through a carefully calculated food deficiency. In short, they were starved to death without cost to the regime, and without publicity.

The overwhelming majority of East Germans was well aware of the existence of these camps and mortally afraid to be some day inside one of them, or in a Soviet prison or labor camp. This fear seized even the leaders themselves, some of whom disappeared into the nameless mass.

Most people sent to such a camp or prison in Siberia or East Germany were convicted by the "People's Courts." Fifty-five per cent of the judges, and 71 per cent of the prosecutors on these courts in 1951 were workers or peasants whose sole legal qualification was a short training in special Communist schools as "People's Jurists." The other, more traditionally educated judges and prosecutors, were all SED party members in good standing, bound by the German Communist secret police, the SSD (State Security Service), and the Soviet Russian secret police, the MVD. It was standard practice for the "People's Courts" automatically to convict with the maximum punishment anybody who had been denounced or arrested by any of the secret police services. Hilde Benjamin, vice president of the Red Supreme Court, who personally conducted the prosecution in more important cases, explained in 1952 that the law alone could not determine what constituted a crime. It was enough for an act to be "dangerous to society; jurisdiction had to be founded on the fight for the party and the working class in the sense of Marxism-Leninism-Stalinism." In appreciation of her "special contribution to the new democratic science of the laws," the East Berlin University awarded her the title of *doctor honoris causa*. In her acceptance speech she declared that she was proud of never having felt pity for any of the 346 men and women, boys and girls whom she had condemned to terms of more than twenty years in prison or to death.

The prison population of the East German dictatorship consisted of a cross-section of the total population. Among them was the wife of Wilhelm Zaisser, the old Communist who became chief of the new Gestapo and wanted to marry his younger secretary. Or the wife of Nazi Major Bernard Bechler, who, returning a convinced Communist from his Russian PW camp, decided he was weary of her and set her off to a slave camp. These unfortunate women were simply victims of personal misfortune, but most prisoners were genuine political opponents. They included the eight hundred or more boys and girls under seventeen who were guilty of "grimacing" while listening to a speech in honor of Stalin, or of writing, printing, and distributing leaflets, or of secretly painting "F" (for Freedom) on city walls at night. They included, furthermore, the thousands of militant Christians, Social Democrats, liberals, fanatics of freedom who had survived the hard years in the Nazi concentration camps to be liberated and fight for the ideals for which they had been persecuted and then be sent back to the same concentration camps by the Red Reich. Here they met again many Jehovah's Witnesses, called in Germany "Serious Bible Students," who were rounded up wholesale by the East German government in 1950. The Communist denunciations of this strange sect repeated verbatim those made against it already under Hitler. By the end of 1951, there were 774 Jehovah's Witnesses in East German prisons; 13 were convicted to life sentences; 454 to a total of 3,180 years of hard labor; the rest disappeared and were presumably dead.

Among the other prisoners in the Red Reich were those who had, for one short moment of their lives, inadvertently perhaps or in an upsurge of human dignity, behaved like free men, such as the fisherman on the island of Ruegen, aged 68, who, before a speech by Pieck was to be broadcast in the local inn, said ("with a vicious smirk," as the prosecutor stated and as the judgment confirmed), that he "preferred to sleep at home"—two years for disturbing the peace; the Leipzig worker who read a West Berlin newspaper somebody had left in a trolley car, and gave it to a comrade on the job—"four years for sabotage work at American orders"; the party member of old standing who went to a saloon one night, got drunk, and "called the leaders of the state obscene names"—one year in prison. In this case the innkeeper, the waiter, and five other guests, who had (as a secret policeman on the spot reported) grinned rather than called the police, were each sentenced to one year. Another drunk was overheard saying at a bar: "You know what Socialism is? Herr Pieck's belly that gets fatter every day." He was sentenced to six years at hard labor—for sabotage work in the interest and on orders of the enemy. There were many thousands of "cases" of that kind; almost every day, new ones were reported in the East German press. Many of them were heroes.

Other members in the class of "outcasts"—3 to 4 per cent of the East German population—included workers in the labor force of the Wismuth-A.G., the Soviet combine, which mined uranium first in Aue, and, after its mines were robbed of their precious atomic raw material, near Saalfeld in Thuringia. In addition to an army of "free" workers, these forced laborers had to work under the bayonets of 11,000 Soviet MVD troops twelve to fifteen hours every day.

About 90 per cent of the people of East Germany were neither enemies of the state (though a false step might make them so) nor members of the state party. They were organized in one or more of the so-called "mass organizations," the Communist-controlled, yet allegedly independent "progressive groups": the League of German-Soviet Friendship, the German-Polish Society, the Cultural League for Germany's Democratic Reconstruction, the trade unions, the consumer's co-operatives, the youth and the women's organizations, the Partisans of Peace, the Association of the Victims of Fascism, and the SED's satellite parties—the ex-Nazis' National Democratic Party and the German Peasants' Party. A host of other organizations, such as the German National Committee for the Defense of Paul Robeson, Howard Fast, and other "Victims of American Fascism," and the National Association of Freethinkers and Atheists, was available to people of special tastes. Not to belong to any of these organizations made a citizen of East Germany suspect.

That almost every East German was pressed to enlist in one or more of these groups had a double advantage for the rulers. The totalitarian dictatorship must control all its citizens all the time. As members of auxiliary organizations, they could be continually watched, investigated, tested. And some who had to join such organizations, even under duress and with mental reservations, came to experience a sense of complicity with the rulers until they inwardly submitted to them. Forced to ally themselves with the devil, or at least to pretend to have joined the devil's army, they sometimes convinced themselves that this devil—seen from close by—wasn't actually so bad. Others more cynically hoped that his rule was going to last so that they themselves would profit from, rather than be punished for, their alliance with him. They well remembered the injustice done to many by the denazification programs, when technical membership in Nazi organizations, for whatever reason and however it may have been outweighed by anti-Nazi acts, carried automatic condemnation. After they became outwardly at least followers of Communism, though it was only by force and fear, they felt that from now on they must stand or fall with their Communist rulers.

For some East Germans, especially the young, an inner conflict and sometimes a tragedy developed from their membership and participation in the rulers' front groups, which they had joined only to cover up their convictions and activities directed against the rulers. The German proverb saying "if you give the devil your little finger he wants the whole hand" proved often to be true for the *"illegalen,"* the underground fighters who had to camouflage as supporters of their enemies. "I joined the Free German Youth because that gave me a better chance to do conspiratorial work," an eighteen-year-old student told me, "yet after a year of membership I was asking myself every night whom I was actually betraying now—my convictions, while I marched in my blue shirt, or my comrades in their blue shirts, while I secretly pasted leaflets on the walls. I came so close to a crack-up that I had to give up underground work—one can't carry two heavy loads on both shoulders all the time." However, others of a less highstrung nature, who were camouflaging their opposition by active membership in a mass organization, felt no scruples about their dual role. They considered it rather as a necessary training in toughness.

Totalitarian dictatorship, it seems, tends to stimulate even, and especially, among the best men exactly those qualities which are alien to the morality of a sane and decent society. The conflict between non-totalitarian convictions and totalitarian actions weighed heavy on many East Germans, whether or not they were active in secret anti-totalitarian work. At the great Berlin convention of Protestant laymen in 1951, an East German boy of seventeen rose spontaneously from his seat to say: "What is so unbearable is that we have to lie all the time—I can't go on lying forever."

Those who excelled in the mass organizations because of their "enthusiasm and devotion," were soon promoted to the group of candidates for party membership. They had shown themselves to be loyal and trustworthy, but must undergo further "political education" and a more thorough-going personal observation before final admission to the upper class. This "candidacy" took one year for workers, two years for others. Those already in the upper class, who for some reason had been stricken from membership, might be paroled into this transitory stage to regain perhaps in time their lost standing.

The select 6 per cent of the East Germans admitted to the Communist SED, stood at the top of the East German Red Reich's society of three classes. While there was almost no hope for the members of the lowest class (the "outcasts") to rise to this height, there was constant danger that the members of this upper class might fall from it. Subjected to continuous tests and purges, perpetually fearful that somebody might denounce them, that they might make one false step, that they might clash with a superior or a jealous rival, they rarely enjoyed their aristocratic standing.

In April, 1952, the SED announced that in the previous eighteen months 150,696 were ousted "because they either did not belong to our ranks or were found guilty of inimical and disintegrating activities." Actually, this was only a fraction of the party members who were dropped from its ranks. Altogether, more than one out of three party members was forced, from 1949 to 1952, to leave the party, whose membership fell from 1,774,000 in January, 1949, to only 1,100,000 at the beginning of 1952. The great purge, decided upon in 1950, officially termed "the investigation and exchange of party membership cards," cleared the ranks of the party. Every member had to undergo the ordeal, after supplying the investigators with a handwritten autobiography, a completed questionnaire with more than ninety questions about his past, and three passport photos. In the following months, his case was investigated, private and official spies dug into his past and his present, and confidential information was gathered from the political agents, the party captains of his house, street, and block, on his job, and in the mass organizations to which he belonged. In addition, a ledger was kept for every party member, in which all positive and negative information about him disclosed the trend of his political development. This was checked against the files of the secret police. Finally, he was interviewed by special party boards.

"The criterion for the evaluation of every member," said Hermann Matern, chairman of the ZPKK (Central Party Control Commission), "is his attitude toward the Soviet Union." Therefore, the first questions asked of a member concerned "the meaning and role of the Soviet Union," and his "attitude toward the just war." Pacifists who extended their condemnation of war to the "just wars" of the Soviet Union were ferreted out.

Matern had to admit in his report to the party's central committee that the investigation showed that there were still anti-Soviet, and also pacifist, trends within the party membership. Furthermore, according to his report, the majority of the party was confused about the doctrine of "just and unjust wars." In short, the majority was not yet reliable.

In the most harmless charge of "unreliability," the member could try to cling to his upper-class status by making public "resolutions" of atonement, and by announcing special duties he would carry out on his own to show his good will. In Görlitz, some members resolved to pay their membership dues regularly in the future and attend all party meetings—which only provoked "hilarity" (according to one report) among the party leaders, since this was taken for granted anyway. Others resolved that they would henceforth read the daily papers—also greeted with "great hilarity." A chairman of the party shop in Görlitz, one Gehrnke, resolved to study for an hour each day the writings of Stalin. Yet when his house was searched one month later (by "a control group of the

organization and instruction department," as the record put it),
not a single volume of Stalin's collected works was found. He
was expelled from the party.

Several hundred thousand members were stricken from the
membership lists—a decision less drastic than expulsion. Without being found outright "inimical," they simply failed to live up
to party standards, and there was no hope that they ever would.
Typical of these cases was that of Ilse Dorndorf, thirty years old.
She had been a member of the party since 1945. Her family—
workers in a small Thuringian town—were old Communists. In
1948 she had been promoted to a minor functionary's post in the
party. "Why did you join the party?" the examiners asked her.
The report on her investigation records: "No answer." Evidently
the girl was speechless from fear. To the question: "Why did the
two proletarian parties of East Germany merge to form the Unity
Party?" Fraulein Dorndorf stammered that this was the right
thing to do at the time for two proletarian parties. "What are
you going to do in defense of world peace?" she was asked. "I
shall be against war," she said. The examiners shook their heads.
Five more questions like these, and then the final judgment on
her case: "Comrade Dorndorf gave her replies in a highly self-
conscious way; her theoretical insights are non-existent; she shows
no enthusiasm whatsoever. We vote to strike her from membership in the party."

Another old member of the party was expelled rather than
simply stricken from the party because, as the control Commission's sentence stated, three years before the interview, in a bar-
bershop, he had "made a remark which clearly indicated that he
had read a newspaper from West Berlin, although he denied before this Commission that he was, or ever had been, reading any
literature which was not Communist."

Even more devastating was the case of Fraulein Ch. W., a
former girl friend of President Pieck, chief editor of the party's
woman's magazine *Frau von Heute*. When she lost Pieck's affec-
tion, she also lost her job, and found a new, less important one

in the press department of the Ministry of Industries. There the party investigated her and discovered that she had not admitted in her autobiography that she was once a civilian employee of the Wehrmacht. She was expelled from the party for hiding a fascist past. She never found a job again. The classification as "former party member" marked her as an outcast.

Other and higher party members suffered a similar fate. Paul Merker, a former leader in the party's trade union department, a faithful spokesman for the party during his wartime Mexican exile—but a personal foe of Ulbricht—was found to have been "tainted by Western influences to which he had been exposed." He was expelled as "ideologically unbearable." For several months he was employed as a waiter in a state-run Potsdam restaurant, where his former comrades of the Communist leadership used to lunch. Afterwards he was transferred to a small party restaurant in Luckenwalde, from which he was fired when his former party status was discovered. The East German Information Office (whose chief, Gerhart Eisler, once wrote a voluminous Communist history of Germany with Merker as co-author), when I inquired after his whereabouts, replied that nobody had ever heard of a party member, or person in general, by that name. "Must be a mistake, sir—there is no Paul Merker in our country." One year later his arrest as an "American espionage agent" was officially revealed. In many cases of expulsion involving "Social Democratist, Titoist, opportunist, Trotskyist, objectivist, careerist" and similar dangerous influences, the verdict was made before the final interview began.

Although expulsion was only a party matter, it meant social stigmatization and unemployment. The party informed the trade union, the local authorities, the labor exchange, and the secret police of its decision. The expelled member was relegated to the "outcast" group, to slave labor. Every meeting of a party group was permeated by this fear. It was fear of expulsion rather than the rewards of membership that made the party members so totally submissive to the party line.

The rewards of party membership were, in the main, only social status and prestige. A party member was more overburdened with official duties than anybody else in the Communist community. There were few material rewards, except for the highest officials, like President Pieck, who inherited with his office several Prussian castles—a gift from his faithful people, who, though they had never really owned them, used to be allowed in the pre-Communist past to visit them on their Sunday outings. These outings, after the new president had established residence, were denied them by the presence of armed guards. Some party intellectuals, scientists, and writers were bribed to prevent their westward flight. The novelist, Anna Seghers, or the playwright, Bert Brecht, were given new cars, elegant villas, exquisite paintings and carpets. Party functionaries on the middle level received priority in new housing projects. Yet rather severe standards prevailed even for these privileged few. Party control boards kept a sharp eye on luxuries accruing to them because of their party standing. When the director of a large "people's factory"—an old and tried Communist—used one of the factory's cars for transporting a newly-acquired set of china to his home, he was immediately denounced by the driver, who happened to be a party member of equal standing. As a result, he was stricken from the party ranks.

The most precious reward of membership in the Communist Party was the membership book itself—a voluminous "card" showing the individual's good standing in the party, renewable with fresh stamps and signatures after every investigation and purge. It symbolized the elite status of its bearer. A rather animated debate went on in East Germany after the purge of the early 1950's as to whether members should carry their book with them on account of the risk of losing it or having it stolen by "American agents." The best way, it was decided, was to carry it in a special pouch on the breast, fastened by a cord around the neck as well as around the body. In "letters-to-the-editor" of the party press, several girl Communists objected that this would ruin their appearance, especially under thin summer dresses and blouses. They were advised sternly that it was more important for them to protect their membership documents than their good looks. They should be happy if their party membership books showed under their blouses, for "to progressive-minded people, this is the most beautiful thing a girl can own; she should be proud of this bulk under her dress rather than of certain features with which every woman has been endowed by nature." There were no further protests, at least not in public.

Party members or not, all citizens of the Red Reich who wanted to avoid disgrace, public stigmatization, perhaps death, had to adhere to the party line, to avoid doubting even in their minds its absolute "correctness," to prove their "proletarian vigilance" by spying and informing on their fellow-citizens, to develop "Communist ruthlessness" by the self-atrophication of their normal human feelings toward others, and to hate those the party ordered them to hate. Most people—party members and others —were afraid not to live up to these standards. A spark of independence or curiosity might destroy their blind belief; their better instincts might overcome their submission to evil, or they simply might make a mistake. Since practically everybody was a potential offender, everybody felt secretly guilty. Punishment might meet anybody tomorrow and destroy him.

Hardly had the general investigation of party documents, the mass purge of the little members, been concluded in 1952 when the highest functionaries of the Red Reich were forced to begin their individual public confessions of wrongdoings. It began with the old Communist leader of Saxony, Ernst Lohagen, who was criticized in the *Tägliche Rundschau,* the official organ of the Soviet Control Commission in Germany. "How can I correct my failings?" he tearfully asked in a public statement, and answered: "Only through the party, which must educate me and expose the errors of my ways without pity." His errors, he admitted, were that he had been too complacent and bureaucratic, and that he had ignored the "great teachings of the *History of the CPSU (B)."* Despite this admission, Lohagen was removed from office and disappeared. A little later, similar attacks against, and confessions from, other high Red functionaries were published. Fritz Selbmann, Minister of Economics, Karl Maron, Commander of the People's Police, and other scapegoats proclaimed the "error of their ways." Who would be next? What punishment would be meted out after the confessions? What would have to be confessed tomorrow as the "error of their ways?" These fears kept the Communist leaders awake at night.

Fear was the strongest bond in the building of the totalitarian community. In addition to bringing about the blind obedience of the people, it stimulated them to participate actively in its affairs. A totalitarian rule needs accomplices rather than slaves; it forces its slaves to turn into accomplices supporting it by their own will. The Third Reich succeeded to a degree in this goal. The Red Reich, with more widespread violence and less loopholes for the escape of the individual into "non-political" passivity, made greater claims on its people. In continual campaigns it attacked the passivity of the people and warned them that their fate was in their hands: everybody must defend himself against war, exploitation, poverty, by joining this or that front, following the party line, working twelve to fifteen hours a day, ridding the country of its internal enemies, arming against the foreign enemies.

East Germany did not become the Red Reich because the Germans are naturally inclined that way, because they are inevitably Nazis. It became so for the same reason as did Russia, then the Baltic countries, Hungary, Bulgaria, Albania, Poland, Czechoslovakia, China, North Korea:—small groups of men possessed by evil ideas, and holding the concentrated power of their machine age, subdued the unorganized mass of *unpolitische* and ruled them with the threat of total destruction. What they created was that ultimate perversion of a true community, the collective of fear in which the people are compelled to participate passively, and even actively—or else, be killed.

The new Nazis—a world-wide rather than German movement —ruled supreme in East Germany.

VI

West Germany's Kingless Kingdom

BEGINNING in 1949, West Germany had a new, democratic constitution. But constitutions could mean little to a people which had lived under four deeply different and short-lived political systems in the previous fifty years. The period of the monarchy was followed by the fourteen years of Weimar, with the brave attempt to establish a democratic republic; by the twelve years of Nazi dictatorship, which did not even bother to repeal formally the democratic Weimar constitution; and the four years of foreign military government exercised by the victors in the name, though not in the spirit, of democracy.

In the true spirit of democracy, the new constitution proclaimed: "All the power of the state has its origin in the people." On these very words, the old Weimar constitution had been based; but then, the constitution of the East German new dictatorship, adopted twenty-two days after the adoption of the West German Basic Law, contained exactly the same words, although they could hardly mean that government of, by, and for the Germans was established in Russia's satellite Reich.

In September, 1951, and in September, 1952, on the anniversary of this new democratic statehood for the German people, a civilian holiday, I happened to be on a train speeding through West Germany. From my window I could see the flag of the republic—black, red, and gold—waving over railway stations, taxation offices, court houses, other public buildings. I did not see a single flag on the houses of private citizens.

Seventy-year-old Eduard Spranger, a great German philosopher and educator, spoke at the University of Tübingen in celebration of the occasion. "It cannot be denied," he said, "that despite all the changes of the most recent past, it has not been quite easy for the German people to find their way to democratic government. . . . One cannot sense a great and ebullient enthusiasm for democracy. . . . Nobody could say a general moral movement accompanied the new political establishment of the German Federal Republic. For three decades young Germans here have declared that they do not like the existing systems of their political parties; to share these feelings we don't have to be very young." What had prevailed in Germany for a century, the professor continued, was still the general rule: the Germans preferred "to let the precarious public affairs be performed by the few who feel inspired to do so, while the people at large devoted themselves with great industriousness to their production, or hovered in purely intellectual heavens."

In confirmation of this, the German people paid little attention to this uncheerful lecture. Only a few editorials in West German newspapers remarked in their somewhat lofty and academic language that the words of the professor, alas, were undeniably true.

As if to illustrate this truth, and to symbolize the remoteness of the new republic's government and parliament from the West German people, the Federal capital was in Bonn—near the Western border instead of in the center of the country. And as if to stress the point further, the Bundeshaus, where the parliament met, was on the outskirts of Bonn itself, quite apart from the daily life of the town. Bonn itself is almost a small town, with no industry but a famous university and a reputation as a retirement place for old people of the upper middle classes. From its center to the Bundeshaus a pleasant half-hour stroll leads along the shores of the Rhine River. Lacking street lamps, the road is dark at night, and almost deserted by day. After Bonn became the German capital, the burghers of Bonn strolled along the river shore on Sundays exactly as they had always done, looking at the coal barges, canoes, and pleasure boats that passed untiringly along the Rhine. The only new thing was that when the pleasure boats came close to the Bundeshaus, the tourists began unfailingly to sing a song whose words asked: "Who shall pay for all this, who's got all the dough?", expressing in melody their fear that they might have to pay out of their pockets for that eccentric thing, their democracy.

Cars and cops, gentlemen with bulging brief cases and tourists with wonder in their eyes milled about the small complex of buildings housing the new seat of their parliamentary democracy. The Bundeshaus had been a teachers' college before it was re-modelled for its present use; the workmen finished their job only two hours before the first meeting of the parliament commenced. It was constructed around a large garden-restaurant where beer and soft drinks flowed freely; in a great democratic gesture, "the people" were admitted to the beer garden without special passes; from here they could watch through the large plate-glass windows the absorbed motions of their parliament in session. They would not have enjoyed to be told so, but they were a little like visitors at a zoo. They were observing with tolerance the performance of unrehearsed actors.

After this brief visit to their elected representatives, they proceeded to the town's other special sites: the house in which Ludwig van Beethoven was born, the old university, and the house of the fraternity of which the late Kaiser had been an active member. They did not bother too much about the quarters of their various ministries—in old military barracks, villas, an antiquated museum of zoology. They had no interest whatsoever in the modest, tree-protected dwelling of their President. His house seemed to them as removed from their daily lives as he himself.

Representing the new democracy and standing above all parties was its first Federal President, Theodor Heuss, Ph.D. He seemed

almost the living personification of West German democracy—
its aspiration, its background, its values, and its weaknesses. Sixty-
five years old when elected to his high office, white-haired, with
the marked features of an intellectual who has enjoyed his life,
President Theodor Heuss belonged to what Bismarck had once
described as the profession of men who had failed in their profession—he was a journalist with professorial and parliamentarian interests. He had edited a small, solid, and respected political magazine, *Die Hilfe,* which Hitler suppressed, and written
countless magazine and newspaper articles on politics, philosophy, history, travel, and the arts.[1] Immediately after the war he
received an Allied license to publish a democratic daily, the *Rhein-
Neckar Zeitung,* in his native Southwest Germany. The licensing
officer of the American Military Government, Cedric Belfrage,
warned in his recommendation against the "reactionary" Dr.
Heuss.[2] Unlike Germany's last legally elected president (Field
Marshal von Hindenburg, who liked to brag that he had not
read a book since he left the Military Academy), President Heuss
has himself written an impressive and heterogeneous number of
books—biographies of the liberal politician Friedrich Naumann,
and of the democratic, socially progressive electronics manufacturer Robert Bosch; of Anton Dohrn, a zoologist famous for his
explorations of oceanic fauna; of Justus von Liebig, a great German nineteenth-century chemist; and of Hans Poelzig, a German twentieth-century architect. What these men all had in common is revelatory of the author's own character: they were less
remarkable in their personalities than in their work and their
achievements. But in 1932 Heuss published the first German full-
length book on—and against—Hitler, and throughout the Nazi
regime many of his writings contained, carefully camouflaged between the lines, a message of protest.

[1] In the Third Reich, his writings were published in the never completely
Nazified *Frankfurter Zeitung,* under the pseudonyms "Theodor Brackenheim"
and "r.s."

[2] After leaving the Military Government, Mr. Belfrage became editor of the
National Guardian, an American weekly following the Communist party line.

In 1952 his literary inclinations were chiefly confined to a few carefully polished, elegantly-worded remarks on life and liberty worked into an address at the opening of a vintners' convention or a festival of West German Glee Clubs.

Actually, few people in West Germany knew the name of their President. His picture was on the walls of all Federal offices —it was the same with any President anywhere—but seven out of ten office boys, typists, and stenographers did not know whose likeness it was. Sincere, urbane, open-minded, unpretentious, patriotic, and highly educated, Theodor Heuss, first President of the new German Republic, was a typical personification of West Germany's best democratic forces.

If President Heuss embodied the isolated, intellectual, tradition-bound spirit of West German democracy, its real political forces, genuine hopes and frustrations, divisions and conflicts were represented by Konrad Adenauer, the chancellor, and Kurt Schumacher, the leader of the opposition. A sub-drama was played outside parliament by two other men who completed the cast of the German political allegory, Otto Ernst Remer, the neo-Nazi, and Martin Niemöller, the Eastward-looking neutralist. To understand the life-story of present-day West Germany, one has to know the life-stories of these men.

When Dr. Konrad Adenauer was named by the majority of the Bundestag in Bonn as the first head of the first West German Government, he was almost seventy years old. The German *Who's Who* of that year (published, it is true, and edited by Social Democrats) did not even list his name. He had seen four Germanies, actively participated in three. In the Germany of the Kaiser he was a municipal officeholder and then deputy mayor of his native city of Cologne. In the Weimar Republic he served his native city, a traditional stronghold of democracy, as lord mayor. A leading member of the Catholic Center Party, which opposed the Nazis, he was removed from office under the Third Reich, whose reign he quietly sat out in his country home on the Rhine, interrupted only by two short political terms in prison. After the war, American Military Government officers occupying Cologne reinstalled him as lord mayor. Four months later he was again dismissed from office, this time by the British Military Government, in whose occupation zone the city fell. He was too independent to take their orders without critical objections. He soon emerged in the preliminary councils of what was to be West Germany as the strongest personality in his party, the Christian Democratic Union.

As a hobby he cultivated roses in his garden and collected old clocks, himself resembling somewhat the eighteenth-century grandfather clock that ticked away behind his desk in his office—seemingly fragile, actually tough, reliable, indefatigable, and single-minded. To relax, he reread mystery stories for a second, even a third time.

After witnessing the collapse of three governments that seemed to be securely established in Germany, this leader of a fourth obviously weak Germany viewed with jaded suspicion the claims to eternal health of any one system. Judging from experience, he inclined toward the conviction that the masses always follow whatever leader gives them bread, self-respect, and the sincere promise of progress to a better world. In his view, the meetings of statesmen and the caucus rooms of politicians determined a nation's destiny rather than the mass meetings and parades of the people. Remembering the prosperous days of the Kaiser's Reich and the brief flourishing years of the Weimar Republic, when Germany seemed a healthy democratic Western state, the old chancellor would have preferred to remove all the ruins of totalitarian rule and total war and rebuild something resembling the good old times. Nevertheless, he sponsored with skill and shrewdness such social changes as the workers' co-determination in basic industries, which, had they been made by a younger man, would have been called revolutionary. He helped to put an end to liberal capitalism in Germany, whose advocate he had been called, and pushed the integration of West Germany into Western Europe. Altogether, he was well aware that that restoration of the past was at best a partial solution, and that new structures and new ideas must support it if it was to last.

"The old times," Dr. Adenauer told me, "are gone forever, I am well aware of that. To keep our order alive, we must have changes, innovations, improvements." He became visibly animated as we talked of changes he visualized to give peace to the world, social justice to men, and a decent state to the people of Germany.

Adenauer's main and most dangerous enemy was Kurt Schumacher, the leader of the Socialist party, the man who, single-handed, forced on his party a shape and a direction it was to keep even after his death on August 22, 1952. His successor, Erich Ollenhauer, a friendly and skillful parliamentarian, who had risen in the party by scrupulously obeying the orders of his superiors, was primarily the loyal executor of Schumacher's will and wishes.

Adenauer and Schumacher were a study in contrasts. The well-preserved, agile, unpretentious, foxy old chancellor, who enjoyed his bottle of Rhine wine every evening, whose life happily combined both success and satisfaction, who enjoyed the political give-and-take at conference tables, was opposed by the Socialist leader twenty years his junior—an unfortunate man, a chain-smoker, disfigured, crippled, sick, arrogant, pathetic, contented only when he showered a mass meeting with shrill accusations against his absent enemies.

While Adenauer, the Rhinelander, was born in Germany's western borderland, which touched on France, Schumacher came from West Prussia, where Germany met her Polish neighbors on the Slavonic plains. In the First World War, Schumacher participated as a young lieutenant in the famous Langemarck battle, in which regiments of students who had volunteered for the service led a suicidal attack. In that battle he lost an arm. After the war, disappointed and driven by his longing for a warless, class-less state, the young ex-officer joined the pacifist Social Democrats. For a while he edited one of their party newspapers and

represented them in the Württemberg Diet. In 1930 the party
sent him to the Reichstag, and he began rising in the party ranks.
When Hitler came to power he had just been accepted as a young
member of the party leadership. With short interruptions, he
spent the twelve years of the Third Reich in concentration camps.
In 1945, he emerged from their horror a very sick man. His leg
had to be amputated; incurable and painful facial diseases afflicted
him. His manhood was destroyed, any normal pleasure in life was
denied him forever. He hated the world, which seemed to him
responsible for his misery.

If Adenauer seemed to represent the good old times of Germany before Hitler, Schumacher appeared as the symbol of Germany suffering from the worst years of her recent Nazi past. Adenauer recalled restoration; Schumacher, ruins.

Defeated and humiliated by the Nazis, he—like many other
Socialists of his time—brooded over the reasons for the defeat
of his party and German freedom. That his party had left the
propaganda and politics of nationalism to the most radical Rightists seemed to him the key reason. He decided that the Socialists
must learn from their disastrous mistake; they should be as radical, as nationalist, and as ruthless in their political fight as the
Rightists had been. This, it seemed to him, was the lesson of their
defeat and the prescription for future victory. From its founding
under Bismarck to its suppression under Hitler, the Social Democratic Party had always carried the national responsibility, but
never national power; from now on, it would have to strive for
power rather than responsibility.

In 1945, almost immediately upon regaining his freedom, he
set about to reorganize the Social Democratic Party. Its former
leaders who had survived the twelve years of suppression were
mostly old men now, like Otto Braun, living in Swiss exile, who
was seventy-three, or Karl Severing who was seventy. The more
vital younger Socialists had been executed by Hitler for their participation in the resistance of July 20, like Wilhelm Leuschner,
Julius Leber, and Theo Haubach, or killed by Allied bomb raids,

like Carlo Mierendorff. Since the Social Democrats agreed that "a
new beginning" had to be made with new men and new methods,
and that the younger generation was to take over the party, they
accepted the relatively unknown, fierce, concentration-camp alum-
nus Schumacher as their president.

In the seven years left to him, Schumacher imposed on the old
party a temper which almost transformed it into a new party. The
emerging new ideology, policy, and methods had little in common with the party which—from 1875 to 1933—called itself
the Social Democratic Party of Germany. To achieve this switch,
Schumacher built a party machine which he controlled with an
iron fist; when other leaders, or the rank and file, tried to object
to his policies, their opposition was stifled, and their influence in
the party extinguished by shrewd maneuvers. In 1949 an un-
informed visitor asked Schumacher whether he was married. "I
am married to the Social Democratic Party," he answered without
a smile. He was an almost dictatorial husband, who would not
tolerate the slightest suggestion, let alone disagreement. He re-
modelled his mate—the party—in the image of his ideas. The
party soon lost its old internationalist character, and came to represent instead the nationalist point of view.

In the first elections to parliament, in 1949, the Social Democratic Party polled 29.2 per cent of the total vote, which made
it the second strongest party in West Germany. Schumacher de-
clined to participate in a coalition with Dr. Adenauer's CDU,
which had emerged as the strongest party with a vote of 30 per
cent. If he could not get all the power, he preferred fighting for it,
which he could do only as the opposition, removed from the duties
of government and from a position of real responsibility. In his
failure to gain power, he sensed a conspiracy of the victors, extending from the Allied Western governments to Adenauer and
the winning parties. Since, as he felt, they had forestalled his way
to victory as previously the Nazis had done, he hated them almost
as bitterly as he had the Nazis. But now he could fight back with
every means at his disposal—and all and every means were right

in this last struggle for victory. He shouted his opposition to everything the government did; whatever the issue, he denounced the government's position in scathing, often brilliant invectives. Half-carried by his secretary or an assistant to the speaker's chair, he threw his words like hand grenades into the crowds or the parliament. In his excitement he would sometimes rise for a moment from his chair, only to fall back again helplessly, his crippled, tortured body unequal to the task he had set it. He reflected the temper of many Germans, who responded to him with sympathy.

The 402 delegates to the parliament of the West German Federal Republic were elected on sixteen different party tickets. For Americans, accustomed to a system of two major parties, this multiple parliament seemed rather confusing. But the picture was not so diffuse as it seemed: 323 delegates, or more than three fourths of the whole house, belonged to the three major parties—the Christian Democratic Union (CDU), Chancellor Adenauer's party with its Bavarian wing; the Christian Social Union, with 140 delegates; the Social Democratic Party (SPD), with 131; and finally, the Free Democratic Party (FDP), with 52. All important decisions were fought out by the three major parties; the fight was generally settled between the two leaders of the two great parties, with the minor parties joining one side or the other. Adenauer's autocratic ways of party leadership were notorious; Schumacher's "No" was backed up by his party followers, who rarely dared to oppose him. With the exception of Berlin Socialists led by Mayor Ernst Reuter, who differed as much from the West German Socialists under Schumacher as Berlin did from Bonn, the political parties had no genuine opposition, no democratic life within their ranks. West Germany's parliamentarians represented their party leaders rather than the voters who had elected them. In 1951, for example, the Social Democratic expert on foreign politics in the Bundestag, Gerhard Luetkens, made a speech which did not happen to please Schumacher. Hardly had he finished when several Socialist deputies excitedly left the room, consulted with their leader, and came back to announce that Luetkens' speech had not been cleared with the party leader and was therefore without any meaning. Red-faced Herr Luetkens, who had voiced his own considered opinion, remained silent. The few Social Democrats who did not share Schumacher's radicalism and nationalism and were strong and independent enough to voice their dissent—in addition to Berlin's Mayor Ernst Reuter, they were the mayors of Hamburg, Max Brauer, and of Bremen, Wilhelm Kaisen—had lost by 1953 most of their influence on the party at large.

To attain a majority in parliament, Adenauer's CDU had to form a coalition government in which two other parties—the FDP and the smaller German Party (DP) participated. The FDP was—unlike other parties of West Germany—a coalition in itself, formed between old-fashioned liberals like President Heuss and conservative, if not reactionary, elements. To some degree which seemed to increase in 1952, the rightist views of the latter as well as of the DP impeded Adenauer's full freedom of action.

While West Germany's political parties were under the near-dictatorship of their leaders, the people had little voice and influence in their political parties. Elections merely gave the people a choice between parties, in the organization of which they had no voice and no hand. The parties rather than the people elected the President, the government, the chancellor, the supreme judges. The legislative, the executive, and to some degree the judiciary were dominated by the political parties. Before elections, the inner councils of the political parties decided what candidates would run on their ticket; if a candidate showed some independence of the party leader, he was so placed on the ticket as to have no chance of being elected; or perhaps he was purged altogether. "The German Voters Association," in which a few writers, professors, and minor politicians banded together to change this system, found no echo among the party leaders—and almost none among the people themselves, whose political hand it tried to free from party fetters.

Other groups, though not political in their origins, became carriers of political power that challenged the political parties in the structure of the new Germany. In the first place, the trade unions and, to a considerably lesser degree, the associations of manufacturers, won an influence in the new state which far exceeded their original position. To some degree, the churches and the veterans' organizations also became powerful political organizations. However, in all these groups it was also the leadership and the bureaucracy rather than the members that decided political procedures and goals.

On the highest level, that of the state, the authority was vested not in the democratic structure itself, but rather in the non-political, non-democratic group, the bureaucracy—the *Beamten,* that old backbone of German society. After the war, this backbone had suffered somewhat in its inner strength, integrity, and reputation. Scandals involving graft, swindle, various misdemeanors were connected with the *Beamten* to an extent unheard of in Germany before. One reason, of course, was the social chaos of the postwar period, the dismissal of a number of old civil servants who had joined the Nazi Party only in order to hold their jobs, and who were sometimes replaced by adventurers and opportunists. Another was the temptation to break the old code of honor in a society of ruins in which this code seemed a laughing matter. Scandals connected with the police force, the higher judiciary, the municipal administration appeared frequently in the headlines after the late 1940's. As a matter of fact, incomparably more cases of scandal and intrigue occurred among members of the bureaucracy than among the politicians and parliamentarians.

Nevertheless, the bureaucracy, comprising as it did the only non-political representatives of the state, retained their superior standing. As a class, they had a prestige and held a power which was almost independent of both the parliament and the people. Their prestige went back to the century before Hitler and the First World War when the bureaucrats appointed by the supreme rulers formed a solid column in Prussia's authoritarian community; but the other supporting column of the past, the army, had disappeared. Its disappearance changed the whole pyramid of the society it had dominated, in which the ruler had been the Supreme War Lord and the *Beamten,* just second to him, were above all reserve officers. Now this bureaucratic basis of autocratic militarism became the bureaucratic basis of a civilian democracy. After the collapse of the Führer state the bureaucrats alone were left standing above the quarreling political and economic factions of the nation; they alone appeared as an element of impartial order amid the ruins. The existence and power of the Occupation bureaucracy—military and civilian—which preferred dealing with its counterpart, the German bureaucracy, and even delegated some of its power to it, only increased the influence of this actual ruling class of Germany.

A Swabian peasant, so a German news magazine reported in 1951, had for thirty years paid taxes on a piece of land that never belonged to him, but, by some mistake of the taxation officers, was listed as his property. When the mistake was belatedly discovered, the peasant said, "I knew all the time I didn't have to pay, yet I couldn't have done anything against the officials, so I did not protest the injustice."

Another peasant from a village near the Bavarian town of Dachau was called by his village mayor in the course of an argument a "super-idiot." The peasant sued the mayor for the insult, which, according to German law, is a misdemeanor. But the Dachau judge acquitted the mayor, the court ruling that it was not insulting for a mayor to reflect on the intelligence of a citizen. The peasant's attorney protested the judgment, and wrote to the judge: "If I had called you, Your Honor, a 'super-idiot,' wouldn't you have considered it an insult?" For this insulting question, the judge sued the lawyer, who was sentenced to one month in jail. When the wisdom of this judgment was questioned in a newspaper report of the incident, the other newspapers hastened to explain that the equality of the law was upheld despite the seeming difference in the two court decisions. In the first case, a mayor —representing the *Obrigkeiten*—had merely insulted a citizen, as happens in heated arguments, while in the second case, a citizen had insulted a judge and by this had insulted the *Obrigkeiten* itself, a crime deserving severe punishment. After this legal explanation, the case was forgotten.

At about the same time, a man in Stuttgart received a form letter from the Municipal Health Service, instructing him to bring his infant "in a well-washed condition" to the office for an inoculation. He replied that he resented the tone of the letter and the implication that his infant was not always "in a well-washed condition." Rather than apologize, the office replied that he would be liable to jail and fines if he wrote them another such letter.

In a small town, the *Beamte* in charge of the motorized traffic police teamed up with a gang of thieves, whom he supplied with license plates for the cars they stole. When the case broke and the man was dismissed from office, the court ruled that the owners of the stolen cars had no claims to civilian damages against him, since what he had done, although it disqualified him from being a civil servant, was, nevertheless, still done while he was a *Beamte*.

In short, the "civil servants" seemed rather to be civil lords and masters over the rest of the citizens.

Bureaucracy as the embodiment of the *Obrigkeiten* was almost sacrosanct in Western Germany, although German groups similar to the American Civil Liberties Union carried on an uphill fight to remove from the minds of their countrymen the idea that the acts of the *Obrigkeiten* had to be silently tolerated. While this bureaucracy on the whole did a well-trained, responsible, and impartial job, the undue social exaltation in which they were held by the citizenry indicated the authoritarian rather than democratic spirit prevailing in the social life of West Germany.

This bureaucratic class—of which Dr. Adenauer was one of the best representatives—believed in constitutional government and in the equality of the citizens before the law. Its general respect for the law, indeed, made the *Beamten* clash often and sharply with totalitarianism, which bade them overcome their conceptions of legality. Since the Basic Law of West Germany safeguarded the constitutional human rights of the citizens, the *Beamten* were prepared to defend these rights—an authoritarian class to safeguard democracy.

While West Germany's Constitution was democratic, while its parliament and its government, organs of a democratic state, functioned according to democratic rule, and while the political parties, which professed their sincere belief in the democratic order, polled the large majority of the West German vote—there was practically general consensus among Germans that "democracy is weak in [West] Germany." As a matter of fact, this was one of the few opinions shared by sincere and active democrats, convinced anti-democrats, and by the indifferent majority of the German people. What was more amazing, all three groups had the same thing in mind when they spoke of the weakness of German democracy. They agreed that the political parties and the parliament existed in a sphere far removed from the people, if not in a vacuum. True, a large percentage of West Germans had voted regularly in recent years—so many, in fact, that they surpassed the percentage usual in American elections. But this vote meant, in many cases, rather an affirmation of an individual creed predetermined by the social, religious, and economic status than the political choice of the best man or party. The *Obrigkeiten* ordered the individual to vote, and he obediently voted. In the election campaign of 1949, a Frankfurt newspaperman asked the candidates how they would go about reconstructing the ruins and building new houses if elected. An incensed reader complained in a "letter to the editor" that the German voters were not so corrupt as to vote for men with better ideas on such a material question; a good German, he said, votes for the party of his *weltanschauung*.

Politics as seen by most Germans had little relation to everyday life. By his vote, the individual German demonstrated his allegiance to some such all-engulfing belief as Christian Democratic, Socialist, liberal, or conservative. He saw practical politics as the somewhat sinister business of the professional politicians —the party bureaucrats and party leaders.

Since the political parties stood for a world-view rather than a coalition of domestic ideals, interests, and personalities, there was little chance for the give-and-take that makes a democracy work. To most Germans political compromise was tainted by immorality, since it came close to the betrayal of the world-view which must accept only all or nothing; if a politician made a compromise with another of lesser faith, he was called a "cow-trader." Politicians were expected to keep at a distance from their colleagues of the other parties, and it was considered honorable for them to be the enemies of their opposite numbers in parliament. Not even on questions of foreign policy, where a common national interest transcended the partisan division, could the parties agree on a common procedure.

Democracy, in the early 1950's, had an alien accent in Germany. Despite a certain genuine democratic tradition in the political thought and the cultural climate of Germany, especially among many South and Southwest Germans, the democratic tradition in the political reality of Germany was unhappily connected with foreign conquerors. The new democratic ideas of the French Revolution had first been carried to Germany by the Napoleonic occupation army. When a century later, in 1918, democracy was established for the first time in Germany, it was again closely connected with national defeat and the loss of national freedom; many Germans mistook it for another punishment imposed by the victors. When the foreign "re-educators" after the Second World War again introduced democracy, it appeared more than ever before "of alien corn."

Public opinion polls after 1945 showed increasingly that Germans felt vaguely that "democracy is a good thing, but not for Germany." The first reason they gave was their experience under the Allied occupation, whose dictatorial rule discredited democracy in their eyes. Other Germans attributed their attitude to the specific postwar situation. After twelve years of Hitler, with half the country ruined, there was a poor chance for democracy to take root and grow, they said. Still other Germans tried to prove that their discontent with democracy was not a peculiarly German thing, since it only repeated a generally discernible continental European trend. In France or in Italy the failure of the political parties to represent truly the people's hopes and wishes, and of the democratic mechanisms to keep the country in step with the people's feelings, was evident, and even in the United States there were signs of this shortcoming which differed from the German failure only in extent, not in essence.

All this was true enough. Yet it fell short of the full explanation. For none of these views contained a realistic concept of democracy. In the eyes of many Germans, "democracy" remained an ideal based on fantasy, hovering in metaphysical clouds like other absolute ideals; this ideal had little in common with democracy in practice—its labors, disappointments, hardships, shortcomings, necessary compromises, and unavoidable weaknesses. In the eyes of other Germans, "democracy" consisted only of weaknesses and evil, dirty deals and shabby maneuvers, hypocritically hidden behind the claims of an absolute ideal, and a foreign one, at that: "The democratization of Germany would be the de-Germanization of Germany—and I should participate in such nonsense?" wrote Thomas Mann in 1917[3] (when he was still for war and German imperialism, before his many subsequent changes of mind). These prejudices against "Western" democracy remained deeply imbedded in German minds. To most, democracy came to mean a system too lofty and too low, and therefore unacceptable on any basis.

Few Germans understood that the real reason for the failure of democracy in Germany was the lack of democratic citizenship —the fact that the large majority of Germans did not feel responsible for "their government," which was above them as a super-personal state. In the eyes of the *unpolitischen,* the powerful state had to guarantee the unlimited, total privacy of its citi-

[3] *Reflections of a Non-political One.*

zens. Whatever else the state did was none of their business, if it only left them alone and ensured the conditions of their private security and prosperity. After the Third Reich, this was a revival of the liberal nineteenth-century view of the state which Ferdinand Lasalle, one of the first German Socialists, ridiculed as the *Nachtwaechterstaat,* the state as a night watchman. In the early nineteenth-century's quiet little kingdoms and duchies of West Germany, the pipe-smoking, beer-drinking burghers could well indulge in the luxury of total privacy. But the subsequent century, with its machines, its mass society, its social changes, upset this notion. Like the solid burghers' houses of old times, the restoration of the *Nachtwaechterstaat* did not seem very practical in the early 1950's.

In contrast to a democratic society, which cherishes both the private world and the independence of its citizens, while they actively participate in the public affairs, thus directing and themselves representing the state, the new West German society put the state above the citizens in power and independence. It became a night watchman that was the exalted boss of the citizens it had to protect, and whom—as a *Beamter*—they could not hire or fire. But then, they could not keep so far away from him any more as not to be perturbed in their work and rest, and not to be drawn by him into trouble.

For this reason, more than any other, the *unpolitischen* preferred a democratic state to a totalitarian state. A democratic state intruded less into their personal worlds, it left them alone, it did not make "total" claims on their life, privacy, and happiness. Only when it failed completely to give them security and prosperity, or at least credible promises of both, could a minority of the *unpolitischen* be persuaded by the even smaller minority of totalitarians to give them a chance to make their lives happier by whatever means the totalitarians might choose. (After the totalitarians came to power, of course, the private protests and disappointments of the *unpolitischen* had no weight.) Thus the German *unpolitischen* were not democrats, though they were yet farther from being totalitarians. But as German democracy was likely to fail unless the majority of the citizens participated in it actively, felt responsible for their community, and shared in the public life, it could become a good breeding ground for dictatorship, although they disliked it more than democracy. Rather paradoxically, while the *unpolitischen* preferred democracy to totalitarianism, they supported unwittingly and unwillingly the totalitarian against the democratic cause.

That most West Germans were more antagonistic to Communist totalitarianism than to Nazi totalitarianism was understandable, for they had learned that Communism is more totalitarian than Nazism, and makes more demands on more people—claiming practically everything from everybody. The stories they had heard from the thousands of refugees who saw Communism in action and fled to West Germany, were more upsetting than what most Germans personally witnessed under Nazism, which left a good deal of privacy and escape routes to many *unpolitischen*. To become a democracy, Germany needed democrats.

While the West German Republic restored the nineteenth-century authoritarian state based on a non-political citizenry—a form of government decayed in modern times and ruined by totalitarian dictatorships and world wars—several democratic fixtures were built in, and the whole façade repainted in democratic colors. Yet under this democratic façade remained a partly ruined structure and a weak foundation.

As there were too few free citizens to make the state democratic, the authority vested in its leaders did not suffice to carry a healthy, stable, peaceful, authoritarian state of the kind South and Southwest Germany had known a century ago. At that time, the monarch, by the grace of God fortified by many centuries of tradition, had embodied the authority of the state's supreme leadership; his family guaranteed its continuity. As the German people tried to get used to their new democratic West German house, they felt increasingly that something was missing. Looking back to the good old times, many felt that it would have been better to restore the monarchy than to try to construct a democracy from scratch. Thus, after the Second World War as after the

First, many Germans became nostalgic for the monarchy. It was a rather undefined nostalgia, to be sure, for there was in Germany no monarchal pretender of stature, no monarchal dynasty whose authority even a fraction of them would accept, and finally, there was no organized monarchist movement. Many Germans felt rather a desire for the way of life under the monarchy than a genuine political impulse to restore it. They wanted a government in which was vested genuine, abiding authority; this would be more certain if such authority was granted to one family than to a majority of professional politicians.

The question of monarchism, which seemed a thing of the past when the Constitution of the Republic was written, suddenly arose again in 1951. The marriage of a prince of the Guelph House with a family history dating back to 1070 A.D., in the city of Hanover, where they had last ruled, led to passionate demonstrations by the local citizenry. Two Federal Ministers of the government privately took part in the festivities, which were widely publicized all over West Germany by a sympathetic press. The two participating Federal Ministers, Hellwege and Seebohm, were members of the conservative German Party. Their leader in the Federal Parliament, Erich von Merkatz, declared after the wedding that his party stood for the re-establishment of monarchy in Germany. At the next elections in the city and state of Bremen, his party polled almost 15 per cent of the total vote, a considerable gain over its previous records. At about the same time, the last pretender of the Hohenzollerns, the Prussian dynasty which had ruled Imperial Germany, died; the press and public opinion recalled his life and past glory almost as if he had been their ruler. At the same time, the last pretender to the Bavarian throne, Crown Prince Rupprecht of the House of Wittelsbach which had ruled Bavaria from 1180 to 1918, publicly announced for the first time since his family had been dethroned his rights as a pretender and his desire to rule.

"It seems," said Erlangen University's professor of philosophy, Joachim Wilhelm Schoeps, in his speech to celebrate the 250th anniversary of the Prussian State, "that in our people there is increasing insight into the desirability of the idea of the Legitimate State (the *Rechtsstaat*) being realized again by a legitimate bearer of the old crown of Prussia."[4]

When the *Neue Illustrierte*, one of the most popular weekly magazines, ran pictures of the funeral of the Hohenzollern Crown Prince on its cover, it sold every single issue—something unheard of in its history. Other magazines were quick to exploit this discovery. The memoirs of, and revelations on, the Nazi leaders which had been the best-selling features of these popular weeklies in previous years were quickly dropped for memoirs of and about the monarchs. About the Hohenzollerns alone there appeared in 1951 in long serializations the *Memoirs of the Crown Prince*, (*Revue*), *My Grandfather, the Kaiser* (*Münchner Illustrierte*), *Memoirs of the Crown Princess* (*Neue Illustrierte*). Thirty-four years after their overthrow, the former monarchs suddenly furnished West Germany's favorite reading matter.

The EMNID, a reliable German public opinion research organization, asked a representative sample of the people in the Federal Republic how they felt about the re-establishment of a monarchy in Germany. Less than half of the people firmly replied that they were "against re-establishment of monarchy"—26 per cent of those over 65 years of age, 45 per cent of those from 51 to 65, 49 per cent of those from 31 to 50, and only 44 per cent of those from 16 to 30. On the other hand, 48 per cent of those over 65 were "for" re-establishment of monarchy, as were 25 per cent of those between 51 and 65 years, 20 per cent of those between 31 and 50, and 15 per cent of those between 16 and 30. Of this youngest age group, over 40 per cent had "no opinion" on the question (as on most other public matters); of the older Germans, 30 per cent had no opinion.

The nostalgia for a legitimate authority enthroned above the people did not lead to a monarchist movement if for no other reason than that there was no acceptable pretender. The Hohen-

---

4 Dr. Schoeps, this advocate of the restoration of the Hohenzollern to their throne, a German of Jewish descent and faith, recalled the main jurist and philosopher of the Hohenzollern State who was also of Jewish descent, Friedrich Julius Stahl (1803 to 1861).

zollern as a Lutheran family would have provoked the protest of West Germany's Catholic majority; the Wittelsbacher as a Catholic family would have been rejected by the Protestant minority of West Germany, not to mention the challenge to the predominantly Protestant East Germany. There was a shortage of fitting monarchic eligibles as much as of families. The children of the Hohenzollern had in the last thirty years been farming in England, repairing motors on the Detroit assembly line, conducting symphony orchestras in Berlin, or withering away amid the aristocratic dust of their castles. The granddaughter of Saxony's last King (whose family had owned the famous Meissen china factory, now Soviet property) was modeling for a china factory run by a bourgeois competitor. The children of the Wittelsbach were active in medical and artistic professions like other Bavarians, and did not take very seriously the monarchist propaganda of a few barons and eccentric writers (who had suffered heavily for these monarchist convictions in Hitler's concentration camps). In short, no candidate for a crown in West Germany was discovered to ascend to the non-existent empty throne.

To a great measure, the Federal Republic of West Germany emerged as a strange mixture of democratic and monarchic traits; it was not quite a democracy—for lack of democratic citizens, nor quite a monarchy—for lack of a king. The democratically elected government served as the substitute for a monarchic family, and the chancellor for the monarch. Deeply convinced that his office was given him by a Superior being, he was more concerned with the welfare of the people than with their will. He was opposed by the furious vigor of a party which would never have considered itself as "loyal opposition"; it pursued only the overthrow of the ruler. The people themselves resented less the authoritarian structure of their democracy than the fact that the authority of their democratically-elected ruler seemed deficient and doubtful. They themselves remained "non-political," with little desire to be self-governing, and longing to be left alone and in peace—quite literally so.

VII

What Now, Über Alles?

ERMANY did not exist in the year 1841. There was the
Kingdom of Prussia—"an army owning a state rather
than a state owning an army," as Count Mirabeau remarked—and there were dozens of equally sovereign, older,
more peaceful and more civilized kingdoms, principalities, grand
duchies, duchies. By language, geography, and culture, they were
all "German." Other "German" land belonged to foreign sov-
ereigns—for instance, the British-owned island of Helgoland on
the Atlantic coast.

It was on the steep bluffs of Helgoland in the year 1841 that
a young wanderer, the poet Hoffmann von Fallersleben, as he
looked ashore from "abroad" across the bay to the country which
did not exist, wrote the lines of a poem that expressed his dreams:
Forget the petty divisions, ignore the dismemberment of the
nation—"Deutschland, Deutschland über alles"—above all, a
new, united, free, fraternal Germany!

"The Song of the Germans," as it was called, was published
in 1842 as a leaflet, arranged to be sung by one voice accompanied
by a piano or a guitar. One year later the firm that published
the song was suppressed by the Kingdom of Prussia, and the
author sentenced, according to the law of the land, which said:
"Who causes displeasure and discontent among the citizens
against the government by his insolent lack of respect toward,
censure of, or derision of, the government, shall be sentenced
to jail from six months to two years." The song came to be the

protest of lonely liberal patriots against the kings and their servants, civil and military, and their autocratic power.

Thirty years after "The Song of the Germans" was written Germany came into being—but by a victory of the Prussian kings, whose main military servant, Otto von Bismarck, subdued the other rulers, extended his order to their domains, and was not concerned with freedom for or in a united Germany. This Prussian-dominated Germany adopted as its national anthem the song that had called for a free Germany. The words of the song took on a new, very different, jingoist meaning: Germany above all the values and the nations of the world. Outside of Germany, it was only this threatening message which was heard and understood in the new nation's anthem. Many Germans, however, still heard its original call to freedom. When the revolution of 1918 overthrew the Kaiser, and the first republic was established, its first President, the sincerely pacifist, internationalist Social Democrat, Friedrich Ebert, pleaded for the republic to keep the old anthem. For fourteen years, the Germans continued singing it. To many Germans, the refrain asserted, and appealed to, the old hope of a free country; but to others, it still seemed to say that Germany, right or wrong, was to stand above all other nations.

The Third Reich did not abolish the anthem, but it preferred the new Nazi party anthem, the "Horst Wessel Song," which celebrated the memory of a young, tough Nazi slain by an equally young and tough Communist in a Berlin street fight. It became a passive demonstration against the ruling Nazis to sing the old national anthem only, without the new Nazi anthem. Yet the fact that it was always sung at Nazi conventions and resounded from marching Nazi columns tainted it for some anti-Nazis. Among those who wished to relegate it forever to silence after the Second World War was President Heuss, who chose a contemporary poem as the new national anthem. But his effort was wholly unsuccessful. In 1952 less than one out of a thousand Germans was familiar with the words or melody of the new anthem.

While the President failed to popularize the new anthem, the old chancellor, Dr. Adenauer, had a more popular idea—the old anthem could be retained, but only its third verse should be sung, which did not contain the ambiguous words "Germany above all," and which voiced sentiments so inoffensive, so full of democratic sweetness and light that they could please everybody:

> Concord, and the Law, and Freedom
> For the German Fatherland;
> For this goal let all of us strive,
> Like brothers, with heart and hand.
> Concord and the law and freedom
> Are the tokens of Happiness.
> Bloom, shining in this happiness,
> Bloom, oh German Fatherland.

When, after a speech by Chancellor Adenauer, this verse was first sung again in Berlin in 1950, the Allied occupation officers took offense and the Socialist politicians left the meeting in protest. Yet three fourths of the German people wanted to reinstate their old song, at least the third verse. In May, 1952, the entire song—all three verses of it—was restored to its status as Germany's national anthem. "I had thought," President Heuss wrote sadly to Chancellor Adenauer, "that the present deep swath of German history required a new symbol to clarify soberly to the Germans the historic tragedy of their fate. But," he added, he had underestimated "the force and inertia of tradition."

Once again, the song meant quite different things to different people when they sang again the anthem with its refrain, "Deutschland, Deutschland über alles." What kind of Germany? Above what? Other songs, though, with a more definite meaning, competed with the national anthem. There was the Andreas Hofer Song celebrating the memory of a Tyrolese innkeeper, who in 1810 led his fellow-mountaineers against Napoleon and his Bavarian collaborators, and was captured and shot by them. The Andreas Hofer Song, which had been popular in Germany for a long time, became more topical than historical after the Second World War when foreign troops again occupied the country, and West Germans collaborated loyally with the invading conquerors. For it so happened that just three years after Andreas Hofer was shot, Prussia and Russia formed an alliance and within two years defeated the military power of the French dictator and his Western satellites, thus liberating Germany from foreign rule. This became the favorite song of the West German neo-Nazis.

The Andreas Hofer Song, accompanied by military brass bands or by bands consisting only of many drums and a few fanfares, was also the favorite song of the uniformed youngsters who marched through the Red Reich of East Germany every Sunday. At least it was the favorite of the loud-speakers whose anonymous voices led the chorus.

Its meaning was clearly articulated to the people when, at the memorial demonstration for Ferdinand von Schill, a Prussian rebel officer shot by Napoleon's troops in 1809, a leader of the National Democratic Party, one Warsow, declared, according to the report of the official East German news agency in September, 1952: "Let's learn from Ferdinand von Schill, his officers and his troops, that it is the first duty of every patriotic German to rise for his national interest." The national interest then as now, the report explained, consisted of liberating Germany from the yoke of her western conquerors. Stalin himself had, in 1949, set the pattern. "The experience of the last war," Stalin wrote in his telegram to the President of the new Reich, "has shown that the German and the Soviet peoples have made the greatest sacrifices, and that these two peoples dispose of the greatest power in Europe with which to perform actions of global impact." Wishing the men of the Red Reich "success on the new road of glory," he elaborated: "There is no doubt that the existence of a peace-loving democratic Germany on the side of a peace-loving Soviet Union . . . makes impossible that European countries be enslaved by the world imperialists."

In the years immediately after that pronouncement, Stalin's

appeal to a new German nationalism as a partner of the Soviet Union became the repeated keynote of East Germany, where, as every Communist party convention declared, "the revival of patriotic feelings is one of the main tasks of the new state." This "new patriotism" was more elaborately defined at the meeting of the Central Committee of the SED, the German Communist Party, on October 18, 1951, by the party theoretician, Fred Oelsner: "The fight for national sovereignty has gained its greatest importance in this century; it is part of the great struggle of humankind for liberation from the imperialist yoke. This fight resists the realization of the plans for world rule of American imperialism." Just as Andreas Hofer, the nineteenth-century patriot, and his partisans rose against the foreign, Western conqueror and his West German allies, the new German patriots were to rise against the foreign, Western, American conquerors and their German collaborators—"the barbarians of our time."

A German "new nationalism"—encouraged rather than tolerated by Moscow as part of Moscow's "new internationalism" itself—merged into the new supernationalism centered in Moscow. While this supernationalism still made use of nationalist energies, it extended their pathological delusions into a space incomparably bigger than the confines of any one nation. In fact, the supernationalist was made to understand that it was now the Soviet-ruled one third of the globe which was innately and totally superior to the rest of the world, and entrusted by history to conquer the rest by any means of aggression. The sense of the new supernationalism was well expressed by the high East German youth leader who, in a slip of the tongue, admonished the audience to fight the imperialist world "according to the principles of Nazism-Leninism-Stalinism."

"Soviet Power, über alles," was the anthem of the Red Reich; Soviet Germany would, after the final victory, share with Soviet Russia in the domination of the world. But like all the teachings and promises of their Communist rulers, the appeal to nationalism remained extremely unpopular among the overwhelming East German majority. They abhorred Communism too deeply to accept anything identified with it; patriotism for them was identified with the hope for liberation from Communism.

"If the Germans must have a Führer, let's have Adolf Hitler, who is at least a German," I heard an elderly man mumble as hundreds of Stalin's portraits were carried by at a parade in East Berlin.

In general, East Germans tended to develop a measure of nationalistic hatred against "the East." Despite their great campaigns for friendship between Soviet Russia and Soviet Germany, the Soviet rulers prohibited and prosecuted all fraternization between their occupation troops and the East Germans. To drive a permanent wedge between Soviet Russian troops and Soviet German subjects, the former were encouraged to indulge in mass rape, theft, and murder.

Naturally, though unfortunately, the East Germans came to despise the foreign nation that oppressed them rather than the totalitarian idea from which they really suffered. In 1950, therefore, German and Russian anti-Communists joined to counteract this smoldering hatred, and to promote friendship between the Germans, the Russians, and other Soviet-dominated peoples. Operating from West Berlin under the leadership of Rainer Hildebrandt, founder of the famous East German resistance movement, the Fighting Group Against Inhumanity, an effective underground campaign was launched to lessen national antagonism in East Germany's opposition to Soviet totalitarianism.

From the *"Ami,* Go Home" theme to the Andreas Hofer Song, the nationalist message of Communism was directed more to West Germany than to East Germany. Certainly it contributed greatly to the rise of a new West German nationalism. In a seeming paradox, this new West German nationalism reverted to the attitudes which before had by tradition been those of the non-nationalists. It united the "non-political" Germans in the cause of pacifism, quietism, "neutralism."

9

Nationalism is not a German monopoly. An unhealthy hypertrophy of patriotism (itself a healthy attitude, which foreign and German critics have often confused with and denounced as nationalism if it happened to be German patriotism), an inflated and exaggerated love of one's own country without regard for the patriotic ideals and interests of other countries, a myopic, hectic, insecure collective selfishness, nationalism has been a dominating force among all the nations of the West. The ratio of nationalists to non-nationalists was never any higher in Germany than elsewhere on the European continent. As a rule, the *unpolitischen* had in fact little use for their prophets and preachers of nationalism, since nationalism presupposed a sense of community they lacked; many lacked even any genuine patriotism, which is based on a communal conscience.

Yet a specific German nationalism developed in the nineteenth century and with specifically German causes at its roots. Unlike French or Italian and other nationalism, its standard-bearers were not the people with their striving for domestic progress and prosperity. Nor was it a democratic nationalism, as, for example, in America. It was, rather, identified with the Prussian military state —an autocratic nationalism.

While every nationalism is characterized by the arrogant obsession of the nation's own superiority in almost every field, German nationalism added to this arrogance an almost inevitable aggressiveness. This aggressiveness stemmed from the historic and the geographic insecurity in which Germany found herself after her establishment in 1871. Geographically she constituted a kind of border between East and West—in fact, the line went right through her—and she felt, therefore, that her culture and independence were continually threatened by both East and West. (Actually, her French neighbor had harassed her for centuries, as had, intermittently, invaders from the East—both with the aim of dominating her. That cultural influences from East and West often were considered a "threat" came largely from their close connection with political domination by foreign conquerors.) Historically, Germany felt insecure as a nation, since she was composed of a number of different tribes (and since the Lutheran schism, of two different religions), which were not completely unified in a common national conscience. Whenever there were great crises in Germany, such as after the First and Second World Wars, the nation split open at its seams, and short-lived yet characteristic separatist movements sprang up. If Germany felt less certain of her national unity than other West European nations, she often tried to compensate for this feeling, and to overcome it, by a heightened show of aggressiveness toward other nations. For the missing national denominator of religious unity and ethical purpose, which older and more secure nations had, she substituted the denominator of a "racial" unity and an ethnic purpose. Whereas nationalism among the older nations spoke in the name of humanity, in Germany it spoke only in the name of the state.

"The only healthy foundation of a great state is state egotism," Bismarck, the architect of the first Germany, said in a famous speech at Olmütz, and explained: "It is unworthy of a great state to fight for a cause which does not directly serve this interest." He was at least wise enough not to go looking for such fightworthy causes, as the more outspoken nationalists of his day and their successors of subsequent decades did with the fearful arrogance of barroom bullies.

Of nationalist arrogance there remained a great deal in Western Germany after the Second World War, but it lost its aggressiveness. The last war and its great defeat had a deep impact on the German mind. It shocked even the most ardent nationalists into an awareness of the fact that wars were more likely to hurt than to help their "state egotism"; they began to believe, in fact, that for Germany wars were self-defeating. They still accepted the truth of the German proverb "many enemies are a great honor," but had to admit that too many enemies in war frustrated the goal of "national egotism." Learning by losing, they discovered that for Germany war didn't pay.

Militarism was the first victim of this new discovery. After the surrender of 1945 the love of soldiering, the adoration of uniforms and military traditions, the equation of right and the might of the armed forces disappeared from the ranks of German nationalists. By the early 1950's, when German newsreels showed military parades or war games from other nations, the audience would break into ironic laughter. When the Bonn parliament voted in 1952 that West Germany participate in the West European defense organization, the newspapers abounded with letters and suggestions from former officers as well as enlisted men discussing the ways in which the new army could be non-militaristic. That soldiers would wear uniforms only while doing duty, and change into civilian togs in the free evenings; that they should not salute officers, and be organized in free trade unions; that drill should be outlawed—all this was naïvely proposed and generally approved. The large majority of young men of military age were loath to serve in a new army; from eight out of ten unwilling in 1949, the ratio slowly fell to slightly less than seven out of ten in 1952. "If we have to build a new army, we shall have several thousand inactive generals and several hundred soldiers in the whole country who will volunteer," Dr. Adenauer—who heartily disliked Prussian generals and armies—caustically remarked in 1951. Exploiting the anti-militarist mood in its propaganda and policy, the Socialist Party gained considerable voting strength.

What remained was a melancholy pride in German militarism as it had existed in the past, and as it existed outside of Germany. That "the Germans fought best" was a commonplace among former soldiers, and they would prove their point with stories from the last war. They were convinced that it was merely America's superiority in natural and industrial strength, and Soviet Russia's superiority in manpower, which had defeated the superior soldiers of the German army. They also liked to point proudly to the fact that the foreign nations shared their belief that "the German soldier is the best in the world," by letting a great many German expatriates fight in their ranks—for instance, in the French Foreign Legion, in the armies of the Arabian nations, and, as a popular illustrated weekly reported to the amusement of its readers, in the Israeli army. That the Germans invented and developed the atomic bomb a long time before the Americans was a rumor frequently heard and widely believed in Germany; so certain were some Germans that there could not be physicists and researchers better or quicker than their own that swindlers did a splendid black-market business with all kinds of allegedly German atomic bombs and atomic materials, which they said had been made by the Nazis before the surrender and hidden away. American Intelligence services were still kept busy in 1952 tracking down rumors of secret German deals in "atomic bomb parts."

To compensate for the abasement of their defeat, and for the frequent arrogance of the victors, some of whom liked to call and to treat the conquered as an "inferior nation," many Germans were often and easily tempted to develop and stress a new national arrogance of their own. This led to the conviction that "the Germans" were superior to other peoples in a number of non-military fields—a harmless and not at all solely German show of a collective feeling of insecurity, if not inferiority.

From 1949 into the early 1950's every show in every cabaret all over West Germany contained at least one act that was a surefire laugh-getter—gags, songs, or dances all playing up the amusing fact that four years after the Allies had conquered Germany to purge her forever of militarism, the conquerors now competed with each other in an effort to induce the Germans to be soldiers again. By a surprise somersault, which Germans compared with the *salto mortale*—the life-endangering jump of the trapeze artists in the circus—Germany was to participate in the armed defense of the Western world, whose supreme values were threatened by a totalitarianism more threatening and more ruthless than Nazism had been.

For an impressive number of reasons, the old-time nationalists opposed this participation. First, it did not seem to promote German "state egotism" to engage in war or preparation for war, for the time being at least. Second, it was "unworthy to fight for a cause which did not directly serve the state egotism," and after the Second World War, there was no such cause for Germany; the "direct interests" of state egotism were not served in a war for such lofty ideals as the defense of freedom. Third, Germany's allies in this fight would be the Western democracies, for whose military power as well as ruling ideas the nationalists felt contempt rather than affinity. Fourth, the enemy in this fight would be Soviet Russia, for whose military strength and ruling ideas the nationalists felt respect rather than hostility. Fifth, there was the danger that West Germany as a partner of the Western peoples would have to fight against East Germany as a slave of the Eastern rulers, but the solidarity of all Germans seemed incomparably more important in nationalist eyes than freedom and justice for all men. To sum up, the German "state interest" made it more advisable to stay out of foreign wars and entanglements, to be for pacifism and neutralism, to isolate Germany from the international free community, with the slogan *"ohne uns"* (without us) as the German *unpolitische* isolated himself from his national community with an *"ohne mich"* (without me). In fact, neutralist isolationism was the attitude of the *unpolitische* as well as of the new nationalists.

The spiritual leader of both anti-militarist and neutralist Germans was the Reverend Martin Niemöller, who personified the thinking, the development, and the changes of traditional German nationalism as fully as Theodor Heuss personified the tradition of liberal democracy, Konrad Adenauer the trends of restoration, Kurt Schumacher the drama of frustration, and Otto Ernst Remer the hopes of the unreconstructed Nazis in Western Germany.

Born in 1892, Martin Niemöller had been an officer in the Kaiser's navy; in the First World War he served as the commander of a U-boat. As he later protested in his autobiography, he "didn't feel quite comfortable" when he had to frustrate the rescue of the drowning crew and passengers of a French troop transport which he himself had torpedoed. After the First World War was lost, the German fleet scuttled, and the army abolished, Niemöller took up the study of theology to become a Lutheran pastor as his father had been. When some Rightist radicals attempted to overthrow the Weimar Republic in the putsch led by Wolfgang Kapp, he interrupted his studies to join the rebels and to lead a *Freikorps,* a group of armed volunteers. In 1924, Niemöller was ordained, and worked for several years as secretary of the Protestant Mission in Westphalia, a populous part of Prussia. In 1931, his first—and, up to now, only—congregation was entrusted to him in Dahlem, a well-to-do suburb in what is now West Berlin.

In the next two years, he advised his parish members and friends to join either the Nazi Party or the Nationalist Party, while he himself refused to be a member of any political group. When Hitler took power in 1933, he rejoiced. But after some time he learned that Hitler did not exempt the Protestant Church from his totalitarian rule, and to this he strongly objected. He believed in the independence of the Church; in its defense, he joined with a number of Protestant clerics and laymen in "Brothers' Councils" to proclaim a state of ecclesiastical emergency. From this emerged the organization of the "Professing Christians," whom he led in marked and brave opposition to the "German Christians," the Nazi-controlled wing of German Protestantism and to the completely heathenized "German Believers." Niemöller was suspended from office by Hitler, but he continued preaching in the Dahlem church, which became a symbol of Protestant opposition to the Third Reich. As a matter of fact, the church became a center of opposition to Nazism in general, since many anti-Nazis of no religious conviction attended its services to demonstrate their protest. In June, 1937, Dr. Niemöller preached a sermon on the text, "We must obey the Lord rather than man," and four days later he was arrested. The court sentenced him only to a nominal punishment, but the Gestapo stepped in and sent him without further trial to a concentration camp.

Belonging to the upper class in the "concentrational universe," as the French writer and former concentration camp inmate, David Rousset, has called the highly stratified social structure of these camps, Niemöller was spared the ordeals of those who were tortured and murdered. The Nazi leaders wanted the irritating churchman out of the public light, but he had many friends and protectors among the non-Nazis in high places of the Prussian bureaucracy and army. He was permitted by the camp commander to do theological research and to be visited regularly by his wife and friends. Immediately after his liberation by American troops, the world-famous dissenter from Nazism declared that he had resisted Hitler only on ecclesiastical, not on political, grounds.

At the end of the war, Niemöller's son Johannes, "Jan," a junior officer in the army, was captured by the Russians. He was sent by his captors to the "anti-fascist school" for war prisoners in Krasnogorsk, which was directed by Wilhelm Zaisser (later to become Germany's Minister for State Security). Unlike his fellow prisoners, young Niemöller received permission to write to his family once a week; in every letter to his father, written in co-operation with the MVD Commissar Stalkov, the son described with persuasive enthusiasm the achievements of Communism. The letters were sent to Niemöller by special mail—at a time when most German war prisoners in Russia could not even inform their families that they were still alive. After his release, Jan Niemöller was appointed to a professorship at the Walter Ulbricht Academy in Forst-Zinna, one of the Soviet German colleges for Communist party officers.

Dr. Martin Niemöller himself, after the war, was appointed to high office in the Lutheran Church, was placed in charge of its foreign relations, and traveled widely abroad. He became more and more antagonistic to the new West Germany. "With the establishment of the Federal Republic," he said, "which was begotten in Rome and born in Washington, Germany has lost her previous position as the strongest Protestant power on the European continent." He blamed the anti-Communist powers for the condition of Germany, and of the world: "I am convinced that Myron Taylor, as special envoy of Roosevelt and later of Truman to Rome, was a factor in the division of Germany and the threat to peace that is being caused by it." This led to the next step in his thinking: "If there is the alternative between the continuing division of Germany, or the unification of Germany, even under the Russian dictatorship, the Germans must prefer the latter— including the risk of Communism." Nor did this risk seem so disastrous to him: "It is an infamous fallacy," he stated, "to claim that it would be ruinous for the Church to wake up some day in a Communist world." And he promised a reward of one million marks ($250,000) to "anybody who can prove that the preparation of resistance to bolshevism is founded on the Holy Scriptures." What he wanted to resist more than anything, he amplified, was that "Germans kill Germans." Any German, he said, who would take up arms for the Western democracies, which were in his eyes as contemptible as the Soviets if not more so— "any German fighting for Rome and Washington"—"is just a fool."

On January 2, 1952, Dr. Niemöller flew to Moscow for a six-day visit. On his return he published an enthusiastic report on what he had seen there. "With the 'German Christians' of the Hitler period the Russian Orthodox Church cannot be compared in any way. It is concerned with the Christian community rather than with bolshevik propaganda," the old foe of totalitarian interference with church affairs happily reported. "In the depth of the Russian man's voluminous soul there is so much room for everything else as to leave an immense place for religion; people in Russia are of a moral and spiritual-ethical purity which is amazing." Recalling evidences of racism, he explained: "This is caused by their biological nature and is basically a part of the Slavonic type." In short, the former U-boat commander in the garb of an Anglican priest found Moscow as close to his heart as any propagandist could wish.

"This man Niemöller," the political commissar of the Soviet

Military Administration exclaimed at a meeting of East German editors in Leipzig, "is worth ten divisions to our cause." What made him so valuable was that he appealed to so many different groups and led them in the united front of neutralism against the West.

In themselves, his main appeals seemed neither nationalistic nor anti-Western or pro-Soviet. The urge for German reunification was a perfectly natural feeling that every patriotic self-respecting people would feel if a cruel war had split their country into hostile halves. Yet by placing the realization of this urge above all other considerations, above the issues of Western freedom and Eastern liberation, the nationalistic motive was emphasized. Nor was the desire to keep out of war more than the normal reaction of people whose country had just been devastated by war, who were working hard to remove the ruins and to reconstruct their cities, and who feared that a new army would lead to a new war which would destroy everything again. The nationalist element crept in, however, when it was stressed that the war was rejected because it would be profitable to "Rome and Washington" rather than Germany. The priority given to reunification, along with the anti-Western slant of neutralism, obviously led to support of the Soviet strategy of conquest. To rationalize this fact and to justify it in their conscience, men like Niemöller tried hard to find "the good sides" of Soviet totalitarianism and to point to the "bad sides" of Western democracy. They sincerely had no interest in, or thought of, the Nazi hopes for a German share in the Soviet conquest of world power; but when they saw that their attitude actually benefited the Soviets, they had to convince themselves that the Soviets were not so bad, after all, and that the West was worse, perhaps, or at least equally bad. From their confused nationalism to radical Nazism was still a wide step.

Niemöller's record as a soldier in the First World War made it impossible for anybody to accuse him now of unsoldierly, "un-German" cowardice. His record of resistance to the Nazis placed him above the suspicion of totalitarian leanings, and his high standing in the Lutheran clergy seemed to clear him of the taint of sympathy for the Godless Reds. As a former military hero, a former anti-Nazi resistant, a respected churchman, and a fearless spokesman of fearful people, Dr. Martin Niemöller was able to win over to his ideas a great many Germans who neither were nor became pro-Communist, pro-Russian, or German nationalists. A heterogeneous crowd, which had little in common but the desire for peace at any price, followed in Niemöller's steps. Among them were the followers of the high-ranking Protestant layman Dr. Hugo Heinemann, a convinced pacifist, who resigned from his post as Federal Minister of the Interior in protest against "remilitarization"; the intellectuals around Würzburg University's Catholic professor of history, Ulrich Noack, a brilliant historian of nineteenth-century political thought but lost in twentieth-century political realities; a number of other Protestant clergymen and Catholic laymen (the latter organized in the Center Party), who believed that social reforms should be the first task of the Western nations. Alongside these pacifist idealists stood disgruntled businessmen with export and shipping interests, to whom it seemed more profitable to regain and extend trade behind the Iron Curtain than to compete with West European industries, and disgruntled politicians of all shades of opinion, feeling frustrated in the present order. There were also among the neutralists Germans with an anti-Western chip on their shoulders, especially former officers of the army, navy, and police, who were resentful that in the postwar years they lost their jobs and their generals were jailed by the victors, or who simply feared to be on the losing side in the next "war criminals' trials" arranged by tomorrow's dubious victors, and therefore preferred to remain on the safer neutral grounds. Other former officers found civilian jobs which paid more, or promised a better future, than a return to military careers; for them, to manufacture shoes, work in a construction firm, be an accountant, brought greater individual security and material success than army life. In 1952 it was a frequent claim of former German army officers that only misfits unable to adjust themselves to civilian life were still willing to serve as officers.

The youth, the upper classes, and the intelligentsia—which in the decades before Hitler had been the main reservoir of traditional nationalism—followed the neutralist banner with particular determination. Their own personal future seemed more promising in a neutral than in a rearmed Germany—in contrast to previous times when conquest, colonies, domination of others seemed to open brighter individual prospects. The anti-Nazism and anti-militarism prevalent among some of the most responsible young Germans made them reject German participation in the international Western defense community; while their attitude led them in fact toward an uneasy neutralism, they kept—in the struggle of ideas and in peaceful action—supporting the Western democracies, and actively opposing Communism.

·"Neutralism" was above all the program and the hope of the *unpolitischen*. Impressed by the example of Switzerland, which, thanks to her neutrality, has remained peaceful and prosperous for centuries, they found in the prospect of a neutral Germany the answer to their longing for undisturbed, secure privacy. What they did not see was that Germany was a prize incomparably more attractive to any aggressor nation than Switzerland, that a neutral and unarmed Germany could be taken overnight by foreign aggressors, and that even Switzerland had to safeguard her neutrality by an impressive army of her own.

Although neutralism had much influence on public opinion and politics in West Germany, it was an unorganized force, consisting largely of individuals with their spontaneous, passive, and negative resentments, fears, longings. The dozens of "circles," "movements," and "groups" that tried to organize and articulate these individual feelings on a mass basis made little headway. Whenever these groups attempted merely to get together for common ends, such as in the "German Congress" of 1951, they failed before they really began. Aside from profes-

sional politicians, unemployed would-be politicians, and people
with a special ax to grind, few Germans were drawn into the
webs of isolationist organizations, although they approved of
their aims in principle. "Peace and privacy in Germany über
alles" was what they meant and wanted when they sang their
national anthem.

If "bourgeois" neutralism, with its nationalist and militarist
lineage, remained a vague mass mood, there developed on its
side a close-knit, politically powerful, widespread neutralist organization of strongly anti-nationalist antecedents: the Social
Democratic Party became after 1949 the standard-bearer of a
working-class nationalism also devoted to its form of neutralism.

In political terms, the new nationalist resentments and aspirations of the Social Democrats exhausted themselves in negations.
Like the new nationalists of the Right, whose program stood and
fell with their *"ohne uns,"* the Social Democrats based their
politics on an eternal "No" to every move in the international
field made by the government in co-operation with the Western
democracies. They were strongly opposed to co-operation with
the Communists, whose suppression of human rights and of free
labor in trade unions or political parties kept them from a potential alliance. This, of course, made the new nationalists on the
Left differ sharply from the new nationalists on the Right; but
both had almost equal scorn for the Western democracies. The
history of the Social Democratic Party was from 1949 a never-
ending protest against the West German government's road to
peace with the Western powers. At every step they objected
vehemently, marshaling up all the ready-made arguments of resentment, arrogance, short-sighted pride, occasional personal attacks (some lifted verbatim from Hitler's arsenal), permanent
denunciations of *das Ausland* as such—hardly a positive, constructive idea.

Schumacher's personal past, which he had begun as a young
officer in the legendary Langemarck battle, found a faint echo
in these new nationalist tones—men often keep faith with the

values of their early upbringing, however deeply they may have divorced themselves from these values to oppose them sincerely in their later life. On the other hand, his personal sufferings and his conversion to pacifism were expressed in his new stand against Germany's effective alliance with the West against Soviet Russia. That this alliance was initiated by the Western powers made it almost automatically unacceptable to Schumacher, who had despised them from the time when occupation officers had slighted and snubbed him as a "German tainted by the collective guilt of his people." In the first years after the war, the Morgenthau-minded taboo on fraternization with Germans kept occupation officers from offering him a chair or a cigarette when he was summoned to their office. This naturally left a bitter scar on him after his almost twelve tortuous years in concentration camps as an uncompromising anti-Nazi. He did not forget his frequent clashes with high occupation officers—sometimes on his anti-Soviet position, which was considered in the first postwar years by many Americans as rebellion against the Allies. In addition, like most German democrats persecuted or exiled by the Nazis, he had brooded throughout their rule over the question why Hitler had won, and concluded that the German Left had neglected the natural and legitimate national urges of the people and left the Nazis free to monopolize and misuse them for their own ends. Rather than repeat the old mistake, he was resolved to voice national resentments and aspirations as violently as any German of the Right. Finally, in his view, it seemed the fault of the Western Allies that he was in opposition to, rather than at the head of, the West German government. He believed, mistakenly, that for economic, social, and other reasons, they kept him out of power by a sinister plot, and this was a last personal reason for him to hate and to attack in venomous words the French and the Americans—"*das Ausland*."

Schumacher's personal resentments fused in his mind with the interests of the political party to which "he was married," and which he wanted to lead from opposition to power. Aware of the resentments against the *Ausland* and of the nationalist reactions smoldering among his people, he saw a chance, by incorporating them into his party's program, to gain nationalist voters and keep them from following the totalitarian parties, and to strengthen the appeal to the Socialist rank and file. A number of his sub-leaders were secretly perturbed by this plan, feeling it to be short-sighted, since it would soften the traditional stand of the rank and file against nationalism to such an extent that they might fall for the still more resentful, more radical, more nationalist appeals of the totalitarian parties. Socialist leaders who strongly defended Schumacher's line in the Federal Parliament or in their party conventions privately admitted after some prodding how well aware they were of this danger.

These personal and partisan motives of Schumacher would not have been so meaningful had they not expressed a deep and general change in the mood of the working classes whom he led. Since Marx and Engels had published their Communist Manifesto a century ago, the "proletariat" of Europe's industrial nations had become as deeply integrated into the life of their countries as any other class. Even German Marxists had admitted since the beginning of the century that the economic fate of the workers depended on the economic and political fate of their nation. And in the extreme crises of war or economic depression, the Socialist leaders half-heartedly had to identify themselves with their nation—so half-heartedly, however, and with so many reservations and qualifications that on the one hand they could still be accused of betraying their nation, while on the other they seemed guilty of betraying the interests and ideals of the international working class. Many people considered them guilty of both. Following the First World War, the Socialist parties of the Western world acted more in accordance with their national interests than with their international slogans, a discrepancy between program and practice that led to increasing confusion among the rank and file. Speaking as revolutionaries and internationalists in accordance with time-worn slogans, but acting as democratic patriots in accordance with the necessities of the day, the Social Democrats came to feel insecure. When Hitler—after his suppression of the Socialist Party—invited the workers to march with him on his nationalist course, a strong fraction of the German working class followed him—notwithstanding the legend to the contrary that Hitler was backed "by industrialists, junkers, and the upper classes." This legend, of Communist and Marxist origins, ignored the evidence which showed that the dividing lines of rejection and acceptance, resistance to and support of Nazism went straight through all classes, with the ratio of supporters among the workers perhaps higher than among the upper classes.

After the Second World War, the working classes of West Germany were finally convinced that their situation merely reflected the national situation, and that they were losing more than anybody else in the general bankruptcy of their nation. With their factories in ruins and the victors dismantling industries considered of potential military value, the workers saw themselves robbed of the opportunity for employment. The restrictions on the volume of production which the Allies imposed on basic industries meant a further cut in the employment and wage level of the workers. The Iron Curtain, which split Germany into two parts that could no longer do business with each other, deprived German industry of badly needed natural markets and the workers of income. With less chance to compete and advance as individuals than the upper classes, many West German workers set their hope on the collective "national egotism"; their employment, their wages, their prospects depended very much on the peaceful power of production which Germany was to recover.

But in the early 1950's the thinking of the German working class was in itself split. Among their trade unions was a trend toward rejecting Schumacher's nationalism and accepting Adenauer's conception of Germany integrated with a united Western Europe. Their interests as an economic group seemed better safeguarded in a reconstructed nation integrated with the West. Their main task seemed to them to win for themselves the greatest possible share in the nation's management and returns. Something like a split personality developed among the German workers: as unionists, they were decidedly pro-Western; as political Socialists, they were aggressively neutral. Under the leadership of Hans Böckler and, after his death, of Christian Fette, two moderate unionists in conflict with the Socialist Party from which they came, the German trade unions supported the program of European integration. But in October, 1952, a majority of Socialist union bureaucrats voted as their new leader the metal worker Walter Freitag, who followed the Socialist party line.

The great dilemma between Western integration and German neutralism, between democratic internationalism and nationalist pacifism, was not restricted to the German working class. In a less organized, less articulate way, it confronted all Germans.

That from 1949 on the Federal Republic moved steadily towards integration, internationalism, and active defense of European freedom was almost exclusively the work of the old chancellor. Almost alone, weakly supported by his friends, bitterly embattled by his powerful enemies and poorly assisted by the very powers who sought his alliance, he did what few leaders of a democratic nation have done, and what is usually the privilege of dictators—he changed the destiny of a lethargic, unresponsive people by leading it toward action.

In one of his first statements after coming to power Dr. Adenauer declared that the Federal Republic of West Germany would remain on the side of the Western democracies and work for their cause, whatever political prize for desertion the Soviet side should offer. A program like this was perhaps without precedent in diplomatic history, certainly in German history. He rejected all the political gains which the competition of the two foreign power blocs in their desire to win Germany's favor would have been certain to bring. He forsook the opportunity to "play one side against the other," which would have been easy for him and would have forced the Western powers to make more speedily and more thoroughly their already overdue concessions to the new state. Finally, he pledged himself to a line of action that was almost certain to weaken his domestic popularity and to supply his German opponents with ample ammunition for demagogic arguments. In the eyes of partisan politicians, Adenauer's unqualified support of and solidarity with the Western powers—who still occupied the country, had behaved as enemies rather than allies in the preceding years, and still slighted and harmed the country on frequent occasions—appeared as an almost suicidal act. The chancellor seemed to disregard Germany's nationalist interests on the international level and his own partisan interests on the domestic level.

Dr. Adenauer executed his declaration of intent in the following years with a firmness which sometimes made even his closest associates protest. He overcame the economic national egotism of his country by promoting the Schuman Plan for uniting the coal and steel markets of six European countries and shifting their marketing and investment policies from a national to a European framework. With Germany's superiority in Europe's coal production (55 per cent of 220 million tons) and almost a half share in Europe's steel production (40 per cent of some 40 million tons), the Schuman Plan eliminated German economic sovereignty in the two basic materials and removed the possibility of her making arms or wars without the assent of her Western partners. Adenauer overrode the neutralist mood of his people by promoting Germany's participation in the European army with an international supreme command, equally offensive to pacifists and to militarists, to Rightist and to Leftist neutralists. He was accused of making advance concessions to the West before the allies had made concessions on their side, he was denounced for giving away Germany's manpower and raw materials to foreign countries, he was attacked for entangling Germany in the wars of other nations. The Socialists, nationalists, and pacifists were sometimes joined by members of his administration in their condemnation of Adenauer. Before signing the contractual agreement with the Western powers which was to give sovereignty to the Federal Republic while the occupation forces remained in the country, he was even accused of putting his signature to "a new Versailles Treaty"—an accusation which had been the political death sentence of his predecessors in the Weimar Republic, and the literal death sentence of one of them.

Adenauer explained his position with a simple argument to show that he acted in the interests of Europe, and that Germany's "national egotism" was subordinate to this greater goal. The main threat to Germany and the Western world, he said, is war; Soviet Russia will start an aggressive war unless she finds the defense of the Western world too powerful. If Western Europe unites in economic, military, and finally political forms, and if Germany is part of this Europe, it will be so powerful as to keep Soviet Russia from attack. If the West does not succeed in this, West Germany will be overrun by the Soviets with or without war, and will be destroyed. If she joins in the Western integration, she will save herself. Therefore, he saw only one choice for Germany—a united Europe; "only then can my country be free."

"German nationalism is on the downgrade now," he told me when I visited him in Bonn, "because a new, greater, more vital view takes its place, the view of a United Europe." As a matter of fact, the first chancellor of West Germany put the self-preservation of Europe consistently above the national egotism of Germany, and the value of freedom above the idea of the state.

It seems almost ironical that in 1952 Adenauer was called a "nationalist" by thoughtless foreign observers when he protested reluctantly and belatedly against some regrettable acts of French nationalism. In a spirit of short-sighted national egotism rather than of the European unity which France's Robert Schuman promoted among the French people as Adenauer did among the Germans, the French government tried hard to keep from Germany the little Saar district with its great coal treasures, although more than nine out of ten Saarlanders spoke German and felt German. A semi-dictatorial puppet regime had been installed by France,

which suppressed the display of German patriotism in the Saar-
land and prepared its *anschluss* to France. To call such legitimate
requests as the German demand for a plebiscite in the Saar a "nationalist" relapse, to smear so genuine an enemy of nationalism
as Adenauer with the term "German nationalist," to deny in the
name and to the profit of a foreign power German wishes on
which her self-respect, her self-determination, and her security
as a nation was based, was indeed a rather effective way to beget
and strengthen new German nationalism. Adenauer's great de-
sign to overcome once and for all the nationalism of Germany was
threatened by foreign nationalism at least as much as by German
reluctance.

As a matter of fact, the conspicuous lack of responsiveness,
good will, and fair participation shown by the West, which consistently hesitated to treat West Germany as an equal partner in
the European community, did much damage to the responsiveness
and good will of West Germany itself. In the late 1940's the goal
of German integration with Western Europe was the most appealing and the strongest political idea in the eyes of many Germans, especially the young; they were almost enthusiastically willing to participate in such an undertaking. In the early 1950's this
temper cooled down; to many, it seemed another trap in which
they were seduced by idealistic hopes only to be later disappointed
and frustrated. Yet potentially, the "European idea" retained its
appeal if—an "if" which became bigger and more doubtful all
the time—if the unification of Europe was not merely devised to
demand sacrifices from Germany in favor of the other partners,
if equal sacrifices and performances were to be brought by all
participating nations. Many young Germans were willing to follow this guidepost more than any other, and to sing: "Germany
in a free, united Europe über alles."

Undoubtedly and unavoidably, a few genuine nationalists of
the traditional kind found shelter and hope in the European idea.
A small number of older intellectual fellow-travelers of Nazism
banding together around a new magazine, *Nation Europa*, hit on
the idea that Germany could be the strongest national unit in a

united Europe, and thus could win power and perhaps domination by the device of the European organization; Germany would be able to rule Europe (and Africa) by allying with the other European nations in peace, since she was unable to rule them by subjecting them in war. They were a minority compared with the larger group of their nationalist and neo-Nazi comrades who dreamed of a powerful Germany in a Soviet empire, since to them Western Europe looked decadent and the democracies weak. If the "West-oriented" nationalists were a minority among German nationalists and unreconstructed Nazis, they were an even smaller minority among the Germans in general.

From the ruins of their national destiny and the rubble which covered her *lebensraum,* Germany had to clear a new path to a new position among the nations. The overwhelming majority of Germans followed the road which led them away from militarism. What they also abandoned was the idea of a Germany that would conquer and dominate the world. On whatever road the Germans set out now, it was not a specifically German road any more leading to a specifically German goal. There were those who chose to fall in on that great highway on which many peoples commanded and oppressed by the Soviets were already marching, and they dreamed of conquering the world jointly with Soviet Russia under the banner of Communism. The Communists, many unreconstructed Nazis, and a number of non-Communist nationalists took this direction. A second road pointed to German survival rather than German power, and ruled out war with, or domination of, other nations. Many nationalists and most non-political people felt that this path was safer than any other; they hoped to keep a peaceful Germany above all the global struggles rather than push a powerful Germany above all foreign nations. They stood for fearful isolation. Finally, there was a third group, which also followed the guidepost leading to a greater unit, as did the marchers of the East; they wanted to integrate Germany with the Western community which in time was to be the united Europe of free nations.

Each of these roads contained some evident promises and some equally conspicuous dangers to the Germans. Their responses to the three alternatives varied strongly with the general course of events. The trend toward isolationism was strongest when Soviet Russia seemed most powerful and dangerous and the West seemed weak. When the Germans saw that the West was able, and might become as willing to bind itself to Germany as Germany was to bind herself to the West, many began to prefer integration with the West to both other alternatives. But to many—probably most—other Germans it seemed that in the international lineup it was best simply to stand and wait.

VIII

Jews, Germans, Anti-Semites

THE mass murder of Jews in the Third Reich was remembered by many in America as Nazism's most frightening and repulsive performance. It was natural that they should wonder, seven years after Hitler's fall, whether "anti-Semitism was still running wild in Germany." Behind this question there lurked the scarcely-hidden fear that a second racist crusade of hate in Germany might lead to new extermination camps.

Their fear was understandable. In the beginnings of the Third Reich, few people in Germany and abroad had given full credence to the warnings of the coming horrors. The majority of Germans (which included most German Jews) and of foreigners (including foreign Jews), in short, almost everybody, belittled as "signs of a passing hysteria" the Nazi challenge to "world Jewry" and the predictions of German anti-Nazis. But after being shocked from their complacency by the final fact of the murdered millions, they remained apprehensive if not permanently alarmed; they did not want to be surprised for a second time when it would be again too late. Rather, they fell into the opposite error of expecting as almost certain a repetition of the past. And catering to their misgivings, the American press did its best to report every incident from Germany in which Jews were involved, to inflate all such molehills into mountains of anti-Semitism.

After 1945, German-Jewish relations in the Western part of Germany were acted out on three quite different levels little connected with each other. First, there was the official opinion exemplified in the Bonn government's position with regard to Jews and anti-Semitism. Second, there was the public attitude toward the Jews in Germany, sharply divided into two rather distinct spheres—on the one hand, public reaction to the German Jews who were active in and integrated into German public life; on the other hand, the public attitude toward foreign Jews, most of them former Displaced Persons who came to the postwar Germany of ruins and chose to remain.

The official attitude to the "Jewish question" was in complete contrast to that of the Nazi government. From the inception of the Federal West German Republic, in September, 1949, the government and the leaders of practically all political parties undeviatingly and repeatedly condemned the Nazi crimes against the Jews, as well as anti-Semitism in general. According to Article 3 of the Constitution of the Federal Republic all men are equal before the law, and nobody may be discriminated against on account of his sex, descent, race, language, homeland or ethnic origins, faith, religious or political views. In addition, the Bonn government adopted special laws which provide severe punishment for anti-Semitic propaganda or racist activities. It was eager to prove that the new Germany was deeply opposed to the anti-Semitism of the Nazis, and that it hoped for official German reconciliation with the Jews. In this domain, too, it had to remove the ruins of a past which cluttered the way to reconstruction. The removal of the feelings created by the pogroms and the reconstruction of a new relationship between Germans and Jews was a herculean task after the horrible human devastation wrought by Hitler.

Nevertheless, the leaders of the Bonn government were bitterly criticized by Jewish organizations abroad, especially in Israel, whose government led in these attacks. These critics said that in making overtures of peace toward the Jews, Germany was too slow and hesitant. By this they meant mainly the offer of material reparations claimed by Israel and Jewish groups.

If the Bonn government did indeed not offer such payments

as quickly and generously as the Jewish spokesmen requested, it had reasons. For one thing, in a country of ruins, beset by pressing, often desperate economic, social, and political problems, the Jewish "problem of the past," which was how most German leaders came to regard it, simply took second place. Another factor was that the friendly, conciliatory gestures and declarations made by the new German government were eyed coldly and suspiciously by Jewish spokesmen, who usually responded to them with hostile recriminations and rebuffs. If it was quite understandable that Israel was not given to a posture of supreme forgiveness, it seemed oblivious of any middle way between such forgiveness and collective hostility, if not hatred, toward all Germans. But it was the unwaveringly hostile attitude which Israel chose, thereby barring the way to a reconciliation which was of equal interest to Germans and Jews alike. The pattern first appeared in 1949 when Konrad Adenauer, just elected as the first chancellor of the newly founded Bonn Republic, happened to be staying at the same Swiss summer resort as Chaim Weizmann, just elected first president of the newly founded Israeli Republic. Dr. Adenauer, whose personal record as a lifelong foe of anti-Semitism was spotless, wanted to pay Dr. Weizmann a courtesy call; he was told that the Jew did not want to see the German. Similarly when Theodor Heuss as new president of the republic publicly declared that all Germans, Nazi and anti-Nazi, had a share in the "collective shame" for what the Nazis had done to the Jews, he was violently attacked by Jewish organizations abroad for "trying to evade the collective guilt of all Germans." As late as the summer of 1951, when the Inter-Parliamentarian Union met in Istanbul, Turkey, to discuss the world-wide refugee problem, the Israeli delegation protested against the presence of the German delegation, which consisted of a number of lifelong anti-Nazis.

In August, 1951, forty-six countries formally ended their state of war with Germany. Israel (which had been founded only after the war with Germany ended) refused to join with them. The news induced "in many Germans feelings of mourning, sadness, and also sympathetic understanding," Erich Lüth, director of the Senate of the City of Hamburg, wrote in a full-page article that was reprinted in many leading German dailies: "One thing which threatens to happen must by no means happen: that the Germans, whether from shame or out of embarrassment, whether out of not knowing what to do or out of despair, should attempt to evade the Jewish issue." He concluded with an appeal to his people: "It is we who must be the first to talk to the Jews . . . We must *beg* Israel for peace."

Chancellor Adenauer expressed his full approval: "The Jews," he told me, "have suffered the most bitter injury and injustice. Please believe me that the greatest part of the German people was and is truly filled with revulsion against the deeds of the past. We must find a way to let the Jews know it—they have a right to it."

Soon afterwards, on September 27, 1951, the Federal Parliament in Bonn met to listen to the governmental declaration, which not only restated Germany's spiritual shame and revulsion about the past crime against the Jews, but declared her willingness to make material amends, as the Jews demanded. "The Federal Government is prepared to co-operate with the representatives of the Jews and the State of Israel to solve the material problems of reparation in order to ease the way toward a definite indemnity for the infinite suffering of the Jews." At the conclusion of this statement, the whole house rose quite spontaneously to its feet to demonstrate its sympathy for the Jewish victims of Nazism. The leaders of all political parties—except of the Communists who remained silent, and of the neo-Nazi SRP who were not present—spoke up in favor of the government's action.

This impressive declaration was accorded a most sceptical welcome by Jews abroad. Jewish organizations hastened to formulate a set of demands that would "test the good faith" of the German offer—demands for the outlawing of the expression of anti-Semitic sentiments and opinions that it would have been deemed too extreme to present to an American or British government, and which no constitutional regime could really carry out. In the Jewish communities all over the world, acrimonious debate broke out whether or not reparations should be accepted from Germany; those who wanted to accept the reparations and those who pleaded for their rejection outdid each other in their professions of irreconcilable hatred against Germany. The Israeli government, which advocated accepting payments offered by Germany and even bargaining for more, though rejecting at the same time the German offer of reconciliation, assured its parliament that no Israeli would be permitted to enter Germany, and no German to enter Israel, in order to negotiate the extent and forms of Germany's material amends. No political, social, or other relations except these negotiations would take place between Israelis and Germans. "The Government remains firm in the belief," Israeli Foreign Minister Moshe Sharett stated in the Jerusalem parliament, "that the responsibility for the destruction of masses of Jews in Europe falls upon the entire German nation." With a close vote, Israel's governmental proposal to accept reparations from West Germany was adopted against the Israeli opposition, which consisted of the extreme right-wing Herut party, the fellow-traveling Mapam party, General Zionists, and the Communists.

Starting under these auspices, there seemed a fair chance for the emerging sun of good will soon to disappear again behind financial, diplomatic, and legalistic clouds. "Whatever we do," I was told by a German official close to the Government, "it can never be enough. We know that. We cannot make material amends for the loss of somebody's parents gassed in Auschwitz. We cannot even make amends for, say, the loss of 'his' mountains by a refugee from Bavaria who used to climb them every week end before he had to flee his native land. Of course, we have to try and we shall try our best. But then, there is another limit to our doing everything that ought to be done—our financial situation. With the millions of refugees and expellees from the East whom we have to support, with the millions of war victims who cannot support themselves, with the ruins still all over Germany, and with our economy precariously close to crisis all the time, we just cannot afford to be as generous to the Jews as we know we should be."

All this was undeniably true. Yet it was no matter for surprise that many Jews should have read into such explanations a preliminary attempt to evade full responsibility, and should have seen German ill will in a situation that was created only because of German good will.

The question would have been complicated enough if there had been only the individual Jewish claims for restitution and compensation with regard to damage or loss of property, money, or goods, which amounted to $600 million. Individual Jewish property expropriated or sold at a loss under Nazi rule had to be returned to the Jewish owners, or their heirs. In 1952, 85 per cent of all these Jewish claims had been settled in cash or through the restoration of property.

The matter became more involved with the claims for "collective reparations" to the amount of $1,500,000,000 (one billion dollars from West Germany, and $500 million from East Germany) filed by the State of Israel in a note to the four occupying powers in March, 1951. In addition, it was claimed that heirless property demands of $500 million should be paid through a special organization to Israel. Although the financial as well as the legal basis on which these Israeli claims were computed may have seemed debatable, the Germans accepted them without objections. But the weird horse-trading over these "reparations claims" which began in The Hague, Netherlands, in March, 1952, could not promote a genuine atmosphere of reconciliation.

Dollars-and-cents restitution could never be the measure of repentance for the Nazi crimes, nor the price of reconciliation on the Jewish side, as most observers felt. In an atmosphere poisoned by the past crime, the very attempt to make amends was bound to create new distrust and hostility.

After six months of negotiations, which were twice broken off by the Israelis, the restitution treaty was finally signed on September 10, 1952, in neutral Luxembourg. The German Federal Government agreed to pay three billion marks to Israel, and 450,000,-000 marks to the World Jewish Organization. After the treaty was signed, no speeches by the contracting parties—as is usual on such occasions—were made; the signers did not even shake hands with each other. The Israeli representatives, whose country was badly in need of money, insisted on omitting these gestures; while they accepted the German offers of payment, they did not accept the German offer of reconciliation; they did not want to make it appear as if the treaty was a first step to such a reconciliation. Rather than to the goodwill of the new German Republic they attributed the treaty to their own national power: "The signing of the treaty," Israel Foreign Minister Moshe Sharett declared, "shows the changes brought about by the founding of the Jewish State."

Chancellor Adenauer, who signed the contract for the Federal Government, said: "I hope that this event shall essentially contribute to strengthen the principle of right and justice in the conscience of the peoples."

How serious the new German leaders were in their desire to make amends for the crime of the Nazi era was tested later in 1952 when the Arab countries—still technically at war with Israel while Israel was still technically at war with Germany—protested with vigor against the treaty between Germany and Israel. For several reasons they considered this treaty as an unfriendly act of Germany against the Arab states; and they announced that as a reprisal they would break off all trade relations, and cancel all commercial contracts, with West Germany. This was a serious blow against West German economic recovery; it had been particularly these undeveloped Arab markets on which the German export industry with its vital interest to the German economy had set its hopes since 1950. But West Germany remained firm and told the Arabs that she would live up to her obligations and that the reparations to Israel would be paid, whatever the consequences.

When Israel's President Weizmann died in November, 1952, the West German parliament in Bonn rose again to its feet to honor his memory in silent mourning.

The mood of the Bonn government reflected to some degree that of most Germans so far as anti-Semitism was concerned. The overwhelming majority wanted "peace with the Jews," though for many this meant only the absence of enmity made possible by the absence of contact. Even the ruthless, avowedly anti-democratic leaders of the neo-Nazi SRP, though they exploited every popular grievance and were undisguisedly nostalgic for the Third Reich, had no use for anti-Semitism. This represented no moral revolution on their part; they simply felt that Hitler's anti-Semitism was a gross political error, and, besides, that the issue had lost its demagogic value. Fritz Dorls asserted that he and his party stood for "full and equal rights for the Jews," and that Hitler's Jewish policies had been "fundamentally wrong." Anti-Semitism, he said, is "rejected by the SRP as a matter of principle." Dorls' second-in-command, Count Wolf von Westarp, added that there was "one full Jew and two half-Jews" in the party's central executive committee, and that "anti-Semitism has no place in its ranks." Insincere as they probably were, their remarks certainly indicated how unfashionable anti-Semitism as a *weltanschauung*—the way of the Third Reich—now was in Western Germany.

The only public statement defending Hitler's anti-Semitism was made in 1950 by Fritz Hedler, then deputy of the DRP *(Deutsche Rechtspartei)*, the mother party of the SRP; in an election speech, he said that "there should have been better ways to get rid of the Jews than those used by Adolf Hitler." He was promptly expelled from his party, soon faded from the political scene and was sentenced to nine months in prison. The first— and while this is being written, only—anti-Semitic speech, a veiled one at that, in the Bonn parliament was delivered fifty days after the governmental declaration on restitution by "Franz Richter," who was later exposed and removed from the Bundestag as the old Nazi leader Fritz Roesler. He claimed that for Germans to offer reparations to Israel meant trading with an enemy who had not yet ended his state of war with Germany, and that therefore the Bonn deputies who advocated these reparations were "collaborators who, according to the usage of our liberators, must be punished, as you well know, as you have approved, and as they deserve." The rest of the house answered with protest, and Richter was immediately silenced by the chairman. (Less than two months later, the same attack of collaborating with the enemy was hurled in the Israeli parliament by the spokesman of the extreme right-wing Herut party, the successor of the officially suppressed terrorist organization Irgun Zvai Leumi, in a demonstration of identical thinking among the fascist-minded, whatever their differences of "race" and nationality.)

That racist and aggressive anti-Semitism in the Hitler tradition had disappeared from German public affairs was shown most convincingly by the fact that not a single voice was raised to attack as Jews those Germans of Jewish descent, or the substantial number of Germans called by Hitler *Mischlinge* (people with one to three Jewish grandparents) who were active in the political or academic life of the new Germany. In the Weimar Republic, when such a man was elected or appointed to a public office or professorship, the rightist press, not to mention the Nazi press, was quick to denounce him as a Jew, and to slander him on the grounds of his race as inimical to German interests. Two candidates of purely German origin—in Hamburg and in Hanau— were elected in 1949 as deputies to the new parliament; in the election campaign, tough and vicious as it was, no anti-Semitic arguments were used against them. When a German of Jewish faith was in 1951 appointed vice president of the *Verfassungs-gerichtshof*—a kind of Federal supreme court—in Karlsruhe (after serving as Secretary of Justice in Schleswig-Holstein) not even an allusion was made to his being "Jewish." And few people either knew or were interested in the fact that the government's Associate Federal Secretary of Justice, or the legal adviser to the new Foreign Office, or the city treasurers of Hamburg and West Berlin were "Jews." They belonged to the twenty thousand native German Jews still living in Germany, to which they had returned from foreign exile after the fall of Hitler, or where they had managed to survive the Third Reich with the help of their non-Jewish wives, relatives, or friends. Hitler murdered 190,000 German Jews out of 500,000 who, when he came to power, had been living in Germany.

Throughout their rule, the Nazis had never ceased complaining that the majority of the German people did not participate in or "understand" their anti-Semitism. The press and literature of the Nazis written in these years bear abundant evidence that they failed indeed in making pogroms popular. When Hitler came to power in 1933, the Nazi propaganda speaker F. M. Dose reported: "My attention was drawn to the Jewish question. The views and opinions that I heard expressed on this matter simply do not bear repetition. When responsible men in Germany's social and economic life, teachers, people in every section of the community, hold an opinion which differs from that of the Führer, then it is certainly necessary that one should try to remove these phenomena." Two years later, in 1935, Dose reported that "I realized that not only did there exist an insane view and attitude on the Jewish question in intellectual circles, but also that the broad masses of the people for the most part simply did not know how to approach this question," and "that the lowest classes constantly talked of the poor persecuted Jews."[1]

After the first five years of Nazi rule, a great many Germans continued to resist anti-Semitic indoctrination. "This talk about the decent Jews," wrote one of the most popular party papers, "is like a contagious disease that is hard to stamp out. Again and again one meets blockheads who will repeat this dangerous non-

[1] F. M. Dose, *Sind 500,000 Juden ein deutsches Problem? Ist der Jude auch ein Mensch?* Köln-Kalk, 1935.

sense like parrots. Also there is no end of people who simply cannot forego their private intercourse with the Jews."[2]

A few months later, when the deadly violence of Nazi anti-Semitism had been demonstrated in public, *Das Schwarze Korps,* the official publication of the SS, stated: "We have experienced how difficult it is to mobilize the powers of defense of all strata against the Jews. The volumes of the *Schwarzes Korps* are a chronicle of this our martyrdom of untiring and inexorable monitors."[3]

After the war and the subsequent extermination of the Jews had begun, the official publication of the Hitler Youth wrote: "Reich and Party went unperturbed along the road which they deemed necessary against the Jews. The understanding of the German people lagged behind the course of events. . . . Except for those to whom our aims are a matter of course, there remains the host of people who feel embarrassed when they hear the word Jew. . . . In wide circles of the intelligentsia anti-Jewish discussions continue to be very unpopular."[4] Native anti-Semitic forces were induced to start pogroms against the Jews . . . "though this inducement proved to be very difficult," an SS brigade leader reported in a letter to Supreme SS leader Himmler.[5] In short, anti-Semitism remained under the Nazis the movement of a minority, as it had been before; the majority neither understood nor approved of its teachings, and even less its pogromistic practices.

That Hitler "committed a crime" against the Jews, or that his anti-Semitism was *"eine ganz grosse Schweinerei,"* was quite a commonplace for older Germans to say whenever the subject came up after the end of the war. Usually they stated this in a mild, very matter-of-fact way which left no doubt as to their sincerity, but which did provoke some misgivings as to whether

---

[2] *Westdeutscher Beobachter,* Köln, January 19, 1938.

[3] *Das Schwarze Korps,* November 17, 1938.

[4] *Wille und Macht,* September-October, 1943, Berlin.

[5] *Nazi Conspiracy and Aggression,* Vol. I.

they were fully aware of what Nazi anti-Semitism meant and did. Most Germans, when they spoke of Hitler's Jewish policies, condemned the *Kristallnacht*,[6] the evening of November 9, 1938, when the SA and SS burned the synagogues, looted Jewish shops, destroyed Jewish property, and arrested many Jews "in retaliation for the Grynszpan murder in Paris" (where a young Polish Jew killed an attaché of the German Embassy)—while silently passing over the extermination of millions of Jewish persons between 1942 and 1945. As a matter of fact, while the "six million murdered Jews" became the stereotyped, emotion-loaded symbol of Nazi anti-Semitism in foreign eyes, in German eyes its symbol rather remained the *Kristallnacht*. This difference was revealing.

The first, and most obvious, reason was that most Germans witnessed the *Kristallnacht* personally. It meant for them the first frightening, shocking experience of the Nazi will to destroy, and the Nazi power of destruction. But few Germans, on the other hand, witnessed personally the incomparably worse crimes of the war period when, instead of sacred buildings, shops, and merchandise, Jewish lives were destroyed. At the beginning of the war, before the murders began, after many Jews had already emigrated, the ratio of Jews to non-Jews living within the borders of pre-Hitler Germany was 1 to 300—in the United States, the ratio is 1 to 30. Therefore, considerably fewer Germans had an opportunity to be aware of the disappearance of the Jews in their midst than many Americans, applying their own standards, assumed.

While many Germans could or would do little but close their eyes to the crimes which their totalitarian rulers committed in their names, some Germans did more. Outstanding among these were Karl Friedrich Goerdeler (who resigned as Leipzig Mayor when the Nazis ordered him to remove the statue of the Jewish composer Mendelssohn-Bartholdy from a public square), General Ludwig Beck, Johannes Popitz, the Prussian Minister of

[6] Literally, the "Night of Crystal," i.e., the night when the crystal glassware owned by Jews was smashed by the Nazi troopers.

Finance, and other men of July 20, who were induced by the pogroms and persecutions of the Jews, among other crimes, to take their heroic course. They all paid for it with their lives, as did also Elisabeth von Thadden, headmistress of an aristocratic Prussian girls' school, Otto C. Kiep, former German Consul General in New York City, and a number of officials in the German Foreign Office, who were executed for having shielded Jews. There was also a considerable number of unknown people who helped Jewish relatives and friends at the risk of their own lives. Neither their number nor their kindness and courage can be summed up in a statistical figure. Yet the large majority of Germans lacked either the opportunity or the kindness or the courage to take any such action.

Of those Germans who witnessed, or heard of, the arrest or disappearance of Jewish friends or acquaintances, many tended to believe what the Nazis told them—"the Jews were resettled in the Lublin area," a district in occupied Poland. It was the time when large migrations and dislocations were the order of the day in Germany as a whole. Some rumors and reports on the real fate of the Jews trickled back to Germany, mainly from enemy broadcasts, occasionally from letters of German soldiers. Yet most Germans, while they saw the *Kristallnacht* themselves, learned about the death camps only after the war when their whole world was, physically and morally, collapsing about them, when they were completely taken up with the problem of sheer survival, when nine million Germans arrived as fugitives from the East where two million Germans had been killed after the war; when atrocity stories were a dime a dozen. The very particular case of the murdered Jews merged in their minds with the destruction of millions of other lives in the war and the postwar period; there was little room left in the consciences and emotions of many Germans for the Jewish case; after they were acquainted with all the facts, the facts still lacked full status as reality.

But as the years went by, their minds still resisted accepting these facts as reality. This had been predicted in December, 1939, a few months after the outbreak of the war, when the German Catholic philosopher Theodor Haecker noted in his secret diary, one of the few great literary documents written under the Third Reich and published posthumously after the war: "One may assume that the Germans, consciously or subconsciously, will do everything to forget as quickly as possible what is being said, written, and done today in Germany. Memories of guilt are lasting, therefore they are painful. Man gets rid of them whenever he can. But God has still to decide whether he can."[7] This explained indeed why twelve years later, many (perhaps most) Germans preferred to forget, to suppress in their minds the memory of the murder. On the one hand, they felt an embarrassment which often grew to a vague, helpless sense of shame—"how could they do it, in our names." On the other hand, they wanted to protest their innocence—"there was nothing I could do against it." Both the sense of shame and the sense of innocence were authentic, although they seemed to conflict with each other; the conflict exposed the basic tragedy of the individual under totalitarian rule when crimes are committed in his name, without his will, making him simultaneously guilty and innocent, a helpless accessory to the crime and a passive, unwilling accomplice. This conflicting, unhappy feeling was well expressed in a phrase of the philosopher Karl Jaspers which became quite popular after the war among German intellectuals: *"Dass wir leben, ist unsere Schuld"*—That we are alive is our guilt. The phrase was as ambiguous as the feeling which produced it, and in a less articulate, less precise way, the feeling took hold of many *unpolitische* in Germany.

The more particularly German tragedy of the *unpolitische* individual accentuated this totalitarian tragedy. He meekly accepted the course and the actions of the state, democratic or totalitarian. Whether it pursued politics or committed crimes, he neglected privately the *force majeure* for which he did not feel responsible,

---

[7] Theodor Haecker, *Tag- und Nachtbücher*, München, 1947. *Journal in the Night*, New York, 1950.

and which he, being "only a little man," could not change. He felt especially so in the matter of racial persecution, from which (if and when he could secure the proof of his "Aryan grand-mother") he individually was rather safe; it was none of his busi-ness. But beneath and despite this good, sincerely proffered alibi of the *unpolitische,* the individual suffered on occasion from the pangs of his bad conscience. Although—as a *Privatmann*—he would not understand his responsibilities in the political com-munity, neither could he quite suppress his awareness of the di-vine commandment to love his neighbor and to be his brother's keeper.

He had voiced his subconscious guilt in the bomb shelters dur-ing the war, when he had said, faced with death and destruction: "That's our punishment for the *Kristallnacht.*" Even a cynic like Ernst von Salomon, who had participated in the murder of Walter Rathenau in 1923 and remained a hard-boiled nationalist, ad-mitted in his best-selling autobiography, published in 1951, that this feeling overcame him in the seclusion of his apartment, in the midst of the looting and the destruction of the *Kristallnacht:* "We shall remember this day when everything else will be for-gotten; it's an eternal curse on us." For not having been their brother's keeper, the non-Nazi Germans felt in their souls the curse of Cain. Unable to understand their own past failures and therefore unable to resolve never to let it happen again, they pre-ferred to black out as much as possible the memory of their sin, to repress the feeling of shame, to remain unaware of the reality, and rather to debate whether the facts of the past were true facts.[8]

---

[8] The unreconstructed Nazis denied the truth of the fact altogether. Some played a shocking numbers game, pretending that "merely" one and a half mil-lion, or two million or three million Jews could have been murdered—a statisti-cal claim which seemed to absolve the murderers of their guilt. Others went farther, and pretended that Jews had not been murdered at all—the photographic and cinematographic evidence to the contrary, since it presented only posed American horror pictures. In an obscure mimeographed news-letter addressed from Berchtesgaden to former SS men I read the most cynical explanation: The Jews were racially less tough than the Aryans, and therefore less able to with-stand the hardships of the war, in which they died in great numbers a perfectly natural death.

Totalitarianism encouraged, and almost made unavoidable for many, the passive toleration of its public crimes. The unadmitted guilt in the backwash of totalitarianism still tended to corrupt vast areas of the succeeding society and to obstruct the necessary epuration.

That a feeling of guilt persisted for a long time was shown in many remarks one could hear all over Germany—for instance, the frequent saying, "We lost the war in November, 1938, when Hitler burned the synagogues." Oddly, this was said without any hate, even with an appreciation of the right of the Jews—or "world Jewry"—to retaliate. A driver in Berlin, to whom I commented on the ruins of the Kurfuerstendamm before our eyes, answered: "Yes, that's where the Jews lived before the war. They specially instructed the *Ami* bombers to bomb their houses first." When I said that I thought things were different, he replied angrily: "You don't know how furious the Jews were against Hitler—perhaps you don't even know what Hitler did to them."

In September, 1949, a majority of the aldermen's committee of the industrial city of Offenbach near Frankfurt voted to appoint Dr. Erwin Lewin of Cologne as senior physician of the municipal gynecological hospital. The mayor of the city objected to the appointment on the grounds that a man who had suffered as badly under Hitler as the Jewish Dr. Lewin, who had been in a concentration camp and whose family had been murdered by the Nazis, could not be expected to be a good doctor in a German hospital; he might some day be overcome by understandable resentments and the impulse for revenge. The appointment was cancelled, and the latter fact was reported in the foreign press as a typical and shocking instance of resurgent Nazi anti-Semitism. The reasons that had led to it, which were guilt feelings, though misdirected and confused, were not even mentioned in these reports. Neither was it reported that the Hessian state government suspended the mayor from his office, and that the municipal council of the city of Offenbach, with a vote of all its delegates from all political parties, approved this suspension and voted again for Dr. Lewin's appointment to the job.

The young—that is, most Germans who were still under thirty in the early 1950's—had little awareness of, or interest in, the whole tragic matter of Hitler's crime against the Jews. They grew up after it was over, and while they had the overpowering memories of the chaos that prevailed at the end of the war and in the first postwar years, few had any personal experience of Nazi anti-Semitism in action, or even any personal contact with Jews. Among several smaller groups of younger intellectuals, there developed a sort of violent philo-Semitism. Among them were university students who met visiting professors of Jewish descent after the war and by this encounter became aware of the whole problem. Quite a few young Germans became fanatical anti-anti-Semites as a result of their experience with Jews such as Victor Gollancz, the British publisher and politician connected with the Labor Party and Zionism, who had been one of the earliest and most energetic foes of Nazism and after its defeat visited Germany and appealed to the world to help the Germans in their ruins and starvation. That members of the "race" they had been told was plotting their destruction actually came to save and support Germany persuaded many young Germans to fight the anti-Semitic teachings of Hitler.

Most often, the young anti-anti-Semites of Germany were also very active in the general political struggle for democracy. They felt that the fight against anti-Semitism was a test case and an educational catalyst of this more general struggle, and that, after all the injustice done to the Jews, they had a special obligation to go to great lengths, and sometimes lean over backwards, to show their sympathy with the Jews. In several cases, they proved how serious a task this fight seemed to them. When, in 1951 and 1952, two new non-political motion pictures, directed by Veit Harlan, an old actor who, although he had directed and played in the notoriously pogromistic Nazi play "Jew Süss," had been legally cleared by denazification courts, were shown in their cities, hundreds of students in Berlin, Freiburg, Göttingen demonstrated excitedly against the reappearance of the tainted man. When in 1952 leading West German professors, artists, and writers publicly appealed to their countrymen to buy olive trees for Israel as a lasting and productive gesture of their bid for forgiveness and their wish for friendship with the Jews, they found a large response at the West German universities. A nationwide group of Catholics, affiliated with the Caritas Association, the Catholic Welfare group led by Gertrud Luckner, who herself had suffered in a Nazi concentration camp for her heroic attempts to save Jews, called indefatigably for "friendship between the old and the new peoples of God, in the spirit of both Testaments." Protestant, political, and professional groups did similar work. But for most young people, neither anti-Semitism nor anti-anti-Semitism was important. Their interest in politics was in any case peripheral, and all their passion was involved in their personal futures and their private worlds.

What passed for anti-Semitism in West Germany after Hitler's fall, what the American press got so agitated about, and what most foreign observers viewed with alarm as surviving or resurgent anti-Semitism had actually little to do with Nazi anti-Semitism, from which it differed completely in its motives, its character, its appearances, and its goals.

An instance of this was given in August, 1949, when the world press reported that the Möhlstrasse in the city of Munich had been the scene of the "worst anti-Semitic outbursts since Hitler." Most dispatches gave the impression that a Munich newspaper had published an anti-Semitic item, and that Jewish DP's who assembled in protest against it were run down and shot at by the police and the people of Munich. Here, it was implied, was the avenue leading to a new Auschwitz. What actually occurred was rather different from what the correspondents reported.

To understand the story and its meaning, we must go back a bit. In the essentially rural city of Munich, the Möhlstrasse was once a quiet pleasant street of semi-suburban, well-to-do villas, just four blocks long and bordering on the Isar River. Its new career began after the surrender, when the international relief organizations for Displaced Persons of Jewish and other origins were billeted in the requisitioned houses of the Möhlstrasse and its neighborhood, which happened to be less ruined than the rest of the city. People from East and Southeast Europe, swept in by the thousands, came to these offices in search of immediate help and a more promising future.

The little streets around these offices soon became the meeting place and the market place of these DP's. They stood around in the street, exchanged rumors, gossip, information, made deals of all sorts among themselves and soon with the German population. In the first postwar years, such rare goods as cigarets, coffee, food of all sorts, could be freely bought at the Möhlstrasse, as everybody in Munich knew. The Allied Occupation Military Governments formally protected the DP's from any control by the German police. Practically free to do as they pleased, the DP's became, in a real sense, the black market.

Most of these DP's tried to leave Germany as soon as they could, and during the first postwar years most of them succeeded in migrating to Palestine, to America, or other overseas countries. In 1949 only a minority of approximately ten thousand Jewish DP's remained in Munich, still milling around the Möhlstrasse, which became a strange new settlement, a booming shack town such as those in the America of the gold-rush years. The Möhlstrasse and the four little side streets leading to it were now the shopping district, where almost everything was for sale. The stores were a little different from the usual run of shops. Some of them consisted only of a table crudely set up on the street, with some merchandise spread out on it and the rest hidden in a cheap suitcase over which the owner stood guard. The next stage of economic progress was marked by an umbrella protecting goods and salesman, perhaps with a cart replacing the more primitive table. The next shop would have a primitive booth around the table, giving the first hint of a real store. Then a display window was added, and often a small back room was finally built and the raw wooden structure improved into a small con-

crete hut. In the Möhlstrasse—as in many streets of German cities
where similar makeshift shopping avenues grew up after the war
in and before the ruins they were hiding—one could find all
these types side by side, in free competition and unsystematic
mixture, demonstrating like a living museum the development
of retailing from trading post to modern stores.

What made the Jewish Möhlstrasse different from the many
German shack-town streets mushrooming over the cities was that
it was openly devoted to the black market. When the shortage of
goods was overcome after the currency reform in June, 1948, the
regular stores had everything to offer, and the black-market business with its exorbitant prices had to close down for lack of customers in normal competition, the Möhlstrasse competed by selling a variety of goods at cut-rate prices, which attracted shoppers
from all over Munich, especially the poor. Food stores dominated,
offering everything from Argentine beef to French brandy, and
on the tins of American cocoa amply displayed in the windows
one could read the labels saying "A Gift from the American
Jews" and the name of a relief organization. As a matter of fact,
wholesale black marketeers ordered and received large amounts
of foreign foodstuffs from relief organizations, some of them
fictitious, which, since they were paid for by foreign charity, entered the country customs free and could be sold tax-free, at a
price that was considerably under the current German market.
There were also in the Möhlstrasse many stores selling silverware,
clothing, shoes, and furs—usually smuggled into the country.
From early morning to late evening trading went on between the
men who spoke Yiddish, Polish, Ukrainian, other Eastern languages, and their customers who answered in the Bavarian dia-
lect. Every few steps in the Möhlstrasse neighborhood one ran
into a little group of men who, in a secretive manner, traded in
bills and bank notes of all countries—which was strictly forbidden under Allied currency regulations—as well as forged birth
certificates, passports, entry permits, affidavits, doctors' diplomas,
documents attesting the bearer to be a priest, and so on. The

newsstands at the corners displayed only foreign-language newspapers, and the waiters in the restaurants refused to translate their menus into German.

A few days before the Möhlstrasse made the headlines of the world press, I happened to talk with several inhabitants of the little foreign colony in Munich. Most of them did not want to leave Germany because they saw better business opportunities here than anywhere else in the world. Some of them had already done very well, and hoped to do still better. Others wanted to save money so they could emigrate overseas with sufficient capital. There was a young Jew from Poland who had survived the horrors of a Nazi concentration camp, studied medicine after the war in Holland, had an immigration visa to the United States, and planned to go there as soon as he had earned the ten thousand dollars which, his relatives in America had written him, he would need to get started in his profession. There was an elderly man from Latvia who sold silver candlesticks and cigarettes; he had heard that people were starving in the States, that business was bad in Israel, and he was quite happy here in the Möhlstrasse. Most of the people of the Möhlstrasse, uprooted from their former homes, able to survive only by highly developed toughness, and without family and community ties, considered that they had a moral right to get the best out of life, and especially out of Germany, which, they felt, had pushed them into their present state. Except for the exchange of goods and money, there was hardly any relation between them and the German population. They distrusted each other, but found each other economically useful. The people of Munich disliked these Jews, exactly as every rural society dislikes a group of foreigners in its midst, but there was no actual hostility.

Now for the more immediate background of the unhappy events which led to the "worst anti-Semitic outburst since Hitler," according to the American newspapers. At the end of July, 1949, John J. McCloy, the newly appointed United States High Commissioner for Germany, met with a number of American and

Jewish leaders in charge of Jewish affairs, and asserted in his speech that the gauge of the democratic regeneration of Germany would be the development of a new attitude on the part of the Germans towards the Jews. Taking up this point, the *Süddeutsche Zeitung,* the largest morning newspaper in Munich, published a long editorial stressing McCloy's statement, elaborating on it from the German view, and strongly condemning all forms of social or subconscious anti-Semitism which some of its readers still might consider "legitimate."

A week later, the *Süddeutsche Zeitung* printed in its "Letters-to-the-Editor" column four letters referring to the editorial; three emphatically approved its message, a fourth objected in vitriolic language. It told the Jews to "go to America, but there they don't have any use for you, they too are fed up with these bloodsuckers. I'm employed by the American occupation authorities, and some of them have already said to me that they forgive us everything but that we haven't gassed all of the Jews, who are now enjoying themselves in America. . . ." The letter went on explaining that "we"—those who think about the Jews as did the writer of the letter—"are a very small circle. . . . Please publish my letter if you're really a 'democrat.' "

The editor of the "Letters" column, who happened himself to be the author of the anti-anti-Semitic editorial in question, published this letter, thinking of it as an educational document which would repel his readers and warn them that pathological anti-Semites still existed in their midst. He tried to act as the American press does, opening its columns to the free expression of every opinion. However, he did not note that the signature under the letter, "Adolf Bleibtreu, München 22, Palestinastrasse 33," was a transparent pseudonym; it meant "Adolf, Remain Faithful, Palestine Street," and "33" was the year in which Hitler came to power.

The news of the publication of this letter soon reached the Möhlstrasse, where German newspapers were not usually read. A crowd of two to three hundred offended Jews gathered immediately and decided to march on the offices of the "Nazi paper" and smash or burn them. Their belief was that it was the editorial opinion of the *Süddeutsche Zeitung* rather than that of a protesting letter to its editor that "all the Jews should be gassed."

The American Military Government in Germany had a ruling that all public meetings and demonstrations must be licensed by it; here was undoubtedly a case of a spontaneous, unlicensed demonstration. Spokesmen of the Jewish Committee representing the DP's tried to talk the demonstrators out of their folly, but to no avail. The six Munich policemen on duty in the neighborhood also tried to stop the demonstration, but were swept away by the crowd.

When the inflamed crowd had moved on a few blocks to the Statue of the Angel of Peace, which stands at the point where the Möhlstrasse district leads to the main part of the city, it had grown to more than 750 in number. Here the Munich police tried again to stop them, again in vain. At this point a detachment of Munich mounted policemen arrived and galloped toward the advancing mass. They were greeted by a volley of stones from the ruins surrounding the Angel of Peace.

Precisely what happened in the next few minutes has never been established with absolute certainty. At least one policeman, perhaps more, got panicky and fired into the threatening crowd. It is certain that the police had not received permission or orders from their superior officers to use their guns. Later they claimed that they were surrounded by the furious mob and acted in self-defense. On the other hand, the Jews wounded by the shots of the police were wounded from behind, which proved that they were not the attackers, unless the police fired blindly into the crowd. A short struggle followed, fought with clubs by police, with stones and sticks by the Jews. Only a few German civilians participated in this fight on the side of the police; even fewer fought on the Jewish side.

In the next thirty minutes two companies of Military Police of the United States Army were rushed to the scene and drew a cordon between the Jews and the Munich police. American officers, including a Jewish army chaplain and an executive of a Jewish relief organization, spoke to the Jews from loud-speakers mounted on trucks and asked them to disperse. When quiet was finally restored, at least six Jews had been hurt by shots and six more beaten up; the police said that twenty-six of their men were wounded. There were no deaths. The investigation which ensued, and in which the authorized representatives of the Jews took part, led to the conclusion that "no anti-Semitic tendencies had played a part in the Munich police force." The German press protested against the mistake of publishing the letter, of sending mounted police against the demonstrators, and against anti-Semitism in general. The American press carried the picture of a car with a big swastika amid the crowd of excited Jews to show the organized onslaught of the Nazis against the helpless victims—who in their fury had themselves painted the swastika on the car.

If this was anti-Semitism, it bore little resemblance to the anti-Semitism of the Nazis, nor was it a recrudescence of it. It was anti-Semitism of a newer—and yet older—breed. What really happened in the Möhlstrasse, and what as an extreme situation indicated the relations between Germans and Jews in Germany since the end of the war, was a sudden outburst of mass hysteria that explodes occasionally when there is a state of underground tension between what social psychologists call an "in-group" majority and an "out-group" minority. Ethnically, socially, economically, in language, habits, appearance, social status, the Jews of the Möhlstrasse, like all the displaced Jews of the postwar period, undoubtedly formed a typical out-group. The mere mention of the word "gassing" and of Nazi atrocities in the past was likely to startle them into a precipitate reaction. Foreigners in a country they had every reason to distrust, and which distrusted them, they could hardly be expected to react rationally to such incitement. The backwash of the great crime of the past poisoned the present. The Germans acted defensively against these Jews, not aggressively as Nazi anti-Semitism had done. As a German effort to eradicate anti-Semitism was misunderstood and rebuffed in hostility by the Jews, and as this was the reason for the riot, it well symbolized the tragedy of German-Jewish relations amid the ruins of the Third Reich.

If the German historian Theodor Mommsen referred in the 1880's to the German Jews as "another German tribe," half of the Jews in Germany in the 1950's were, admittedly and undoubtedly, a very foreign tribe in the midst of the Germans. This was brought about by Hitler. Although, after his fall, the German Jews were accepted as Germans, "Jewish" became synonymous with "foreign" in German eyes. Distrustful and defensive attitudes toward these foreigners were different from the racist and aggressive attitudes the Nazis had promoted against Germans of Jewish origins.

In Bavaria or Franconia, Germans often made the odd comment: "What a mess the Führer made—he hounded away our good Jews, and now we have instead all these bad Jews." An elderly woman in Frankfurt, after telling me how she had hidden her Jewish neighbors until she ended in a concentration camp, advised me with friendly concern that I should not walk alone late at night on the Bahnhofstrasse, the Möhlstrasse of her city, since "the Jews" there were dangerous people who attacked strangers and robbed them. A pastry baker in Fürth, who had been sent to jail because he had brought his fresh pastry as a gift every day to the house in which old Jews of his town were kept prisoners by the Nazis, explained to me that it was a matter of course that he should have done so. A little later he had hard words for "the Jews" in a nearby displaced persons camp. A high official in the West Berlin police who returned to her job after surviving a Nazi concentration camp, and whose Jewish descent was generally known, told me that occasionally policemen reported to her raids against "the Jews," by which they meant the black-market centers of Jewish DP's, without realizing that they were talking to a "Jew."

The situation deteriorated considerably after 1950, by which time the great mass of the Jewish DP's had left Germany altogether. Of those who remained, a very small number established respectable businesses. There were also approximately a thousand who married German girls and fused into German life. There was still in 1951 a somewhat larger group of Jews living in the last Jewish DP camp, for the most part sick people waiting to be sent to Israel by agreement and payment of the United Nations-sponsored International Refugee Organization (IRO), and so-called "returnees," Jews who had returned from Israel after living there for one or more years and not liking it. Hidden away from public view, living a rather autarchic community life (except for shopping or bartering in the nearby village, employing local cleaning women, and having clandestine relations with their Bavarian neighbors), these DP's remained practically invisible to the Germans.

It was different with that unhappily larger and more conspicuous group of Jewish DP's who preferred to stay in Germany because it seemed to afford them an opportunity to live lawlessly on the fringes of society. The Möhlstrasse had outwardly overcome its lowly black-market beginnings, looking more prosperous with new coffeehouses and restaurants, normal stores, and cars parked in front of them. But rather tough-looking groups of young men now watched every passer-by suspiciously, and police raids turned up large quantities of stolen or smuggled goods. Along with smuggling on a big scale, various other rackets flourished.

Similar situations had developed in other big cities, and some smaller ones. In West Berlin, the big-time smuggling across the Iron Curtain was mainly a Jewish DP business. A nationwide band, calling itself "The Strong Ones" *(Die Starken),* and its offshoot, "The Rebels," *(Die Aufständischen),* both with methods very similar to the American gangs of the Prohibition era, succeeded in dominating most DP crime. When one of its members was "taken for a ride" and knifed to death, or when others were arrested, police and press referred only cautiously to "X, an alien," or "a member of the alien gang, The Strong Ones," but the common assumption was that a Jew was meant. Even when "alien" referred to a Greek, a Ukrainian, a Slovak, or another national of Germany's great underworld with the gangs lined up along strictly ethnic lines, it was usually taken for granted that he was a Jew.

Only a few thoughtful Germans remembered that it was Hitler who threw these DP's, both Jews and others, into the path of crime, first by uprooting them from their native communities, then by forcing them to dodge and break the law continuously if they wanted to survive, finally by making them believe that laws were made for others and that they had no duties toward them, in this case mainly and particularly, the Germans. That so few Germans asked for the reason why these Jewish DP's had become the unpleasant, parasitic characters they were, and that therefore few Germans exculpated them, showed mainly that Germans are human. There are few people anywhere in the world who sympathetically ask for the reasons why a cutthroat is holding them up at night with a knife, and then forgive him because he comes from an "underprivileged," perhaps persecuted, group, with experiences of lynch law and "in-group" arrogance behind him. And given the regrettable, yet world-wide tendency to undue generalizations, it seemed equally human that few Germans took the time to recognize the fact that these Jewish DP's were only part of the last small residue of a large group that had left Germany, and that they constituted a tiny, very abnormal selection from "the Jews" as a whole. To many Germans, especially the young, these Jews—the only Jews they had ever seen—almost necessarily appeared as "the Jews." They feared and despised them, first as the shady, dangerous outlaws they really were, rather than as Jews; but eventually, both images tended to fuse into one and to supply the basis for a new antagonistic stereotype of "the Jews" in German eyes.

Whether to call this new stereotype "anti-Semitic" or not is a question of semantics—at any rate it was not the stereotype that led to pogroms. It lacked the irrational, pathological features of the Nazi stereotype, which saw the Jews as political, social, intellectual, cultural, spiritual, national and even sexual threats to Germany in particular, and to humanity in general. It lacked the delusional fear of a Jewish conspiracy for the riches, the power, and the domination of the world, and the racial basis as well as the aggressive character of the Nazi stereotype. It was only a rational defense against an actually alien and asocial group whose members would be the first proudly to confirm that they were foreign and dangerous to Germany. Compensating themselves for the humiliations and outrages they had suffered less than a decade ago from Germans, this was exactly what they wanted to be. If the Jews, like the Germans, were neither more nor less than human, unfortunately quite a few spokesmen of both groups tended to grant the privilege of being human only to their own group, whose behavior thereby became "completely understandable," while they censured and condemned the equally human behavior of the other group.

The stereotype of the Jew as a parasitic "enemy of society" was widespread all over Europe before the rise of capitalism when there was also a very small, very foreign group of Jews living among the peoples, doing business with them, selling commodities and exchanging money in more expert ways than their native competitors, sometimes practicing usury, or smuggling, or forming gangs of robbers because the society in which they lived forced them onto these ways, living in hypertrophied *commercium* and without *connubium* with other peoples. Before Moses Mendelssohn opened the spiritual intermarriage between Germans and Jews in the eighteenth century, before Heinrich Heine and Ludwig Börne appeared as masters of the German language half a century later, the Jews lived in Germany exactly as the displaced Jews did in the new Germany, looking back to recent martyrdom, a foreign tribe feared by, and fearing, the Germans. The Jews in Germany stood in the 1950's where they stood two hundred years ago, as if there had been no Hitler, or rather, because there has been a Hitler.

The old stereotype of the Jew as an economically and socially dangerous outsider of society, after being revived in West Germany in 1945 by the mass invasion of the displaced Jews, was reinforced after 1949 by several rather sensational scandals that were front-page news and became topics of general conversation. After the so-called Morgenbesser case in Frankfurt, where the director of the Jewish Restitution Bank and some of his co-workers fled abroad after embezzling the capital of their bank—for the most part "Jewish money"—the Auerbach case in Munich became from 1950–52 the center of national and international interest.

Philipp Auerbach was an ambitious, impressive, perhaps mentally disturbed adventurer of the kind that rise in disturbed times and fall with the normalization of society. Born in 1906 in Hamburg, where he attended the Hebrew High School without being graduated, then going into business, he left Germany for Belgium when Hitler came to power. There he was sentenced and fined for unlawfully working as a drug manufacturer. He was arrested by the Nazis when they invaded Belgium, and was sent to several concentration camps, where he became a Nazi-appointed "barracks chief." In 1945 he was liberated by the British and employed for a while by their Military Government which finally dismissed him for incompetence.

At the time, Bavaria had just fired its first—non-Jewish—State Commissioner for the Persecutees of Hitler and was looking for a new one. On the recommendation of the Social Democratic Party, which Auerbach had joined, and vouched for by Jewish relief organizations, Auerbach was appointed to this important job. In his *curriculum vitae,* which nobody bothered to check, he described himself as a doctor of science, a hero of the resistance against the Nazis, and a man sentenced to death by a Nazi People's Court—none of which was true. As State Commissioner for the Persecutees of Hitler, and later as president of the Land Compensation Office, Auerbach gave weekly sermons over the Bavarian radio, acquired influence by involving himself in Bavarian politics, acted as assistant rabbi of the Jewish communities in Bavaria as well as their political representative, and was a public speaker on every occasion at which Hitler's victims made themselves heard. Within his jurisdiction were those Jews who after the war had crowded into Bavaria, as well as the claims of all other Bavarian persecutees and their heirs. He had the power to decide what claims going through his office should be approved, and whether there was to be immediate payment or none. The settlement of these claims involved complicated deals with Bavarian authorities and banks.

Although there were persistent rumors about strange things that went on in Auerbach's office, ranging from bribery to blackmail, forgery, perjury, theft, and large-scale smuggling, they provoked no action. But finally, in the summer of 1951, the Bavarian Minister of Justice raided Auerbach's office and arrested him. Auerbach promptly protested this "act of anti-Semitism." The minister was Joseph Müller, himself a colorful character, three times arrested by the Gestapo as a secret agent of the Allies, active during the war in the German army intelligence and simultaneously in the plot to kill Hitler and overthrow Nazism, sentenced to death by a Nazi People's Court. He now led the minority group of the Bavarian Catholic Party (CSU, *Christlich-Sociale Union*), which opposed its majority in favor of German participation in the military Western defense, this majority being led by bearded, medieval President Dr. Alois Hundhammer, who became known for his advocacy of caning in schools and his opposition to equality of the sexes. A Machiavellian with the shrewd, friendly manners and features of a fat Bavarian peasant, Minister Müller was a long-time foe of Auerbach.

The Munich Court sifted the accusations and the evidence of the Auerbach case for seventeen weeks. In August, 1952, it pronounced its sentence. While many charges against Auerbach could not be substantiated, he was found guilty on several grounds: demanding and accepting bribes and embezzling small sums. He was sentenced to thirty months in prison. Two days later, Auerbach, now a very ill man in a hospital, took his life.

The big and ugly Auerbach case could be—and was—"explained," of course. After all, German officialdom as a whole in the first postwar years was not so pure and spotless that the Auerbach case could be viewed and judged in isolation. And then the business of compensating a large number of penniless foreigners for losses the actuality of which could rarely be proved, at least not in a hurry, while payments had to be made in a hurry, was something so unheard of that only a non-bureaucratic "bohemian" like Auerbach could have tackled the job at all, and it was not too astonishing that he used unusual methods. Jews experienced perhaps greater temptations than others. After all the injustice done them, many felt no sense of responsibility toward the German community. Moreover, they could act with a certain measure of impunity. Many Germans—not to speak of the occupation authorities for whom a Jew was often innocent even when proven guilty—at the time gave a kind of general absolution to anything done by a Jew. Thus, among some unscrupulous Jews, the feeling could easily develop that "anything goes."

Yet most Germans—as would most people anywhere—did not think about the juicy scandal surrounding Auerbach, or the crime chronicle of the DP's and "The Strong Ones," in the large terms of cause and effect. Nor did they trace the chain of guilt which reached far back to the past. The great grafter in his luxurious office and the little racketeer on the street corner were "Jews" to be distrusted and disliked. As a result, anti-Semitic insinuations and innuendoes that would not have been listened to in the first years after the war were heard again after 1950; they did not intrude into politics, were rarely made explicit in print, and certainly were completely different from the anti-Semitism before or in the Nazi epoch. Yet they tainted the atmosphere. Auerbach was neither a victim of new German persecutions, as some legend builders claimed after his death, nor was he the great supercriminal, as some hate-mongers tried to depict him. The tragic chain which started with the totalitarian Nazi assault against the moral order destroyed him in the end, with the monstrous guilt of the murderers leading to the petty guilt of the victim.

It was probably inevitable that, in the backwash of crime, the corruption of the past should still be visible like the ruins of the past, and should infect the atmosphere. What in American eyes are "normal" standards of community relations and group tolerance could not yet be applied in Germany, where the aftereffects of totalitarian rule and total war still dominated all physical, moral, and spiritual existence, notwithstanding the great achievements of reconstruction. Since so few Jews were left, and since the few who were left formed an increasingly abnormal group, German attitudes toward them did not indicate much about the index of real tolerance prevailing today in Germany.

In the Franconian town of Aschaffenburg, an empty lot of ruins was transformed into a little park. At the center of the saplings and flower beds there stood in 1952 a simple white tombstone on which were engraved two lines written by Friedrich Hölderlin more than a century ago:

> *Alas, the dead you cannot bring to life*
> *Unless it is love that does so.*

In smaller letters, the legend continued: "Here stood the synagogue of the Jewish Community, which, on November 9, 1938, was destroyed by criminal hands."

Hölderlin's verse, chosen by the town fathers of the little German town for the memorial stone, might well serve as a melancholy motto and the quintessence of any and every survey of the postwar relations between Germans and Jews. They were still dominated by the dead whom murderous hands destroyed.

In Eastern Germany, where totalitarianism was re-established after its overthrow, anti-Semitism was officially outlawed, as in

West Germany. The situation of the Jews under the Soviet dictatorship was one of the few things in which East Germany seemed truly to differ from the previous Nazi dictatorship. Yet this was a deceptive surface impression. For one thing, there were almost no Jews living in East Germany. Except for convinced Communists of Jewish origins, the few non-Communist Jews who returned from foreign exile, or who survived the Nazis and did not flee to the West, were imprisoned and sent to concentration camps—as "Western agents" if they came from a Western country after the war, as "economic criminals" if they tried to build up a new business.

In contrast to West Germany, East Germany did not offer reparation payments to the Jews or to Israel. And while East Germany herself did not admit any Jewish DP's, its press, in denouncing the conditions in West Germany, described the DP's as a symptom of Western decadence and corruption. The most blatant anti-Semitic attack of that kind was delivered by Anna Seghers, winner of the Stalin Peace Prize in 1951, herself of West German-Jewish origin and a Communist novelist, propagandist, and old-time party hack.

A small number of Communists of Jewish origins were still employed in 1952 in the propaganda departments and the universities of the party, though none was given a standing in the party hierarchy itself. But they shared this disregard with the non-Jewish Communists, who had also spent their years of emigration in Western countries and were suspected of being tainted with Western influences which made them unbearable for party leadership although they were still useful for party work.

Whether they were neglected as Jews or as "Westerners," anti-Semitic stereotypes became identical with anti-Western stereotypes, when the leaders of the Red Reich—in accordance with orders from Moscow which had been given to all the countries in the Soviet sphere—opened their great crusade against the "cosmopolites" in cultural and political life. The *Tägliche Rundschau,* a daily newspaper published by the Soviet Military Administration for Berlin and the Soviet zone, commissioned Arnold Zweig, an old, near-blind novelist who returned from his exile in Tel Aviv to East Berlin after the war, to write the keynote attack against the "cosmopolitan" German writers. The order was quickly and suddenly cancelled after the author delivered his piece, and the editor was told by a secretary that Zweig was "himself a Jew." The published article was written instead by the Communist party writer Bodo Uhse, a former Nazi and "of purely Aryan descent."

After 1951, the Red Reich's persistent and acrimonious denunciations of the "passportless, rootless cosmopolites, the bearded and hook-nosed enemies of national sovereignty, the international disintegrators of a true people's culture," clearly took up the Nazi stereotype of the Jews. Since Communism reverted to open and venomous anti-Semitism when it sentenced to death the Jewish Communist leaders of Czechoslovakia in November, 1952, and lashed out against the "Jewish world conspiracy" which it identified with the "American world conspiracy," the instigation and exploitation of hatred against the Jews became a basic tenet of Communist totalitarianism.

If there were few spectacular attacks against the Jews in East Germany, it was because her few Jews were oppressed like everybody else—with the racial equality of the dungeon democracy. If there was an occasional sign of anti-Semitism in West Germany, it was a by-product of the ruination brought about by the totalitarian past, which can be removed only slowly, and which can be removed completely only after a new order has been firmly established.

IX

Soviet Man of German Make

STALIN remarked to President Roosevelt at Yalta early in 1945, three months before the Third Reich's unconditional surrender, that "it may take twenty or thirty years for Germany to recover from her defeat and to restore her power." Six years later, the then Minister of Foreign Trade of the Communist government of East Germany, Georg Handtke, declared in a speech that it might take twenty-five or thirty years "for us to produce the German *Planmenschen*—planned men—after the Soviet pattern."

In the first seven years of their rule the Soviets achieved the first stage of their goal in East Germany. Midway in their production of "planned men after the Soviet pattern" they succeeded in transforming the East Germans into a strange, contradictory, ambivalent people. Their success was demonstrated for the first time in the summer of 1951 when millions of East German girls and boys were shipped to East Berlin to participate in the "World Festival of Youth and Students for Peace."

The parades, games, and demonstrations seemed on the surface a repetition of Hitler's yesterday. But there was a new, even more frightening overtone, which, rather than pointing back to the recent past, pointed forward to the nightmarish future George Orwell depicted in his last book, *Nineteen Eighty-Four*. In one of the spectacles several thousand young workers from an East German steel mill, all dressed in baggy gowns of different dull colors, assembled on a gridiron and arranged themselves to portray a giant steel-working machine. Then the wheels and cogs of the machine, each a small group of young men and women, began moving with technical accuracy, first slowly and then quicker and quicker, until you forgot completely that human beings performed the complicated act. The guests of honor, German Communist leaders and Soviet generals, applauded with a happy grin as the human machine moved and worked in exact imitation of a real, factory machine.

In another presentation of what was called People's Culture, thousands of school children in bathing suits arranged themselves to form a giant head. It was the head of a man with a familiar mustache, pipe, and epaulets, whose name was continually shouted by the loud-speaker and echoed by the children transformed into his likeness: "To the greatest friend of the world's children, the great Joseph Vissarionovich Stalin, hurrah, hurrah, hurrah!"

Each of the countless units of the parade "for peace and against the Western warmongers," as they marched along Berlin's former main boulevard, Unter den Linden, was preceded by an immense poster bearing the portrait of some great Bolshevik —most often, of course, Stalin himself. There were thousands of these posters, some so gigantic that the youngsters carrying them broke down from the weight. But that was not all. Every member of the thousands of units held high above his head a smaller reproduction of the same Communist leader whose portrait preceded the group. Thus it seemed that the paraders had ceased to exist individually and had been molded into an octopus with a thousand heads. They were nothing but floats conveying the exalted rulers forward.

Yet through all the long hours of the big parade I could not detect a sign of passion on the marching faces—neither happiness nor hatred, never a laugh, rarely a smile, almost no cheerful or jocular remark from one to another. When, between marches, they walked in little groups through the bombed-out streets of East Berlin, they just walked side by side in utter silence, searching for nothing. Their faces all wore the same expression; all

showed the same premature feeling of ruin and of emptiness.
But despite this general, almost painful lack of enthusiasm and
animation, they marched according to plan, in passive obedience
to their rulers. For this reason the Festival was considered a
success.

What was missing to make these submissive youngsters full-
fledged Soviet men was an active, deep-felt faith. Of the three
totalitarian virtues—"believe, obey, fight," as Mussolini's fascism
had once proclaimed—they knew only two; they would obey and
fight, but they could not believe.

"You know," a leading German Communist intellectual confided to me, "we never expected that these kids from the People's
democracies could be real 'Soviet men.' The next generation,
perhaps, but not this one. They are ruined by the war and the
first postwar years, and by their bourgeois background and their
reactionary ideology. It takes longer to create 'Soviet men.' For
the time being, though, they serve our purpose. Whether they
like it or not, they march in step."

It was notorious, incidentally, that at the Youth Festival Soviet
functionaries and hand-picked foreigners were given excellent
meals, good hotel rooms, private cars or busses, whereas the
youth from East Germany and other satellite nations had to live
on a few slices of bread and gumdrops a day, sleep in billets of
concentration camp style, and stand in line for hours before their
triumphal parade. It was disturbing to see Soviet German boys
in their Free Youth uniforms staring with resigned envy through
the window of the state-run luxury restaurant, Intourist, where
young Soviet Russian soccer players were merrily wining and
dining.

While the majority of the young delegates to the East Berlin
Festival functioned as a passively obedient mass, those few who
had the opportunity to express themselves as individuals rejected
the mass of which they had become a part. Actually, the majority
of the East German youngsters over fifteen or sixteen rejected
the collective into which they had fallen and despised the appeals

and ideas of Stalin and his German satraps. Of this strange split personality under totalitarian rule, not even George Orwell in *Nineteen Eighty-Four* seemed aware, let alone the Western strategists of "psychological warfare."

What this captured youth was really thinking became known only after some of them came to West Berlin. The Communist organization failed in preventing them from this expedition, although the street crossings were barricaded, police cordons drawn at strategic spots, potential transgressors warned of what severe punishment awaited them after their return, and what they might expect in West Berlin (the boys would be poisoned by the "American Secret Service"; the girls would be raped by the American GI's). Still, one out of four managed to get through.

True, quite a few came out of pure curiosity, others because of hunger. Remarkably enough, many came simply to do things they could just as well have done in East Berlin—swim in a West Berlin lake, watch a dance, walk through the streets. Just to enjoy themselves for a brief moment, to feel free, they came westward. While following them, it was strange to see how, after crossing the border, after scrambling over the ruins and dodging the People's Police and the Communist voluntary vigilantes, in West Berlin they became all of a sudden real people. They talked with each other, laughed, flirted. When they were offered a banana and a soft drink in the stands near the border, they answered questions, at first with a shy, suspicious, frightened voice. Then they themselves started asking questions. They wanted to know about life and liberty in the West, and they also wanted to know what the West was going to do to liberate them and let them partake of its blessings.

The Allenbach Poll of German Public Opinion[1] posted interviewers in West Berlin to question a sample of 501 East German Festival visitors. In answer to the question: "What is the

---

[1] Das Institut für Demoskopie, Allenbach am Bodensee, *Gesamtergebnisse der Berlin-Umfrage,* August, 1951, mimeographed.

main difference in the condition of East and West Germany?"
60 per cent said that there was in the East "totalitarian life." As
the main hardship of totalitarian life 7 per cent named "lack of
freedom," 28 per cent, "force and fear," 46 per cent, "the general
politicalization [*Politisierung*] of life," by which they meant the
pervasion of their lives by politics in general, totalitarian Communism in particular. A somewhat smaller fraction—38 per cent
of the East German youth questioned—mentioned the material
hardships of life under Soviet occupation; of these, 20 per cent
objected to the economic system of Communism as such; 16 per
cent, to shortages and the poor quality of the goods on the market;
and 5 per cent, to Soviet reparations or dismantlement. Only 8
per cent held or gave no opinion, and only 5 per cent preferred
the situation in the East to that of the West.

Of those polled the majority of East German youth disliked,
even hated, the Communist regime because of its pressure on
private life through political force and material hardships. The
phrases and slogans of the Communists glorifying exactly these
conditions had practically no hold on their minds. While they
were ready to admit that many things were bad in the East, and
good in the West, most of them took this as much for granted
as they did the fact that there was nothing for them but *mitmachen*
—to go along with the Eastern dictatorship and to accept passively the orders of the rulers and the regime. They collaborated
with what they disliked, marched for what they hated, and resigned themselves generally to what they rejected in their hearts
and souls.

Sensing this, the Soviet rulers decided to produce new generations which would have to accept their orders after undergoing
their "new education." Since Communist theory had taught that
the mind of man is merely a "superstructure" over the economic
condition, and that the basis of the ownership of the means of
production must be socialized to create the new man, the Soviet
man, and since this theory apparently did not work in producing
Soviet men, it had to be abolished, and a new theory be put in its

stead. It was Stalin himself who proclaimed the new theory, according to which the Soviet man had to be produced by the machinery of "new Education."

A "theoretical conference" took place in 1951 in the Karl Marx Party University at Klein-Machnow, led by Hanna Wolf, an old German Communist who had returned from her Moscow exile in the uniform of an MVD officer. For four hours she and Fred Oelsner, the party theoretician, lectured the assembled Communist party leaders, thinkers, and professors on a fine point of Marxist science, so fine that few people could understand what it was all about. According to Stalin's treatise on philology, published in 1950, the party teachers said, Communists had discovered that they were mistaken if they had assumed that "the thinking and culture of man is nothing but the superstructure of the distribution of property, and that the change from capitalism to socialism and Communism would automatically change the ways of man. Even after this change, production had to be separated from the 'mode of production,' and therefore man had still and independently to be changed after the 'mode of production' has been changed."

Everybody applauded the unintelligible. The applause continued when a very old man named Herman Duncker rose. He was almost a contemporary of Marx, and revered by his fellow Communists as a relic. On the speaker's stand he rummaged through his brief case, extracted a plump one-volume edition of Marx's *Das Kapital,* without which he never left his home, and with an accusing finger pointed to page 88, volume one, where Marx had said the contrary of what had been said just now. How could such a misunderstanding occur? And then he quoted— "from memory since unfortunately I did not bring the relevant books with me"—that Lenin had repeated what Marx had said, and that Stalin repeated it again as late as 1938. He concluded his speech with the puzzled words: "What does this contradiction mean?" Back to his seat he went, not applauded by anybody this time. The leader got up quickly to state that the aged comrade had not understood the profound discovery of the great Stalin. The fact was that it had been scientifically proved that whatever the conditions of property and production, man and his mind had to be revolutionized by itself, notwithstanding previous Marxian belief. There was puzzled, but obedient, general applause again.

The education of the Soviet man began before his birth. According to a general order of the East German Office of Public Health, large pictures of Stalin and Wilhelm Pieck must be hung in every maternity ward "in such a way that every patient can see them and know that she is protected in her pains."

As he grew up, the young East German soon learned to cut off all ties binding him to his parents. In every city and town of East Germany "Family Counseling Services" were opened; their task was explained in their publicity: "If you have difficulties with your family on political or social questions, or if your parents need to be enlightened on the problems of the day, visit us." The family counselors were members of the secret police and party faithfuls. Their job was to support Communist-educated children against parental authority, to threaten the parents if they opposed the Communist education of their children. From this the children were to learn that the state is superior to the family.

Positive indoctrination began at the earliest age. Kindergartens became "collective social institutions" built and run after the pattern of large factories. In 1952 East Berlin opened its fourteen-floor skyscraper Children's Paradise, where working mothers could leave their children to be cared for by Communist youth builders. They made sure that the three- and four-year-old children were shaped according to the Soviet pattern. For instance, the government ordered all kindergartens to see that "the celebration of Christmas should be beautifully replaced by the celebration of Stalin's birthday." The Ministry of Education issued a Christmas play for its kindergartens with the following outline:

FIRST SCENE: In America. White children torture Negro children.

SECOND SCENE: In England. Boy Scouts play war.

THIRD SCENE: Children from Soviet Russia and Korea sing peace songs.

During the year in kindergarten, the children received political lectures, mainly elaborating on the virtues of obedience to the Soviet leaders; they played "productive games," such as shooting at targets in the likenesses of Chancellor Adenauer and Uncle Sam; and they learned the little prayers to the great Stalin which they must say before going to sleep.

At the age of six the machinery to sovietize these little subjects began to run full blast. As of 1952, grammar schools in East Germany were exact replicas of those in the Soviet Union— dictatorships to which the children were to submit with eager enthusiasm. The formation of personality, the education to independent thinking and responsible action, which are considered goals of modern and democratic schools, were sharply rejected. To use the official words of the Red Reich, the ultimate goal of its schools was "the education of physically and intellectually healthy men." To be healthy meant to be an enthusiastic functionary and follower.

What was called "progressive education" in the West was anathema to education in Soviet Germany. The Second Teachers' Congress in 1949 resolved that "progressive education" meant a "regress to nihilistic and anarchistic ways of thinking," that it "renounces the dissemination of learning and the formation of children in favor of an arbitrary and irresponsible 'freedom' for teachers and pupils," and that it "corresponds to the tendencies of dissolution of the rotting society of monopoly capitalism." Instead, as many orders and directives of the Ministry of People's Education repeated over the last years, "the role of the teacher as a leader," the "continuous control and direction of the pupil by his leader," had to be upheld. As in an old-fashioned school, the teacher held full authority over the children, who were trained to submit—an attitude they could transfer to the rulers of the state itself. Yet, while full and unrestricted power had to be reserved to these rulers, the teacher remained—unlike the old-fashioned schoolteacher—subject to, and permanently controlled by, the children themselves, whose "political councils" had to keep watch on his political reliability and to report on him whenever he seemed to deviate from the party line. In addition, the principal of the school, his trade union's local, the parents' council, and the Young Pioneers' representatives (the youngest Free German Youth members) were given the task of keeping close watch on the teacher's political line. This intricate system of cross-vigilantism coupled with autocracy was called "democratic penetration of schools."

While the teaching methods had to be carefully controlled, since the teacher himself was not a Soviet man and therefore open to error, deviation, and heresy, if not inherently suspect of subversive intent, all teaching matter was prepared and elaborated in every detail at the educational center, and handed to the teacher in a ready-to-use package. Based on the experiences and prescriptions of the Soviet Union, teaching was alike all over the country: it combined the three R's with indoctrination in the current political slogans and aims of the regime, and with dissemination of the general ideological ideas and word plays which convinced the pupil that he had to learn and to memorize exactly what was presented to him by his superiors—the teachers and the government. Doubt or reluctance to go along with this program was frowned on as the sinister sin of "objectivism"—the Soviet term for "concern with non-approved theories, be it only in order better to repudiate them." Not to accept a Soviet doctrine such as, say, Mitchurin's and Lysenko's theories of genetics and materialist atheism, exclusively and without the admission of possible errors, constituted "a regress to the most dangerous reaction."

"Recently I listened to the radio," a boy of fifteen started his composition on the subject, (Our Government in Defense of

World Peace) "and I heard Adenauer and other warmongers. From their criminal nonsense I saw again that only our government defends peace." "Very bad," said the teacher. "This is objectivism, and surrender to the class enemy. You should not have listened to the West, but written instead why our government objectively defends peace."

"If we have a bottle marked 'cyanide,' " said East Berlin's Municipal Education Director Ernst Wildangel, "everybody believes us, and nobody wants to first taste and make sure it's really cyanide, or he would be dead. But as concerns the products of Western thought, everybody wants to taste them first, and after a person has done so, it's too late; he is lost." This sordid crime of "objectivism," a capitalist trick to poison the minds of the Soviet men in the making, be it only by a Western newspaper or broadcast or a book, was considered the contradiction to "true objectivity," which could be found only in the words and works of Marxism and Leninism, as interpreted by Stalin and his satraps.

The theory and practice of "objectivism" was indeed the very core of the Soviet man, the transmission belt between physical, intellectual, and spiritual terror, the basic lever by which the raw material in the production of the totalitarian mass was made or broken. Hand in hand with education to automatic deafness in response to non-totalitarian voices went education to automatic submission under the totalitarian rulers.

Russian was the only foreign language obligatory in the schools of East Germany. The Russian language teacher "has to be supported ideologically by all the other teachers," a directive of the Ministry commanded. Another directive excluded from high school any elementary school graduate with bad marks in the Russian language. All other teaching was equally "politicized": biology, German history, nature (including biology, zoology, chemistry, geography, gymnastics). But the chief subject was *Gegenwartskunde*—the knowledge of current history, consisting in 1952 altogether of fourteen carefully prepared topics, such as "the American aggression in Korea," "Stalin, the leader of the world peace front," "the Five-Year Plan as the road to plenty and peace." This subject was taught twice a week in the high schools of East Germany.

On special holidays, celebrated in all the schools of East Germany, political events were highlighted by speeches of students, teachers, and party functionaries. These celebrations included a Day of Peace, a Day of Resistance Fighters against Imperialism, a Foundation Day of the German Democratic [Soviet] Republic, a World Youth Day, an October Revolution Day, a Day of Foundation of the Young Pioneers, the birthdays of President Wilhelm Pieck and Stalin, an International Women's Day, May Day, the Day of Liberation (changed in 1952 to Day of Defense), and Day of the Child, in addition to regular school celebrations, such as Graduation Day and Commencement Day.

One regular task of East German students was to compile weekly "wall newspapers" made up of newspaper clippings and articles they wrote advertising the achievements of their youth groups, taking a stand on political questions, and criticizing their fellow students or teachers. Another classroom project was "Stalin corners," with Stalin's picture and a new quotation from his collected works each week, decorated with flags, flowers, and ornaments made by the pupils. There were nationwide competitions for the "most beautiful Stalin corner worthy of our beloved leader, the great Stalin."

Beginning in October, 1952 (when the "People's Police" was extended to a full-fledged "People's Army"), an ordinance of the Ministry of Education ordered that one hour a day was to be devoted in every school class to military education. Boys as well as girls had to take shooting lessons—firing small-bore rifles if they were twelve to fourteen years old, and army rifles and revolvers if they were over fourteen. At the age of fifteen, all children of both sexes were, in addition, instructed for two hours a week in the commando techniques of street fighting, hand-to-hand fighting, and sniping.

More intensive military education was provided for the university students. The universities of Soviet Germany—East Berlin's Humboldt University, Jena, Halle, Leipzig, Greifswald, and Rostock, as well as the special colleges, all looking back to a proud academic history—were turned into Soviet agencies as regimented as the primary and secondary schools. Professors who did not belong to the SED, or at least to several of the party auxiliaries, were forced out, with the exception of a small number of experts in special fields, who were retained *pro tempore*. The number of these specialists decreased so considerably after 1950 that there developed a shortage of well-trained engineers, physicists, chemists, agriculturists, and other technological experts. Therefore, the rulers advised all their party and police functionaries to go easy in their treatment of "the technical intelligentsia," whose important members suddenly were presented with cars, food packages, and villas by their devoted government. Many of them, however, preferred to flee to the West.

No such considerations, of course, protected the "non-technical intelligentsia." A large number of philosophy, sociology, history, language, or literature professors had to leave their chairs to make place for so-called "people's professors," faithful party members who often had not even graduated from secondary school or gone to college, but had attended a six months' training course at the party's Karl Marx University near Berlin, or at the Marx-Engels College in Leipzig.

The State Secretary for Higher Education in charge of colleges and universities, Gerhardt Harig, was under orders of the two Communist party education officers, 42-year-old Ernst Hoffman, and 31-year-old Hans Gossens, a former Russian prisoner-of-war; neither ever attended a college or a university. It was their job, as Harig said, to "develop the universities into the military academies of the class war."

Every university student had to take sixteen hours of "political science" every week, with the main courses the History of the Communist Party of the Soviet Union, the Theory of Marxism-

Leninism-Stalinism, and Applied Marxist-Leninist-Stalinist Theory, the latter an indoctrination course in the political issues of the day. (Prescribed subjects in 1952 were the Korean War, the rebellion of the colonies, German unity and Western peacemongers, and the decay of the Western world under monopolistic capitalism.) Special Communist commissioners grilled university students before each term; those who turned out to be "ideologically intolerable" were sent to the local labor exchange to be drafted for the People's Police or some labor project, such as the uranium mines of Saalfeld, where students could prove their "earnest will to contribute to socialist reconstruction."

"Whatever the field of study, our main subject is the fight for the Marxist dialectical materialist school of thought against the claptrap of the decadent West, such as the so-called idealist philosophy," the State Secretary for Higher Education proclaimed.

Fifteen hundred "progressive textbooks and primers" in seventeen million volumes—most of them translations of Soviet works—were printed and distributed in 1951, according to the Five Year Plan. A professor of theology in Leipzig was dismissed from his post because he told his students: "There are several theories about the creation of the world: one is the fundamentalist belief in the genesis as described in the Bible, a second the Christian doctrine that God is the creator of all life, the third is the Soviet theory of materialism." This was "objectivism": whether elementary school children or university students, East German youth was permitted to know only "the correct concept" of life, as discovered by Soviet Professor Oparin: "Life originated from matter in a materialist way of chance when co-acervate drops mixed in the ocean with organic solutions."

Approximately one half of the student body consisted of the so-called "worker and peasant students." They had to be of purely proletarian origin—if their father was not a factory worker, he had to be a peasant owning less than 15 hectares (37.065 acres) of land; and they had to be members of the Communist Free German Youth. Their scholarships were graduated upwards, like Stakhanovite wages, according to their political enthusiasm. In addition they, as well as other students, got a medal, "For Good Knowledge," coined in bronze, silver, and gold by the Free German Youth, if they came out well in the political examination. They had always to be uniformed in the blue shirts of the Free German Youth. Some were commissioned to spy on their fellow students and professors. They had to keep "development files" in which the behavior of every student and professor was recorded in detail, bringing up to date the questionnaires and "autobiographical histories" which students and professors had to fill in before being enrolled.

The so-called "bourgeois· students" who had no satisfactory proletarian background were admitted to higher education only if they could prove "special excellence in their political education." Proficiency in their military training also helped. But when the political education of one boy whose father happened to own two hectares more than a proletarian was allowed to own, and who therefore was classified as a "kulak," seemed considerably less excellent three months after he had been admitted to college, he was not only expelled, but sent to a prison for "deliberate fraud in his exams."

The future Soviet man was educated to think and act as his rulers wanted him to think and act—neither to see, nor hear, nor believe what they did not want him to see, hear, believe. It was the first undertaking of such a thorough-going nature in German history. Though Nazi education was certainly totalitarian, it was never so expert as the Soviet system; after it reached its peak it flourished no more than five years, too short a time to affect the majority of German youth irreparably.

Like education, the new culture became a carefully planned, uniformly controlled, comprehensive machinery for the production of Soviet men. The creation as well as the consumption of art and entertainment was strait-jacketed along Soviet lines, to bar routes of escape for the people at large and to build up the enthusiasm with which the young zombies were to obey their masters.

"The culture of the Soviet Union is the great example for the cultural development of all peace-loving peoples," Hans Lauter of the Central Committee of the SED and its cultural commissar outlined the pattern of Soviet Germany in a programmatic speech. That this great example was, however, less "Russian" in its nature than totalitarian, was demonstrated by the almost twinlike similarity between the Soviet and the Nazi patterns of culture. Both were formed by the common goal to transform men into active particles of a passive mass, and to forge the unique individuals into one single collective, a goal intrinsically hostile to culture itself, and particularly to a national culture.

"From now on," Adolf Hitler had said in 1937 when he solemnly opened the *Haus der deutschen Kunst* (to be ten years later a club for United States army officers and civilians), "we shall lead a merciless war of epuration against the last remainders of our cultural corruption." By this he meant the suppression of all art that did not meet his personal taste in a personal antagonism which some amateur psychologists explained as his revenge against his youthful injury of not being admitted to the Vienna Academy of Fine Arts. Yet Stalin, who had no such experience in his past, had almost the same taste in art, and as a totalitarian dictator, imposed it also on all those in his empire. His satellite Red Reich's President Pieck echoed Hitler's as well as Stalin's—in short, totalitarianism's—artistic party line when he declared in 1951: "From now on, we shall mercilessly eliminate all formalism in the arts, since it is a sign of corruption and stands in the way of truly progressive culture." Formalistic, he explained, is everything "that emasculates and discourages the vigor of the people, that serves to corrode genuine patriotism, that distorts and uproots the sense of the nation."

"Art for art's sake," Dr. Paul Joseph Goebbels stated in July, 1939, before the Reichsschrifttumskammer (Chamber of Literature of the Reich), "is not a thing in itself. Art is a function of national life, and to relate it correctly to the people, without regard to the so-called interests of culture, is the superior political task." In 1952 the Red Reich's Otto Grotewohl echoed: "Literature and art are subordinate to politics. . . . Art for art's sake does not exist. He who does not recognize today that the principles of art have to be dominated by our politics is opposing the fundamental need of the working class." Art for art's sake, which originates when the artist follows only his impulses controlled by his conscience (unlike art for a Cause, when the artist uses his abilities as a means to justify or promote an extraneous end) was taboo under totalitarianism for two reasons: first, the artist himself would then demonstrate his uniqueness as an individual, his freedom as a creator, and therefore show that he was a person rather than a particle of the passive mass; second, he would communicate to the other people his uniqueness, and therefore break them away from the mass with his message against all "messages" for which art was a vehicle.

The Red Reich cleaned house by removing and destroying that kind of non-political, anti-totalitarian subversiveness. In 1951, a "State Commission for the Arts" scrutinized the East German museums for works of "modernists," "formalists," "reactionaries," which abroad were called modern art, and which had been stored away already in the Third Reich. Otto Dix, Oscar Kokoschka, Andreas Feininger, Paul Klee, Marc Chagall, Bechmann, Kandinsky, Xaver Fuhr, who had been exhibited proudly after the "liberation," were again hidden away from the public eye. A painting by the great artist George Grosz, banned under the Nazis, had been bought by a museum of the East Zone in 1949; in 1951, the State Commissars for Art threw it on a garbage heap as a "dangerous case of degenerate Western formalism." The same happened to all the other paintings of all the other "formalists."

"Formalism," as Hans Lauter explained to the "cultural functionaries" of party and youth organizations, "does not help the active fight of the people against war; the followers of formalism support, whether they themselves know it or not, the Western warmongers. Therefore, there is only one art which can successfully supply the toiling masses with the knowledge of reality, and which therefore successfully leads them to the final victory over the enemies of humanity: socialist realism."

According to this Moscow-invented and imported slogan, art was acceptable if the paintings clearly depicted the story of people at work, machines and tools as lifelike and detailed as possible (substituting for the Nazis' peasants and German land-scapes), or if they portrayed the great Führers. Stalin, for instance, looking from a tower over his army as Hitler had done ten years ago, was the great favorite story of "socialist realism."

The "progressive painters" of the Red Reich were ordered to spend a few hours every day in factories and to observe "the beauty of life which is the free life of a people constructing a free society in the image of Marxism, Leninism and Stalinism." Traditional "proletarian artists," such as Kaethe Kollwitz, were outlawed, since their social protest made the workers look ugly and miserable, giving dangerous ideas to the new society in which the proletariat was always happy and beautiful. At the Great Arts Show of East Germany in 1951, I counted 87 portraits of muscular men at work in all kinds of factories; 38 portraits of almost identical-looking, serene, strong-bosomed women with kerchiefs on their straw-blonde hair at work in fields; 55 scenes from the Bolshevik Revolution, in 48 of which Stalin was the central figure; and a dozen scenes depicting the oppression and the suffering of the workers in the West and in America.

All Soviet German writing was produced along similar lines, since young poets, essayists, and novelists were convoked to a "four weeks' training course" and taught what were desirable and objectionable styles and stories, how to form and work in teams, how to support the political fight. Writers of "socialist realism" encountered many new problems. Take, for instance, the case of the young Communist whose first novel was the story of a new road being built in East Germany; dutifully, he came every morning to the building ground to observe every detail; but he was slower to put it into words and fit it into his plot than were the workers on the job. "Work quicker, and work in shifts with the other writers," was the advice given him by the leader of his training course. When eighteen outstanding and state-supported writers met with the government and party delegates on July 28, 1952, in East Berlin, to discuss their work in progress, one after the other chose as the subject of his next novel, poem, or play an economic story of industrial or rural production.

"It doesn't matter at all," asserted a speaker at the great German Writers' Congress in East Berlin in 1950, "whether one of our young writers happens to make mistakes of grammar, so long as his work shows a progressive ideology." "The literary artist," another speaker said to great applause, "is a dangerous man who loves the words and hates the people, as shown from Goethe to Sartre."[2] Of those who applauded the resolution, some had been prisoners in Himmler's concentration camps, some had been high officials in Goebbels' propaganda ministry ten years before.

In 1952, over 8,000,000 volumes were purged from the libraries and shops of the Red Reich by the Soviet cultural advisers, in an operation incomparably more thorough and more radical than the notorious burning of the books by the Nazis. The publishing companies, among them such famous firms as Reclam, Brockhaus, the music publishers, Breitkopf and Hertel, and the book shops were expropriated and nationalized. The so-called "Eisler index" contained titles of 19,562 books to be banned and destroyed. Only three copies of each book were to be saved for special use by the highest party leaders. In addition, millions of other volumes published before the Communist rule, or abroad, were kept off the shelves, since the librarians and book-

---

[2] Like the painter Pablo Picasso, the writer Jean Paul Sartre was held up to Communist contempt abroad despite his fellow-traveling with Communism at home.

dealers feared somebody might find a reference in a novel, children's book, or a historical work considered reactionary by a controlling commissar. Fifty-nine thousand out of sixty-nine thousand volumes in the old Municipal Library of Leipzig, once Germany's book publishing center, were "sorted out" by the local SED commissar.

Most new books published in the Red Reich were translated from the Russian, with some occasional translations of other foreign Communists and fellow-travelers and the few party hacks accredited as Soviet German writers—Bodo Uhse, Hans Marchwitza, Anna Seghers, Kuba, Stephan Hermlin—mixed in. The people were put under great pressure to buy and read these books; the mass consumption of the manufactured culture served to help the manufacture of planned men. As very few people seemed inclined to consume the Communist novels, poems, and theoretical treatises, large-scale distribution centers were set up, with monthly purchases compulsory for the rank and file of trade unions and other "mass organizations."

But to build Soviet men who willingly, actively, enthusiastically melted into the obedient mass, the human raw material had to be given a more active role in the "People's Culture" than merely that of consumers. The people themselves had to participate actively in the production of their entertainment, as was possible in folk dances, group singing, amateur theatricals.

In 1951 Hans Lauter admonished his culture-makers that "our dances, our songs, our music must be much gayer; our people's culture must be merrier." Soon after, Johannes R. Becher, an aging Communist hack poet and commissar of the intelligentsia, chimed in by denouncing the "sterile, boring" activities of his own apparatus, and calling for "joy and gladness."

Being trained by education and culture to say, think, see, and hear what his makers and masters thought useful and proper, the Soviet man was controlled even in his dreams—his daydreams, at least. In modern times motion pictures have become for most people an escape into a world of ready-made dreams.

Even in the totalitarian society of Nazism, *unpolitische* movies, wholly unrelated to the realities of political life, by far out-numbered political films. The Soviet society was eager to shut off this brief escape. Whether by mass media or individual en-deavors, the dreams and fantasies of the individual had to be directed within rather than without the collective society. Rather than permit self-reliant individualism, the new Soviet state shaped man in the mold designed by the dream factory.

The movies of Soviet Germany were planned to make the audience see "the true political background of the terrible situa-tion in the capitalist world," to make them dream of their own duties, performances, and subsequent progress in the Soviet world. In 1952, the production program of DEFA, the movie-making monopoly of the Red Reich, consisted of eighteen com-edies and tragedies, sixteen documentaries, two musical pictures and over a hundred shorts. According to the governmental pro-gram, each picture had to be "close to our times, its problems and its tasks."

Popular theatre was propelled along similar lines. The musi-cal comedy, "The Heart as Meeting Place" *(Treffpunkt Herz)* presented by the Metropole Theatre in East Berlin in 1952 and generally applauded as "the first positive step on the road to a renewal of the musical comedy," involved a station master who, as a good Communist, had worked out a new timetable which would let the train stop for five rather than fifteen minutes at his little depot. After his telling the passengers for three acts how much coal and labor this saved, the musical comedy ended on his singing together with a lady passenger: "Don't work more hastily, but more efficiently. Let all of us think how this can be done." At the same time, a new musical comedy opened in Leipzig with the title "He Who Loves His Wife." The plot revolved about a question that had been discussed in the "Letters-to-the-Editor" columns of Soviet Germany for several years—whether workers should take their wives to proletarian celebra-tions in their factories. In the first act, the quarrel between a husband and his wife, who was not taken to the Communist shindig, was described; in the second act, the shindig itself was shown—the women workers refuse to dance with their male comrades in protest against their "male imperialism." The war of the sexes was won by the Red Lysistratas on a wifely chorus: "From now on we will work as hard as male workers in our factory." The End.

In a much publicized new Communist movie, the pretty star fell in love with a boy. The crisis came when the local party chairman observed them aimlessly walking hand in hand through a wheat field; he told them that as good Communists, they should rather put in voluntary shifts at the harvest than be lazy like bourgeois lovers. The young couple mended their ways; Kurt rolled up his sleeves, ably assisted by Erika, the star; a number of other couples arrived to help them until the boys and the girls had mowed the wheat harvest and loaded it on an empty truck. The happy ending did not grant a kiss to the meritorious hero, but a speech by the party chairman telling the young people how well they deserved of the republic. In another successful movie, the heroine promised the hero—her co-worker in a textile factory—to marry him as soon as he doubled his production— "or," she added with a coquettish wink, "if you increase it by one hundred and fifty per cent." He did, they got married, and both slaved happily ever after.

Sex was banned from these productions of totalitarian culture. As another escape from reality, as something the totalitarian masters could not control for their own ends, as a human rather than a mass activity, sex was regarded as subversive. "Good" Communists were as vigilant about "sexiness" as about detecting a saboteur in an atom-bomb plant. "Our director in charge of culture," one reader complained in a "letter-to-the-editor" of a big Saxonian paper, "permitted last night at a People's Culture meeting a singer to appear and to lift her skirts so high above her knees that her garters were plainly visible. What have garters to do with socialist reconstruction? Does a woman have her thighs to show them to workers, or to use them for work? The singer should never again be allowed to insult the working masses of our country and the cultural director in charge should be thoroughly investigated." Three days later the paper reported that both the cultural director and the singer had lost their jobs.

The manager of the H. O. state-run department store in Potsdam was severely taken to task for letting a girl model a nightgown at a fashion show. He had to apologize publicly for his "offense against the new rhythm of life in our country which can well do without the decadent exploitation of female workers usual in the West, and of which I have been guilty." The most popular cover girl of the Red Reich fled to the West in 1951 because, as she explained upon her arrival in West Berlin, she "could no longer stand that political talk about how proletarian and good, or how seductive and Western and therefore bad, my smile would come out in the picture."

Many young people hid their interest in sex behind passive obedience, as they did with other forbidden fruits. Yet under this apathetic surface there was actually a more lively, and probably less healthy, obsession with sex among the satellite youth than among the Western youth, who, as will be shown later, met the problem in a new, mature, detached manner. When Communist-educated boys came to West Berlin or West Germany, the first thing they bought—after the soft drinks and food delicacies—was the photo magazines made up exclusively of pictures of nude women; girls from the East seemed far more inclined to promiscuity than those of the West. An East German humor magazine, *Ulenspiegel,* specialized for several years in depicting and denouncing the sexual depravity of the West in often salacious pictures and cartoons, which turned out to be so attractive to Eastern readers that the magazine became a bestseller; the rulers suppressed it when they discovered why their magazine was so popular among their subjects.

"He who owns the youth owns the future," was a favorite

slogan in Soviet Germany. The quotation goes back to the Third Reich, which in turn inherited it from the Communist leader Karl Liebknecht, whom the Nazis murdered in 1919. In its great campaign of conquest aimed at the generations born under the Nazi dictatorship and, since the war, under the new Soviet dictatorship, the totalitarians made considerable progress. Uniformed, disciplined group life with its marching and singing, of which there was as much in the Free German Youth of Stalin's Germany as in the Hitler Youth, had a fatal appeal to a number of boys and girls. It compensated them for their feeling of loneliness, and gave them at least an *ersatz* comradeship in the community. It also gave to the less sceptical-minded a faith and a hope, an enthusiasm and self-abnegation, a sense of release and solidarity. That many young people search for a meaning of life beyond self-interest, and wish to belong to, and do something for, the community was fully and skillfully exploited by the Communist rulers.

In the name of Adolph Hennecke, a former coal miner, who, after one record shift, was made a director in the Ministry of Production and who became Soviet Germany's counterpart of Soviet Russia's Stakhanov, young workers were driven to achieve incredible working performances "in the interest of socialist reconstruction." For example, when the blonde and pretty seventeen-year-old Communist shock-worker Marga sorted 20,000 cigarettes in one day, her picture decorated for weeks the front pages of the Communist press. Previously, even the most experienced workers had never sorted more than 14,000 cigarets a day. Sixteen-year-old Communist brigade worker Reinhold won his laurels by installing twenty radio tubes per hour. These young heroes were accorded such glamorous titles as "Hero of Labor," "Distinguished Worker"—they might even receive the National Prize of the Republic, meted out each year to a selected few in East Germany.

This kind of "heroism" strongly appealed to some youngsters. "It gives us the sense of social usefulness which no worker had before," one of them explained. Among other youngsters, though apparently only very few, there was the same glory in the very privations, sacrifices, and material difficulties the Communists imposed upon them. Convinced that their sufferings served the cause of freedom, peace, and plenty, they proudly bore their hunger, and looked with contempt at the full shop windows, the boasts of material well-being, the "bourgeois satiety" of the Western world.

Less masochistic-minded young people were attracted by the preference the rulers gave to youth itself in filling glamorous and responsible positions in the community. In a state in which many mayors of big cities, police presidents, and university professors were under thirty-five years of age, and quite a few "people's judges" and police colonels younger than thirty, a promise and a chance seemed to be presented to a whole generation which had finally won the centuries-old ever-frustrated German struggle of the young against the old. All they had to do to claim such an elevated position, it seemed, was to be outstanding in Communist enthusiasm and ruthlessness. The same was true for the female sex, which in the Red Reich ascended to heights unheard of before in German public life. In 1952, there were four female secretaries of state, two female land ministers, 626 female city, town, or village mayors, and the president of the State Bank was a woman. (But then, of course, the equality of Communist women with men did not only prevail at the top of the social pyramid: several hundred thousand girls and women did men's work in the coal and uranium mines, in the factories, on the railroads. The same was true again of young people in general.)

To win the wholehearted support of the young, however, the rulers resorted to the whip and the carrot. For a young East German not to give himself up completely to the dictatorship was certain to overshadow his future life with great dangers and hardships. He would most likely not be admitted to higher schools or specialized training, probably never be able to earn an adequate living. On the other hand, if he gave his all to the regime, he could look forward perhaps to great rewards. In this way the Soviet German rulers gained the overt allegiance of a majority and the inner allegiance of a small minority.

There was no doubt that among sincere East German Communists those under twenty-five outnumbered any other age group. Most East Germans estimated the ratio of "true Communists" in the total population at a little less than 5 per cent; but the estimates of this ratio among the young people was generally higher. The members of the Communist Free German Youth usually estimated the Communist percentage in their ranks at 10 to 20 per cent. All students at the six East German universities whom I queried, assumed that 20 per cent of the total students' body were genuinely convinced Communists.

If the Communists won most of their following among the youth, it was also from the youth that there came most of the active opposition to Soviet Germany. In the high schools and universities, particularly, acts of resistance against the occupying dictatorship were committed on a wide and continuing scale. It started in 1948 when Wolfgang Natonek, then twenty-nine years old, a student of philosophy at the University of Leipzig, survivor of a Nazi concentration camp, became the first post-Hitler president of the Leipzig students' council. He promptly opposed the Communist claim to total control of East Germany. He was arrested and disappeared into a prison.

In the next three years, over three hundred high school and university students were arrested for opposing the makers of the Soviet man and sentenced to an average of twenty-five years at hard labor. In Jena, 68 high school boys were sentenced to ten and fifteen years at hard labor because a stink bomb had been thrown at a school festival celebrating the birthday of President Wilhelm Pieck. Arno Esch, a Rostock University student, and Peter Ueschel, a student at the Berlin School of Political Science, were arrested and sentenced to death because they had distributed West German magazines among their fellow students. "You are like young trees which we have got to bind so they will grow in the right direction," the thirty-eight-year old principal of the Werder High School said to eighteen-year old Joachim Göbler. "In that case," the student answered, "take care that we won't hit back in the opposite direction." The Zwickau County Court sentenced the boy (who was also guilty of playing an American jazz song at a school celebration) to fifteen years at hard labor.

A boy of eighteen named Hermann Joseph Flade was sentenced to death because he refused to become a Soviet man. Flade was born in the Bavarian town of Würzburg on May 22, 1932, eight months before Hitler came to power. Both his parents died, and he was adopted by a couple of Olbernhau, an industrial town in the East German Erz Mountains. When he was ten years old, he was drafted into the Hitler Youth. After two years, at the age of twelve, he left this Nazi group, which he had come to despise. A year later Soviet forces occupied the region where he lived. When they established their East German dictatorship, "he refused," as Communist authorities later reported, "to be a member of the Communist Free German Youth; he preferred to renounce the financial aid granted its members to pay their way through school, and chose to earn it by menial work." To pay his high school tuition, he worked in the Soviet-owned uranium mines in Saxony, along with politically convicted slave laborers and other "volunteers," many of them boys of fifteen or sixteen who had likewise refused to join Communist organizations.

Flade's Communist teachers testified that he was "very intelligent, with good intellectual abilities" and "much more serious than his classmates. He was quiet, retiring, and never talked much to anybody." But, they added, "he was a fanatical Catholic and tried to prove with all his means that Catholicism teaches the right doctrines." Evidently an individualist, "he did not attend the Catholic youth meetings."

"His former teachers," the Communist report on Flade continued, "stated that, when politics and sociology were discussed in the classroom, he never used aggressive language, but smiled in a superior and cynical vein. It was evident from his attitude that he rejected the [Communist] state. According to his opinion, the only true democracy is American democracy."

Flade was scheduled to graduate from his *Oberschule* in 1951. During the night of October 15, 1950, he made his way cautiously through the dark, deserted streets of Olbernhau, a bulging brief case under his arm. Every few minutes he stopped at a house door, a fence, a lamppost, carefully looked around to make sure whether anybody was approaching. Then he took a crudely printed leaflet from his brief case and pasted it on the wall. While he was engaged in this work, a man and woman in the uniform of the People's Police appeared from one of their ubiquitous hideouts. As usual, they were heavily armed and accompanied by a vicious police dog. When they tried to arrest Flade, he drew his small pocketknife. The People's policewoman hit him several times over the head with her heavy wooden club, and he slightly wounded her colleague, the People's policeman Drechsel.

Flade was arrested. Four months later he stood trial before the Twenty-second [Great] Chamber of the Dresden Criminal Court. It seemed that his judges were sure they had broken down the boy, and that he would admit his guilt and ask the court for forgiveness. So confident were they of his repentance that they arranged for the whole trial to be transmitted by loud-speakers to the people of the Eastern zone.

The prosecutor read the accusation. Flade had written and printed on a homemade printing set leaflets containing the most treasonable ideas: "The fight of the Americans in Korea is a righteous war"; the Oder-Neisse line which cuts off the Polish-annexed German territories "is an unjust frontier"; the Communist rule in East Germany "is inhuman." This, the prosecutor said, made Flade guilty of the crime against peace, the crime of reviving Nazism, and the crime of espionage for the Anglo-American imperialists, warmongers, and dividers of Germany.

"What have you got to say in your defense?" the judge asked Flade. Everybody expected that the boy would stammer an admission of his crimes and errors, a plea for mercy, and a denunciation of the people who had corrupted him. Instead, with a clear, firm voice, he said: "Marxism-Leninism is not the truth. God is the truth."

The loud-speakers went dead. The rest of the trial was held behind closed doors. But a transcript of the trial was smuggled out of East Germany. Quietly, without hysteria or hatred, the young defendant explained to his judges why, in five years of watchful silence, he had become more and more antagonistic to the Soviet system. He enumerated "the expropriation of the peasants, the scandalous mistreatment and exploitation of the workers in the uranium mines which he had witnessed, the political dismissal of teachers," and finally—a significant point—"the uncomradely attitude of the Russians toward the Americans to whom they were bound by honor to be deeply grateful for all the help they had received." So he had fallen for the American propaganda? "I learned," he replied calmly, "to believe only ten per cent of what the Communist radio said, while I believed at least fifty per cent of what the Western radio said."

The judges did not succeed in proving that Flade was only a tool in the hands of sinister background forces. What he had done, he insisted, he had done alone; no older or other people, let alone any "Anglo-American agents" or "clerico-fascist schemers" had helped him. In the past five years he had had close relations only with his girl friend, now sixteen, and a Catholic priest named Lange from Upper Silesia, with whom he frequently played chess. He had confided to neither of them his decision to print and distribute the leaflets. "Only my parents," he said, "learned, against my will, of my printing the leaflets; I did not discuss with anybody my plan to distribute them . . . I took the decision by myself. I was aware that it might lead to a very heavy punishment. I was convinced that it was right and just to resist the acts of the Soviet government. It took me five years to arrive at the decision that we have to resist the Communists actively as well as passively."

All he admitted before the court was that he "undertook the action perhaps in a somewhat light-handed manner." On one or two points of political fact which the judge held against him, he conceded that he "might be mistaken." He deeply regretted having wounded the policeman which, as he knew now, was not necessary, since he would have been caught at any rate, and which did not further his just cause. But that this cause was just, the boy concluded: "I was quite certain that we must resist the Soviet dictatorship actively and passively. I still think so, and I do not regret what I have done."

The court psychiatrist confirmed what a lay observer would gather from these minutes: "Flade's attitudes and actions showed psychologically an orderly pattern. His strong inner excitement was compensated by self-controlled good outward behavior. I found no indications of mental disturbances or psychotic experiences in Flade's personality."

The Communist court condemned Hermann Joseph Flade to death. After judgment was pronounced, Flade called into the courtroom: *"Die Freiheit ist mir mehr wert als das Leben"*— "Freedom is worth more to me than life."

Other young people in East Germany, inspired by Flade's example, chose this sentence as the slogan under which they took up the fight for freedom against their Soviet masters. So long as freedom existed on this earth, one boy who escaped from a Soviet prison said to me, there would be some who resisted being turned into Soviet men.

And as long as such a minority exists, demonstrating the survival of the free, the great experiment of turning people into collective masses of Soviet men is bound to fail.

X

Land of Lonely People

"THE Bathtub" was installed in the cellar of what had been the biggest, most elegant, most pretentious German night club, a five-story building once devoted to high life, dancing and expensive champagne, but then reduced overnight by bombs to an empty shell. "The Bathtub" was Berlin's first literary cabaret; young non-professionals entertained their crowded audience by reading Kafka's dark-tinted, despair-filled diaries and the Paris-imported Existentialist manifestoes of vociferous weaklings who felt deserted by God and the world and day-dreamed of being Tough Guys. The short one-act plays written by the "Bathtub" poets, of which almost a dozen were shown in an evening, attacked the joy of life as a silly, old-fashioned illusion and usually ended with the leading characters committing suicide. The audience was particularly enthusiastic about one wordless scene in which for three minutes the increasingly desperate convulsions of the unkempt hero on the stage were syncopated with the merry giggles of girls hidden behind the wings; when their distant giggling mounted to loud laughter, the hero stabbed himself to death. The audience was amused. That was in 1949, at the end of West Germany's first postwar period when many young Germans had reacted to their defeat, destruction, and disillusionment with an attitude of romantic despair. "The essence of our time," wrote the young writer Walter Heist in 1948, "is ruin." The sense of ruination penetrated deeply into the young elite of "that gigantic desert which we call Germany," to quote another young writer, Wolfgang Borchart, in his postwar "Manifesto of a Young Man."

In the year 1951, however, "The Bathtub" changed into a center of boogie-woogie and more recent imports from jazzland. While the audience, clad in a Hollywood version of American teen-age styles, still indulged in their convulsions and cynicism every night, they expressed now their individual, hectic, off-balance joy. The young painter who had stabbed himself to death in response to laughter two years ago now wore a violent-colored cowboy shirt and elegant new slacks; he danced with one of the girls whose off-stage laughter had driven him to suicide on the stage, and who was now his real-life wife. She wore a flaming red sweater as tight as a snakeskin, was about to take a degree in romance languages at the university, and made her living by working six nights a week as a barmaid—this was her night off.

When an American opera company came to Berlin on its European tour in September, 1952, to play "Porgy and Bess," the cast went to "The Bathtub" every night after its performance; so little seemed left of the former despair that, as one of the actors from New York put it, "This was like home, right in Harlem or in Greenwich Village."

New literary cabarets sprang up in which young actors, writers, musicians entertained their audiences in backrooms, basements, and barnlike lofts. The programs of these cabarets of the early 1950's were amazingly alike, and depressingly traditional; most could have originated in the last years of the Weimar Republic, as quite a few of their topical songs and gags actually did. With tired satire they ridiculed the military, the governments of West Germany and East Germany, taxes and high prices, the Nazi leaders, the Church—in about that order. The only new objectives in the repertory were the foreign occupation powers, with Americans and Russians as equally obnoxious targets. These cabarets of the young were called "The Porcupines," or "The Small Freedom," "The Penny Gaff," or, most fittingly, just "contra"; so apt seemed the latter name that young students and actors in several

German university towns founded "contra-circles." Their jokes fell flat because they lacked the fire of an ideal or a cause in which they believed, because they were only against everything, because their cynicism barely hid their basic bewilderment, and because the objects of their satire had been attacked, denounced, made fun of for decades—except for the twelve years when Nazism had suppressed that kind of innocuous joking altogether, and sanctified some of its subjects while exterminating others.

If ruin was still the essence of the time, young people had so well adjusted themselves to it that it was banned from articulate expression, and retreated into those subconscious depths where it showed itself only in fears and sporadic panics. Hunger, which in the "zero" years had been their daily experience, was now a memory, though a dread and traumatic one. The times were past when they had to freeze through one winter after another, and to rack their brains how and where they could get some warmth; yet they still shivered in traumatic fear when they remembered those winters. Most of them had again a roof over their heads, even vases and bookshelves, and real homes; yet the memory of the years when they had been homeless, roofless, hopeless, when they had trekked through the country without faith or food, remained painfully close. While the first reaction to the collapse of their world, their values, their security, their most basic human existence had been cynical or romantic despair, the next and probably more lasting reaction was the romantic or cynical super-individualism which prevailed among most younger Germans in the early 1950's. "Everybody for himself, don't trust anybody else, don't believe in the others, the community"—this motto of the young desperadoes of 1946 could, with a little more security for them, a more settled social life around them, some of the ruins and the threats removed, turn without much change into the motto of young babbitts. And this was what happened.

With the wide gulf remaining between "real" hunger and secure satiety, most West Germans still lived closer to the first than to the second. What they became mostly interested in and concerned about was, therefore, their personal outlook toward their economic future. Their minds were occupied by the fear that insecurity and hunger would come upon them again, and the conviction that they could escape this danger only by individual skill and aggressiveness.

To prepare better against this danger, young Germany took over the colleges. Compared with 1935, when 50,000 students had attended the universities of West Germany and Berlin, the enrollment by 1951 had increased to more than twice that number, to 120,000 students. "Everybody hopes that just he himself will win the race," one publication warned, but a large fraction could hardly expect to make even a bare living in the Germany of the foreseeable future. There were in 1949, for example, as many medical students in West Germany as in the United States with a population three times as large; there were already twice as many doctors in West Germany as there were before the war— or three times as many as in England with a population approximately equal. The *akademisches Proletariat,* the college-graduated paupers, the unemployed and unemployable experts, were probably the most important single force among those that carried Hitler to power. Their re-emergence after Hitler brought about the threat of their becoming again one of the largest social stratum in the Germany of the future.

In 1935, 895 German taxpayers had to support one student (in Germany, there are only state universities supported by the taxpayers), while in 1950–51, the ratio had changed to 460 taxpayers having to support one student (not to mention West Berlin, with 232 taxpaying citizens to one student). Significantly, the greatest part of the increasing studies was devoted to "practical" fields. In 1950–51, there were five times more students of economics, and three times more law students, than there had been in 1935. Five times more students enrolled in the sciences; the number in mining and metallurgy increased three times. Attendance in classes of philosophy, history, languages, history of art, and music multiplied also almost three times. The lowest attendance in any subject—trailed only by the sciences of beer-brewing and forestry—was political science, with but 0.6 per cent of the total enrollment!

The tremendous postwar surplus of women over men, which excluded many girls from the traditional career of housewife and mother, provided an additional incentive for girls to go to universities; in 1951 there was one co-ed to four male students. With the majority of all students still coming from middle and upper-class families, they lacked the financial resources of the prewar generations; many young students took part-time menial jobs. In addition, they worked harder at their studies than any previous generation of students. They wanted to own something they could not lose as their parents had lost their property, and professional knowledge seemed to them an indestructible capital, in addition to its more practical promise of better jobs and preferred social status.

It was with an eye to this interest in their personal security rather than from political and social ideals that many young students—though a minority only—joined again the old "fraternities." Originally libertarian associations of students, many of these fraternities had at the end of the nineteenth and beginning of the twentieth century developed into socially and politically conservative, quite a few even into rightist-radical, groups which exercised considerable influence in various public and academic fields, such as the higher judiciary and the foreign service. They came to stand for a revival of Bismarck's and the Kaiser's Reich in reactionary ways which set them apart from more modern and progressive groups, as did also their outward group symbols, the "colors" and the duel scars. Suppressed by Hitler in the Third Reich, the Conference of University Rectors of West Germany decided after the Second World War not to tolerate their public revival, particularly not their distinctive group signs—the public exhibition of fraternity colors which active members had to wear on their caps and on their breasts, the duels between fraternity members, the appearance of fraternity officers in historical gala dresses at academic ceremonies. But in the late 1940's the fraternities made a comeback, first cautious, conspiratorial, and secret, then aggressive. A substantial part of the student body, probably the majority at most universities, objected to their return, sometimes in public demonstrations and concerted action (such as in Berlin and Göttingen) which showed how strongly they resented it. Significantly, they opposed the color-bearing fraternities on social and economic grounds. Being poor themselves, they protested against organizations in their midst whose way of life derived from a leisurely and wealthy age when few students had been forced to work hard for their education or their living. In addition, they claimed that many students joined fraternities only because of their hope for jobs given by the alumni of these fraternities, many of them prominent in the administration, the professions, big business. Yet in a number of fraternities, quarrels between the "active" new members and the alumni broke out when the latter insisted as a condition of their generous support that their old ways of social exclusiveness and political Rightism be continued. In addition to such lures, fraternities also gave that sense of *Kameradschaft* and of honor, unalterable standards of conduct, and a certain standing of the member within his group, the values of authority and of contact with an old, living, beautifully embroidered tradition—in short, a small community exactly in the image of the greater community for which many young Germans wished, and which they could not find elsewhere.

Fraternity life, occupying much of a student's time for two years, tended to interfere with the routine of hard work normal to West German postwar students. Most of them realized that they must overcome the serious educational hiatus of the Nazi and war years, when free research and instruction had been suppressed in many fields, classrooms and laboratories had been transferred to makeshift shelters, books and technical instruments had become almost unavailable, when the older students had been drafted into the armed services and the younger ones into auxiliary formations of the military, leaving little time for study. There was the loss of time, too, in the first postwar years, with the problems of hunger, freezing, and homelessness more pressing than any studies.

The seriousness of this educational inferiority was indicated by a test given in 1949 to candidates for admission to a newly opened school of journalism in Munich. Only 91 applicants out of 1700 showed enough promise to be selected for the simple final examinations, and even these few proved astonishingly ill-informed. Many of these aspirants to journalism could not identify General Eisenhower, Richard Wagner, Albert Einstein, Friedrich von Schiller; many thought the Allies had concluded a peace treaty with Germany in 1945; many could not say to which political parties the few outstanding politicians of contemporary Germany belonged.

The teaching level in the universities was also far below that of pre-Hitler times. The majority, 60.3 per cent, of the professors of 1933 had died or been murdered by the Nazis, or had left Germany as anti-Nazis, or were not permitted to teach because they had been former Nazis. Many of the younger professors had been handicapped by their long isolation from foreign learning and free research; some were still tainted by a Nazi past, though they had not actually belonged to the Nazi Party. In general, teaching leaned towards that extreme specialization and positivism that began to prevail just before the Nazis set out to politicize German youth. Partly in reaction to the Nazi and the Soviet abuse of science, both of which put a premium on political aims rather than truth, Max Weber's thesis of a science free of values and evaluations became again the officially accepted standard. Though this certainly protected science against political bias and domination, it involved the danger of forming a new generation of socially irresponsible *unpolitische* experts whose narrow professionalism would keep them aloof from public affairs and willing to serve—without political opinions of their own—any government willing to employ them.

The *unpolitische* science, to some degree a reaction to Hitler's political totalitarianism, reflected the attitudes of the *unpolitische* youth—an attitude which went further back in German history.

Throughout the first half of the twentieth century, Germany had its own special class struggle—the conflict between "German youth" and the rest of the nation. At the turn of the century, a German youth movement hoisted the flag of rebellion against the way of life of Bismarck's generation. Unable to integrate themselves in a society which they felt to be stagnating and insincere, young men closed their ranks in a sort of socio-aesthetic revolt against their elders. Like many revolutionary movements, the Youth Movement started with the battle cry "Return to Nature." Contemptuous of the *Spiesser*—the babbitts and the philistines—they went in for hiking and camping and nature worship. The boys wore shirts open at the necks, and refused to smoke or drink—in 1910, this amounted to a serious protest against Germany's Main Street. The girls dressed in folksy peasant costumes. Their ideals and achievements, as a friendly historian summed them up, were "the romantic descent to the depths of the German soul, closeness to folk history and nature, the intention to be clear, true and independent, often a revival of genuine religious feelings, and *Verinnerlichung*—a spiritual internalization fighting against the externalizing culture of the times." In short, the Youth Movement was a romantic escape from responsibility.

Under the Weimar Republic the Youth Movement degenerated into an institution for young people interested in romantic, if not mystical boy scoutism with strong undercurrents of male homosexuality. The more vital elements left it to join the early Nazi and Communist parties, or team up with the less radical parties—where, however, they remained separate groups with their own "youth" programs, ideologies, and demands. The Young Conservatives, Young Socialists, Young Catholics, Young Democrats, and a number of other brands of Young Germans seemed often to have more in common with each other than with the parties to which they belonged. Unlike the Young Demo-

crats and Young Republicans in America, which function as training groups for more or less professional politicians, the "young"
German political activists formed a distinct group, with their
own special political ideas and interests. Inheriting their slogans
from the old Youth Movement, they continued to blame their
frustrations on the "older generation" and clamored for a vague,
romantic "total renewal." Hitler promised such a "total renewal,"
and gave young Germans a new interest in politics and a chance
to participate in it; but it was at best a passive participation, without free choice or creative criticism.

The role of German youth as a frustrated, rebellious group,
opposed to the "older generation" and organized to voice its character and requests as a group, seems to have been suspended with
the fall of Hitler. But nothing replaced it, and what remained
was only a disgust with politics in general as carried on by the
professional politicians of the older generation. The situation
was aptly summarized by Hans Zehrer, who, before 1933, with
his "Tatkreis" (Action Circle), was the leading political spokesman of the German Youth Movement and its trail blazer to
Nazism. Zehrer wrote in 1949: "There no longer exists a generation of the young in Germany. Today, there remain only single
individuals who meet each other like atoms, are able to talk with
and understand each other, but whose last word is the Single
Individual."

But in this atomization, the young Germans only shared the
attitude of the majority of their nation. They dissolved into the
amorphous mass of non-political Germans at large. While they
were younger than the other non-political Germans, they differed
hardly at all from them any more in their passive individualism
with regard to their community.

That most young Germans lost all faith in all communities,
after their faith in the Nazi community was destroyed, was the
main imprint left on their minds by the Nazi educators—a thoroughly negative imprint, as negative as ruins. The failure of
their first political father led the great majority of the young to a

rejection of all new ties with a new political family—this was Hitler's legacy.

One of the few favorite serious contemporary writers of the German youth was Ernst Juenger. In the years before Hitler he had prophesied, glorified, and idealized the coming totalitarian, militaristic, Godless, and therefore dehumanized Germany. But when that Germany came, he loathed its vulgarity. With his irresponsible, often arrogant, occasionally brilliant and usually muddled thinking, eternally fixed in a state of intellectual adolescence, Juenger, now in his fifties, still reflected typical attitudes current among German youth. After the war, he retracted from his old views to a cloudy kind of super-individualism and woolly pacifism; in his widely read war and postwar diaries, *Strahlungen,* published in 1949, he noted: "Perhaps many people in Germany are undergoing my own experiences: the knowledge of The Infamous [i.e., the Third Reich] produces a nausea towards all collective matters in general."

This "nausea towards collective matters in general" stifled among most young West Germans any responses to totalitarian government, Nazism or Communism, favorable or unfavorable. Their feeling was voiced by the writer Alfred Andersch who asserted: "I responded to the total state with total introversion." But, despite almost seven years of "re-education," it also kept their great majority from being won over to an interest, not to mention participation, in democracy. Why this was so, the young Germans themselves were quick to explain, some rather plausibly. Yet behind these "good reasons" it was rather easy to discern the "real reason," beside which the others seemed mere rationalizations.

Their main rationalization, as mentioned earlier, was to blame the occupying powers. The occupation troops came, as their commander proclaimed, as "conquerors, not as liberators," and the procedures of the Military Government, notably in its first years, were closer to being dictatorial than democratic. Either the conquerors were guilty of a double standard, or of hypocrisy; why, the young Germans asked constantly in the first five post-Hitler years, are we told that only the individual counts in a democracy, if the Germans are held collectively guilty and collectively punishable? (They were perfectly right in asking this; they were also right in pointing out the collectivist-totalitarian sense of "collective guilt," doubly repulsive in the mouth of "democratic re-educators.") Why, the young Germans asked, is Germany singled out to be punished for the atrocities of her dictators, when the democracies did not even protest against the similar mass atrocities committed by Russians, Poles, Czechs, Hungarians, Yugoslavs, etc.? (They were again right in asking this question, pointing to the shame of Western democracies, of their governments which condoned these crimes, and of their press which ignored them in a conspiracy of silence.) Why, the young people asked, are Germans blamed for collaborating with Hitler, when their accusers themselves collaborated with him, and under less pressure? They well remembered and gladly quoted Winston Churchill's open letter to Hitler, published in 1938 in the London *Times:* "Were England to suffer a national disaster comparable to that of Germany in 1918, I should pray God to send us a man of your strength and your will." Many questions of that kind were asked by German youth, and the true answers indicated that the moral, political, everyday example of the Western democracies did not serve to affirm the ideals of democracy. Instead, the young people of Western Germany had abundant opportunity after 1945 to collect evidence for a damning indictment of the Western democracies, the allies of peace-loving, democratic Soviet Russia, the signers of the Morgenthau Plan, the victims of their own war propaganda.

But this tendency to emphasize the weakness and failures of the democracies while ignoring their virtues, and this inclination to point out misdoings of the democracies as if by this the crimes of Germany's own past would be canceled out, stemmed from a deeper stratum in their minds; they were disappointed by democracy because they wanted to be disappointed. One German girl, formerly a minor leader in the Nazi Union of German girls and now a student of pharmacology, said to me: "As for politics, I feel like a girl whose first love ended in unhappiness because the man turned out to be a scoundrel; after that she might prefer to be a spinster forever." The analogy, with its implied self-pity, is significant: these "disappointments in love" often conceal an inner unwillingness to assume the responsibilities of a mature relationship. Another student said to me: "I liked your lecture because you are the first American who spoke for an hour without mentioning democracy or dictatorship." The young man had been an active anti-Nazi in the Third Reich.

But the deepest reason behind these alibis (most of them true and valid in themselves), lay in the traditional experience which had shaped the general German attitudes toward public life. When Hitler fell, democracy appeared to the young Germans as something strange, unknown, unseen; and one needs a religious experience to believe in the reality of the unknown and unseen. But even if such a religious experience had been possible, it would have been a very inappropriate and useless introduction to democracy. As things were, democracy was first almost accepted, and then rejected, both in terms and images shaped by the Führer State, or at least of the traditional state as an authoritarian *Obrigkeit*.

When, as they explained it, the young Germans were willing to accept democracy after the war, it was in the spirit of waiting passively for it to reveal its wonders, which were to outdo the promises of the bankrupt Nazi system. Democracy would feed, clothe, and house them, run the country better and make the people happier than Hitlerism had ever done. In addition, it would present them, out of its cornucopia, with what was its star feature and most advertised value, personal freedom—which they understood mainly, if not merely, as longed-for privacy, the total freedom from political participation, the freedom from police and from parties, the establishment of *"man on an islande unto himself."* Accepting democracy passively, as they had totalitarianism, they expected to receive from it what had been missing from their lives.

As noted previously, Germans, especially the young, were accustomed to a pattern of public life in which the government gave things to the individual; the individual, in turn, either approved of the government or grumbled against it in privacy without being willing or able to change it, or he rejected it and hoped for a total change to occur somehow some time soon. The government was fate; its acts and omissions, *force majeure*. After the war the young West Germans were willing, as they put it, to "give democracy a chance." Since democracy demanded, as is its essence, their critical participation and responsible co-operation, not their passive consent, they had necessarily to be "disappointed." And they blamed everything on the Western democracies (which were blameworthy in many respects indeed) as they had blamed everything on Hitler and "special historical conditions." It was not they who had failed—someone had "failed them," and something was missing which was not their doing.

If most young Germans paid any attention at all to their budding domestic democracy, it was to detest it as "dirty politics." The parliament of Bonn was preferably referred to as a "chatterbox where politicos yell at each other in public and then make dirty deals in private." Honest political give-and-take became "cow-trading" in their eyes. The virtues of free discussion, of constructive opposition, and of ensuing compromise were not at all understood. Compromise was regarded as treason, and the very fact of political activity as a kind of disrespectable business. In the minds of young West Germans there remained the fatal split between action and thought, between "dirty politics" and "true *Weltanschauung*." By maintaining this absurd dichotomy, the *Privatmann* kept himself free from public entanglements and "above" politics. The sense of individual citizenship developed in England and the United States existed among the German youth in general as little as among their elders. In fact, even less did it develop among them, to judge from the perpetual complaints of the older German politicians that they had not "succeeded yet in getting the young interested in their political parties," and to judge from the ice-cold contempt with which the young looked at these parties, a contempt which lacked even the violence and the potential political passion which drove them before 1933.

In the introduction to an anthology of German political poems throughout the ages published in 1947,[1] we read the editor's statement: "To no other people in the world was there ever given less liberty than to the Germans; therefore, nowhere else has there been a greater volume of longing for it than in Germany; only the unobtainable is desired always." And one of Germany's most popular songs, from the time of the Liberation Wars, apostrophized freedom as a sweet angel high in the sky: "Wilt thou never descend to this troubled world?" In 1952 the Germans still sang this song, still asked this question. But it is not a question that democratic citizens ask. They themselves strive for freedom.

The "private man" of 1952, devoid of a secular political community to which he could and would belong, was a lonely man, unlike the "private man" of a century ago, who was ensconced in the secure structures and institutions of his society, safely bound to the standards and prejudices of his class. After his desire for food, firewood, a room and a job was satisfied to a modest measure, the young private man of West Germany suffered from his lack of a community, from hunger of the spirit.

How difficult and often painful it was for the new Germany to overcome the ruins that filled her intellectual and spiritual landscape was shown by her creative writing after the end of the war. The so-called "literature in the drawer," supposed to have been written and hidden away under Hitler's rule, failed to come forth after his fall. The few notable exceptions were "literature" written in a terribly literal sense with the lifeblood of their authors. What remained from the Third Reich's writings were

[1] *Die Eiserne Lerche, Eine Sammlung deutscher Freiheitsdichtung,* edited by Carlheinz Schellenberg, Mainz, 1947.

Theodor Haecker's *Diaries in the Night,* that grandiose politico-religious blow-by-blow account of German suffering under, and radical Christian rejection of, Nazi totalitarianism, and the writings of the men of July 20 from their death cells—letters, last wills, the Moabit sonnets of Albrecht Haushofer. Haecker, after being arrested twice and hiding his secret notes successfully from the Gestapo, died shortly before the end of the war; the men of July 20 were murdered by the Gestapo in the last year of the war. Hitler succeeded to a frightening degree in killing off the German elite; by his murder of the best German minds of his generation, he left the intellectual soil of Germany in a state of ruins.

In the postwar years, Germany's spiritual life and artistic creation continued to be severely handicapped by the sense of "the ruins as the essence of our time." German creative writing—and creative expression in general—lacked almost completely after 1945 that feverish yet productive animation which had distinguished it after the First World War. At that time, young talents, new ideas, exciting experiments had appeared throughout German culture, making it seem almost a nationwide bull session of brilliant young men who eventually revolutionized the arts and the letters of their country. But after the Second World War, everything was as quiet as a genteel parlor room in which grandparents lived out the rest of their lives surrounded by the well-worn furniture of their youth, playing solitaire and listening with friendly detachment to their rare visitors.

German postwar creative writing mostly ignored the recent political past, from the beginning of the Weimar Republic to the collapse of the Third Reich. Perhaps that experience was still so near that its fears and shock paralyzed the writers; perhaps even its memories were too oppressive; perhaps it was simply more pleasant to side-step it in favor of surrealist fantasies, mystic allegories, and novels dealing with faraway times, faraway places, faraway problems, or the most timely topics, as most writers did. The only recent experience to concern the writers was the war itself, about which, since 1949, personal narratives were pub-

lished by the dozen. What they had in common was their general
contempt for war (unlike many German war novels after the First
World War, which glorified war as such). What was also new
and noteworthy about the war books of the Germans early in the
1950's was that they stressed the loneliness and individual lostness of the single soldier (unlike, again, the period after the First
World War when the *Frontgemeinschaft,* the community of the
trenches, was discovered and celebrated). But it was perhaps significant that while after the First World War several anti-war
books (particularly that of Erich Maria Remarque) and a number of pro-war books by German authors were sold and read by
the millions, after 1945 no war book got much farther than the
small literary groups. Their general and rather hopeless bewilderment was expressed in the title of one book written by a twenty-
four-year-old university student, Dieter Meichsner: *Do You
Know Why?*

"The books which are better than average," Luise Rinser, one
of Germany's ablest literary critics and herself the author of a
number of noted novels and a diary written in her Nazi arrest
cell, said in an essay, "belong predominantly in the category of
what is difficult to understand and are read only by a very high-
brow—not merely an intellectual—elite. Not only good enter-
taining literature is missing, but—what is more important—a
literature which can be understood by all without losing all claim
to quality. People want to escape from the books taking a stand
on politics, social problems, religion, into the illusion of a healthy,
or easily curable, world."

The accomplished authors of the era were all over fifty years
old. They were educated and had gained recognition in a previous era: Elizabeth Langgaesser, who published several profound
novels shortly after the first war; Ernst Glaeser, a novelist successful since the twenties; Carl Zuckmayer, the only contemporary
German playwright of stature; Erich Kästner, an author since the
20's of aggressive poetry in the idiom of the day. Two of them
had been exiled (Glaeser returned to Germany shortly before the

second war, Zuckmayer, after the war); the other two were not permitted to publish under Hitler. Reinhold Schneider, Rudolf Alexander Schroeder, Gertrud von Le Fort, and Hans Carossa achieved their fame decades before and were too old now to add to their works.

The "young writers," with their first, sometimes second, book published after the war, were in general at least forty years old. With few exceptions, the best seemed influenced to such a degree that their books sometimes appeared to be barely unconscious imitations of Franz Kafka, James Joyce, T. S. Eliot, and Ernest Hemingway. Others used the techniques of sincere, good newspaper reporting in semi-novelistic full-length books.

The majority of books published in the 1950's were new editions of German best-sellers of forty to fifty years ago, much of it what Germans call *kitsch,* and translations from foreign languages. Of the six best-sellers in 1952, four were foreign translations; the reading public had an extremely cosmopolitan taste and was more interested in foreign successes than in German experiments.[2]

Sex, love, marriage were minor themes in German postwar writing. Except as allegory or by-play in books primarily concerned with more weighty subjects, the new German novels ignored these subjects which, before Hitler, had been dominant. This reflected a new and meaningful change in West German life itself. Matters pertaining to sex and love life were strictly private affairs about which even close friends should not talk. To hold hands or kiss in public was taboo among the boys and girls of Germany.

But even in the strictest privacy, sex no longer held the healthy

[2] The same lack of an individual style, and the prevalence of imitations of accomplished masters—either foreign, or of past generations, or both—was evident in painting and sculpture. "This tame youth paints and sculpts in such ways as to make their works undatable, and to make them look as if they had been created fifty years ago, when Matisse painted his first pictures, or forty years ago, at the time of Kokoschka's first masterpieces," a leading German art historian, Ludwig Goldscheider, wrote in 1952.

interest it had previously in Germany, as elsewhere. The young men and women of West Germany witnessed the desperate promiscuity into which many Germans attempted to escape in the first postwar years, sometimes for material gain, more often in the hysteria of the general collapse and in another desperate flight from their lonely lostness. The orgiastic mass rapings of the Soviet occupation soldiers gave sex a rather sinister and repulsive aspect in the eyes of many young Germans. In the Hitler era, sex had been "politicized." With its great sexual freedom and almost bureaucratic encouragement of promiscuous intercourse among the young "in the interest of the race," sex had taken on a nonpersonal totalitarian color. This was only the last stage of a crusade for sexual freedom which German libertarians had led for half a century; with their sexual revolution against Victorian hypocrisy finally won, sex lost for the new generation the flirtatious sweetness of forbidden fruit and became a rather dull matter. The many places all over West Germany after the war presenting *Schönheitstänzerinnen*—girls appearing in the nude and pretending to dance—had audiences composed almost exclusively of people over forty. In the cabarets of and for the young sex was practically non-existent. The young generation considered the serious discussion of sex, as well as off-color stories or eroticism in art and life, as the somewhat boring eccentricity of their elders.

In the place of hectic, promiscuous interest and indulgence in sex, true love, permanent ties, mutual loyalty (with or without official marriage) became again the ideal of young Germans. In a survey made in 1952, 80 per cent of the girls and 75 per cent of the boys said they wanted to get married as soon as possible—the possibility depending on finding the right partner and finding a source of income—and that they planned for a family of two to three children. Young women who were asked what they looked for in a husband answered in this order: unconditional sincerity, firmness of character, unconditional faithfulness, intelligence, masculinity, tolerant understanding, and similar interests. The young men, for their part, stressed good looks, yielding compliance, and modesty. The difference between these two ideas was revealing. It indicated the postwar revolution in Germany of the female against male domination.

The war left a "surplus" of three million women in Germany whose men had been killed and maimed or had disappeared in the Eastern prisoner-of-war camps. The majority of this general "surplus"—113 women to 100 men—however, fell in the age group born between 1918 and 1928. Rather than being able to prepare for marriage—the traditional goal of a German girl's life —they faced the prospect of mass spinsterhood. Only a minority adjusted themselves to this fate, by studying or taking up professions which would grant them the independence no husband would give them. Not unlike the students studying harder to get one of the fewer jobs, most girls began working harder in order to get one of the fewer husbands, or, as they said, "a reasonable facsimile thereof." Sadie Hawkins Day was every day in postwar Germany. This led first to an economic change. What had previously been most unusual and considered rather improper —that a boy and girl, for instance, would each pay his own way on a date, or that husband and wife both worked and shared the family costs—now became the rule. Then it led to a change in the marriage relation. The absolute superiority of the male, which up to that time had been taken for granted in Germany, began to totter. Conscious of the threat to their position, the men—like any ruling class threatened in its superiority by the revolutionary challenge of a new class—tried to oppose it by strengthening their rule. Wherever they could, they resisted the intrusion of females into positions held previously by males. For two terms the West Berlin University students held out against the girl-editor of their college paper by listing a male "editor-in-chief" on the masthead, until at last they had to give in. The same happened in every profession. But in 1952, the Society of German Chemists still advised female high school graduates not to take up the study of chemistry, despite the great need of qualified chemists in industry, for few laboratories would employ women, as they considered their abilities doubtful.

With males the hunted-after species, changes began to express themselves in dress and manners before they did in institutional life. In Western Germany, the girls adopted a more or less uniform way of dressing in dull grey, unsexy, tailored costumes recalling the former fashion in men's suits, while the men themselves discovered the attractiveness of vivid colors, which—from mufflers to jackets and shoes—became their modern standard wear. West German men wore their hair as long as girls had done before, with little boys often going so far as to use barrettes. (This was also a reaction against the totalitarian Hitler past when short, military haircuts for men were obligatory; the unshorn heads symbolized liberation from the dictatorship and the victory of total individuality.)

But inside the family the traditional "superiority" of the man and father was strengthened rather than weakened by this new, weakened position of the male in society. With men at a premium, husbands thought they could afford to continue holding their intramural authority without fear of losing their wives. Yet their authority was often shaken, and the gap became greater. Doctors, psychologists, lawyers, and clergymen agreed that the female revolt had already entered the marital domain. Many German women ceased to surrender unconditionally to their husbands, after they realized that they could lead a life of their own and did not "have to put up with everything." In contrast to previous decades, when divorce had been almost a male privilege, divorce proceedings in West Germany were started by just as many women as men. According to a German Kinsey report,[3] marital unfaithfulness of husbands and wives was practiced to an approximately equal degree—another sign of female emancipation and revolt against the previous era.

What most young Germans of both sexes sincerely hoped and

[3] Dr. Helmuth Gottschalk, *Moderne Eheprobleme*, Flensburg, 1951.

searched for was an authentic community as it forms itself in love and in the family. Remote from the political community, insecure in the spiritual community, fearful of loneliness, young Germany turned back to that most basic social unit, the family.

Even in the private confines of love and family, the ruins of the past still cluttered much of the ground and forestalled reconstruction. Many postwar human dramas in West Germany were reported in the press with less excitement than small fires and traffic accidents in America. In 1951 a man wanted a divorce from his wife because when the Soviet occupation troops arrived in 1944 she had sprung desperately into a lake to drown herself, her two babies in her arms. The babies perished and the mother was saved. The husband returned from the war, and four years later found that he could not live with the murderess of his infants. In 1952 a young man returned from a long absence as a prisoner of war in Russia; his old mother was happy to see her lost son again, and the whole village celebrated his return. Only by chance was it discovered that he was a swindler rather than the lost son, and that for five years he had made his living by playing the same role in five other families. Events like these were everyday routine; month after month such impostors were exposed. Identities had become doubtful, the closest relationships shrouded in uncertainty, moral problems insoluble. Millions of seemingly normal, contented, restored lives had a background of tragedy. With ruins in almost every individual life, the youngest West Germans alone seemed sufficiently healthy to start again, to overcome the loneliness, to find a way to a new community.

If the young Germans on the whole seemed to make little progress in "democratic reorientation" and in the formation of a new community, it must be said in extenuation that their postwar education was begun under the worst conditions possible. In the first postwar years "education" consisted all too often of merely reprimanding the Germans for their crime and exhorting them to be good children of democracy like other peoples. The principle that one learns best by doing—a principle that applies as much in the learning of democracy as in most other fields—was little employed. In post-war Germany the conditions and opportunities for active democratic citizenship were miserably poor.* The appeals of the "educators" seemed to remain in the realm of idle talk rather than to take root in real life.

But many young Germans were not so irretrievably lost to democracy as may appear. The experience of their resistance against the new totalitarianism of the Red Reich, the experience of the Berlin crisis and its aftermath, and incidents in West Germany, such as the Harlan student riots, indicated that, given the right conditions, not a few of the young were, after all, ready to transform themselves from "private men" into authentic citizens—or, even better, to recognize the essential unity of the "private" and the "political."

Undoubtedly, there were a few young Germans who devoted themselves to politics mainly because this seemed to them a career with a good future, and who remained "private men" while they chose the profession of political youth functionaries in political parties or youth organizations. But on the whole most young Germans who became aware of their responsibility toward the greater community chose this path after they suffered from totalitarianism—Nazi, Red, or both—and because thereby they were given a chance to fight for peace and freedom.

First of all, many young Germans in the Red Reich, shocked into awareness of their civic duties and prompted by nothing but their conscience, courageously stood up for freedom. From January, 1950, to May, 1951, over 6,000 youths under eighteen years

* According to a report on a two years' Education Project of Teacher's College, Columbia University, New York City, issued in 1952, based on the study of American school systems in nearly 400 cities, American high school students were learning good citizenship more effectively by practical experience than by formal study. "The many how-to aspects of American citizenship are essentially problems of skill," the report indicated. "If citizenship is to be an active thing, it must be taught by action." These findings may be considered as valid in Germany as they are in this country.

of age were sentenced to jail for political reasons by Soviet German courts. Thousands more evaded the terror police and continued the struggle underground.

Of the great number of Soviet German youths who escaped to West Germany, many remained deeply impressed by their new totalitarian experience and conscious of their personal obligation to oppose it. At the German universities—especially at Berlin's Free University, where in 1952 forty per cent of the students were refugees from East Germany—it was the refugees even more than the native West Germans who actively and aggressively took part in and led the anti-Communist resistance.

The East German refugee youth joined ranks with young West Germans, who had likewise awakened to a sense of political duty. Some of them were in their thirties and had experienced Nazism —such as Rainer Hildebrandt who, as a young student, had participated in the plot of July 20, and in 1948 founded the Fighting Group Against Inhumanity; or, Inge Scholl, whose brother and sister had as students at the University of Munich called for a revolt against Hitler and been executed, and who now founded a local adult school for community education in her native town of Ulm. Many more were in their twenties, like the founders and student leaders of the Free University in West Berlin, the most political-minded youth group in West Germany.

They considered the fight against all forms of totalitarianism as their personal task—the fight against Nazism as well as against surrender to Communism. That there were at least several hundred of them at every university was shown most impressively early in 1952 when two new movies directed by Veit Harlan— *"Unsterbliche Geliebte"* ("Immortal Beloved") and "Hannah Ammon"—provoked the violent and spontaneous demonstrations of protest which were led and participated in by students at the universities of Freiburg im Breisgau, Göttingen, and Münster. The students, who clamored for suppression of the movies directed by the former Nazi actor, were attacked by the police and in several cases beaten. No students came out in defense of the Nazis. "For us it is natural," the rioters explained, "to be active in politics, because we have to do something against the restoration and repetition of the old, dangerous ways." In situations in which action was possible and helpful, the most vital personalities of the German postwar youth (in contrast to the German pre-Hitler youth) acted with a sense of democratic responsibility, even if they were not experienced in the "know-how" of everyday democracy.

One of the main stimuli for their activity was a sense of shame for the past—"We do not want to be guilty a second time of tolerating crimes against our neighbors"—and they made the principle of non-violence essential to their political position. "In fighting violence we do not want to use violence," they often stated. The figure of Gandhi was more meaningful to them than were the leaders of Western democracy. In this they expressed the feelings of many young Germans who, despite a frequent distrust of churches—partly, perhaps, as a subconscious legacy of Nazi propaganda, partly as a result of disappointment with church leadership in the postwar years, which sometimes resembled more the traditional bureaucratic group administration than a pastorate of souls—were deeply concerned with religion. This extended even into the ranks of the traditionally atheist Socialists. At a gathering of nineteen young Socialists, upon the question who believed in God, fifteen hands went up affirmatively, some in bashful self-conciousness, some in proud certainty.

The values of the Christian faith came to be to many young Germans true and lasting values, whereas those of secular ideologies had failed them. Although religion remained a "purely personal," private concern, its social obligations and political ramifications were discussed with genuine excitement. Actually, the issues of theology applied to modern life became one of the few great problems about which conversation among young Germans was carried on. An astonishing number of those young Germans who participated in the community as active democrats, whether as leaders or followers, believed in, were fortified by, and acted according to the teachings of Christianity. (Some modern Protestant teachers, however, most of all Karl Barth and his followers and many "Religious Socialists," tended to appeasement with Communism.)

Significantly, these leaders of young democrats rarely mentioned either "youth" or "democracy" when they talked about their programs. Their key word was *Menschlichkeit,* which means humaneness rather than humanity, and they were in search of a system that embodied this principle above all. Even when discussing the advantages of a planned as against a competitive economy for the new Germany, they ignored the question of the efficiency of the two systems; they inquired rather as to which was more "humane." In other words, what the Anglo-Saxon democracies call "human rights" was a value they discovered by suffering; and they tried to make it central to their thought and activity. The second keyword for these young Germans trying to cope with their political future was "Europe." Disgusted with nationalism, they saw a united Europe (either after the Socialist prescription or Adenauer's) as the greater new community into which they could integrate themselves with enthusiasm. The emotional warmth and intensity with which they talked about this united Europe was strong and striking.

Such ideas and tendencies as these—rather vague and romantic in political terms, rather isolated from the mainstream of Germany, and not at all coordinated with the structure of political parties or popular movements—were espoused by vigorous and practical young people and represented the first genuine postwar steps native to Germany on the long road from lonely lethargy to a democratic community.

XI

Berlin, World in Village Focus

BETWEEN the lonely people of West Germany and the collective mass of East Germany, infinitesimally smaller than both, desperately poor and desperately hopeful, in permanent acute danger of disappearing from the political map and proudly clinging to its unique existence, isolated from the world and cosmopolitan, was a third Germany—the city of West Berlin. Actually, it was only a half-city split off from the hostile Eastern half-city. West Berlin was, like other German cities, a city of ruins. More than any other German city it was threatened by the totalitarians around the corner. Unarmed, powerless, almost forgotten by the Western world, West Berlin alone in Germany had grown to be an authentic community of free citizens.

Between West Germany, with her pathetic flight into the pre-totalitarian past she hoped to restore, and East Germany, with her fearful totalitarian future into which she was driven at gun's point, Berlin alone accepted the reality of our times and its choices; and tried to master the difficulties—almost overbearing difficulties—into which it was thrown by its destiny. Berlin chose freedom, and by this very choice asserted freedom's essence in our times.

While essentially different from the rest of Germany in their politics, the Berliners did not differ too much from other Germans. Actually, the majority of Berliners had migrated from other parts of Germany to the big city, as people of all countries migrate to the big city in search of success, adventure, freedom. If the Germans of Berlin seemed so different from the *unpolitische* of West Germany and the slaves of Soviet Germany, it was mainly because chance permitted them to meet and to make their own fate.

Believing in "One World" in which East and West could peacefully "co-exist" once Hitler was defeated, the Allies decided as early as November, 1944, in London, that Berlin was to be ruled by all the masters of this One World; Soviets, British, and Americans each would reign over one sector of the city, which they would jointly govern. At the Yalta Conference half a year later, the French were belatedly given another slice of the Berlin cake and another part in its One World rule.

Yet this prospect of a One World paradise in which lambs and lions would lie down together soon appeared as the malignant delusion it was: the Soviets alone would rule Berlin, as well as the rest of the world. When those Berliners who did not live in the Soviet sector protested that they did not wish to be included in this totalitarian world, the city of Berlin was split into two hostile halves. The democratic half was West Berlin, which fought against Communist domination and conquest both for itself and its eastern segment.

To visit West Berlin in 1952 was an adventure in time and space. Travelers from East Germany had to dodge frontier police, road blocks, all the obstacles a nation at war sets up against its neighboring enemy. The voyage was almost as adventurous from West Germany, since the traveler had to cross through the cold-war territory surrounding Berlin on all sides, either in a military train manned by armed soldiers, or by air, or over the only highway linking West Berlin and West Germany, the 102-mile-long autobahn. At its entrance, Allied soldiers, West German policemen, Soviet Russian soldiers, and Soviet German policemen scrutinized the traveler and his documents, until the Americans waved him on with a "So long," the West Germans with an *"Aufwieder-*

sehn," the East Germans with a snappy *"Tag,"* and the Russians with cold silence. An American traveler who, in December, 1951, greeted the Soviet guards with a cheerful "Merry Christmas" was detained for three hours. The autobahn constructed by Hitler for his military transports carefully avoided passage through settled areas; it would not have differed much from an American turnpike but for the very few cars that used it, and for the occasional patrols of People's Police solemnly taking down their license numbers or stopping and searching them without explanation. Ragged peasants in the fields, recognizing a Western license plate, waved at the car until it passed out of their sight—after making certain that they were not being watched. From far away the lights and the smoke of large factories could be seen. The drivers were nervous lest they might lose their way. They remembered the two American army nurses who mistook a road sign pointing to Frankfurt an der Oder, an East German town not far off the highway, for their West German destination of Frankfurt am Main, were arrested by the East German People's Police and grilled as spy suspects. Two German newsreel men were arrested on the autobahn and sentenced to long prison terms.

When the West German Republic was founded as a federation of eleven states, the French representatives vetoed the inclusion of West Berlin as a twelfth state. As a result, West Berlin elected its deputies to the Bonn parliament, but they had no right to participate in the vote. The government of Bonn, on the other hand, was represented in West Berlin by a Federal Plenipotentiary, as though the city were a foreign country or a colony. In 1951 a serious West Berlin newspaper suggested a declaration of the independence of West Berlin under United Nations sovereignty, a suggestion highly applauded by many West Berliners.

While West Berlin belonged officially to West Germany, it had much closer ties with East Germany, with which it had no official contact at all. West Berlin newspapers contained five to six times more news from East Germany than from West Germany. In West Berlin a new Communist purge in an Eastern town was a greater sensation than a new law voted in Bonn. As a matter of fact, West Berlin felt itself the free capital of the Eastern country subjugated by the enemy. If it looked contemptuously at West Germany, to which it belonged *de jure,* it looked in rebellious solidarity at East Germany, to which it belonged in its heart. Actually, it stood between both. Resolved not to submit to the collective slavery of the East, West Berlin grew above individualism and collectivism, and developed a character, a purpose, a form of life of its own.

Berlin came to be described with many a cliché. Despite the smell of stale editorial newsprint and the sound of unimaginative patriotic oratory clinging to these clichés, they did describe the situation of Berlin with great accuracy. According to one of them, Berlin was "the free island in the Red Sea." Though literally surrounded on all sides by the hostile Communist empire of seemingly boundless width, West Berlin stood out above it, preserving its profile of freedom—a tiny island against which the totalitarian tides were beating day after day without submerging it. That this half-city with its two million people, garrisoned by less than 20,000 Western troops, crowded into 180 square miles, withstood and kept withstanding the onslaught and the siege of the greatest empire of all time, controlling the lives of 800 million people, a giant army, and one fifth of the earth, was indeed a miracle.

Through its tiny, well-lit hole in the Iron Curtain, West Berlin presented life, liberty, and the pursuit of happiness to the millions from the dark side of the earth. As a "bastion"—another apt and true cliché—the city served as "the great refuge" to which the persecuted and downtrodden people of the East turned as a point of last resort, and as "the dagger against tyranny"—persistently sending messages and messengers of challenge and hope to the East. These images of fight and danger might seem to contradict those other clichés by which Berlin invited its visitors to "sip an aperitif on its gay sidewalk cafés and to enjoy its lively music, theatre, art life," but in Berlin's real life they happened to be just as true. After the war, West Berlin became, to quote the final cliché, "freedom's secret capital."

This last word was coined by West Berlin's mayor, a rather miraculous man himself, who did more than anybody else to make the Berlin miracle occur and to make all the clichés come true until the isolated, forgotten, half-ruined, half-city was actually the show window, the beacon, the refuge, the capital of the free world. While the personalities of Konrad Adenauer, Kurt Schumacher, Ernst Remer, and Martin Niemöller personified the political stratification of West Germany, Ernst Reuter, the maker and the mayor of West Berlin, embodied—in his life story, his personality, and his ideas—the fifth stratum of the new Germany, the nature, quality, and purpose of the West Berliners.

A heavy-set, slow-spoken, genial six-foot man in his early sixties, with a limp caused by a Russian bullet in the First World War, Ernst Reuter had a well-balanced mixture of Berlin patriotism and cosmopolitanism. As much at home in German as in Russian, which he learned in his twenties, in Turkish, which he mastered after his forties, and in English, which he taught himself in between, his lifetime hobby was to translate Greek classics into modern German. Dressed in old tweeds and preferably sporting a dark-blue beret, carefully lighting and smoking his eternal cigar, he looked like a friendly old sea dog rather than the great statesman and the winner of the West's greatest moral victory in the cold war which he undoubtedly was. Unlike most of his colleagues of the West, his war with the Reds began in the early 1920's.

Like most Berliners, he was not born in Berlin. The scion of a family of Lutheran pastors and small-town burghers of Prussia, he passed his examinations as a high school teacher in the Germany of the Kaiser, of which he was so critical that he became a Socialist and a pacifist. After the outbreak of the First World War, he joined a secret pacifist society called the "New Fatherland" and served for a short time as its secretary. In 1916 he was drafted into the army as a private and taken prisoner by the

Russians. In the prisoner-of-war camp at Tula near Moscow where he learned the Russian language, the news of Lenin's revolution impressed him greatly. When he was released from camp and marooned by the revolutionary turmoil in Moscow, he took a job as a miner's helper. He was then twenty-seven years old.

Lenin, the head of the tiny clique which ruled Russia, heard of the strong-willed young German Socialist, interviewed him, and appointed him to the important post of "People's Commissar" in the Volga German Republic. He was put in charge of the political organization of the Volga Republic, the Soviet state of immigrants from Germany who had settled in the Volga valley centuries before. Young Reuter frequently went to Moscow to report to his superior, the Commissar for the Nationalities in the Soviet Government, a certain Djugashvili, whose revolutionary alias was first Koba, then Stalin.

Reuter and Stalin used to quarrel and fight with each other almost every time they met. Reuter resented what he called Stalin's "mind of a drill-sergeant" and his frequent recourse to brute force. When, several months after Reuter's acceptance of the Russian job, the Kaiser was overthrown in Germany, Reuter quit and hurried home. Lenin characterized him in a note to the German Communist party leaders: "Young Reuter has a brilliant and clear mind, but he is a little too independent"—a praise and a warning similar to that which Lenin left in his testament with regard to Leon Trotsky, another early Bolshevik who was to become later one of Stalin's bitterest enemies.

For almost two years Reuter worked as editor and organizer in the German Communist Party; for three months he served as its secretary-general. It was the time when many German Communists still had faith in a humanitarian revolution to be brought about by Communism, and in the independence of their own movement from Moscow's rulers.

Reuter's experiences while working in the inner circles of the party, and the insights he got into the true nature of Communism, freed him soon from such illusions. As early as 1921, he attacked the dictatorial principles that developed in the Communist parties—"only that Communist movement makes sense which is carried and preserved by the workers themselves," he said at the time. He publicly stated that the German Communist Party had become an obedient tool of Moscow and its German underlings. The Politbureau of the German party decided with a vote which showed that the last embers of free opinion still burned inside German Communism—the vote was six to one— that Reuter took "a line inimical to Communism," and that he should immediately go to Moscow himself to be "enlightened there." Reuter refused to go or to change his opinions. Instead, he left the party in December, 1921, publicly denouncing "the fundamental immoralism of the Comintern." This was the first such statement of a Communist who became an anti-Communist and a fighter against the God that Failed.

"Perhaps," Mayor Reuter said in 1950, "only men who once themselves have succumbed to the temptation of the eastern will-o'-the-wisp can know and prove with verse and chapter the magnitude of the threat which Communism means to the world." Reuter's successor as secretary-general of the party was Wilhelm Pieck, who remained in his post for the next twelve years, followed every twist and turn of the party line, spent another twelve years in Moscow, and then was named President of East Germany's Red Reich. Reuter rejoined the Socialist Party. He made a name for himself in Berlin's city management, where he reorganized and extended the municipal transportation system, later became the mayor of Magdeburg, a large industrial city of what is now Soviet Germany, and was elected to the Reichstag on the Social Democratic ticket.

If Reuter learned of the totalitarian evil from the front seat as a young Communist, he was to experience it from the victim's receiving end when the Nazis took over Germany in 1933. As a believer in democracy, he was arrested and sent to the notorious concentration camp of Lichtenburg for almost a year. Two months after a number of foreign mayors had intervened on his behalf, and he was released, the Nazis arrested him again in 1934 and sent him back to the same concentration camp. In 1934 he escaped, and with ten marks (less than three dollars) on his person, he crossed the frontier by foot to Holland, made his way to England, and finally turned up in Turkey. The government of Kemal Atatürk (which gave haven to a small number of German refugees if by extraordinary abilities they could help the modernization of Turkey and if they learned to speak Turkish within four years), employed him as an expert on transportation economics. Reuter soon carved out a new career for himself as a consultant on city planning, a teacher of city government at the Ankara School of Administration, and as the author of the first Turkish text book on municipal finance and traffic problems. In addition, he led the anti-Nazi Germans living in Turkey in their opposition to the Third Reich.

When for the second time in Reuter's life his fatherland lost a world war and the German government was overthrown, he again broke off his career abroad and hurried home. To pay for the trip to Germany he had to sell his furniture and the library he had bought from his modest savings in Turkey. For over a year, he had to struggle with Allied occupation officers for an "entrance visa" to his own country, which they first denied to the "enemy alien." Finally, arriving in Germany in November, 1946, he settled in Berlin. Although it was the most destitute of German cities, and although he knew that it meant danger for him to live as a renegade under the direct rule of the Soviets, "I came here," he explained, "because Berlin today is the key front in the coming struggle for Germany, for Europe, for freedom."

Berlin at that time was ruled by the four occupying powers as Germany was to be ruled by them; each held a "sector" in Berlin as it did a "zone" in Germany; the commanders in joint meetings of the *Kommandantura* were the actual city government. With the tensions developing from this co-operation—and sometimes the mere co-existence—of eastern and western powers, the proceedings of the Allied government were soon taken up by their own intrigues and quarrels rather than by joint action toward the governed people. As a matter of fact, the Soviets—and later the Western powers—began to line up the Germans against their enemy ally in the Government. In the Berlin *Kommandantura*, where the Allies rubbed elbows with each other in their day-by-day decisions, this trend from co-operation to hostile co-existence was more acute than anywhere else.

On October 26, 1946, two weeks before Reuter left Turkey for Berlin, the Berliners elected for the first time their city government. The elections—in which 92.3 per cent of the people participated—resulted in a stunning defeat of the Communists, who received only 26 out of the 130 seats in the city's parliament. The elderly Anton Werner, appointed by the Soviet Military Administration as Lord Mayor of Berlin, had to resign; he was succeeded by Otto Ostrowski, a member of the Socialist Party. Using blackmail and bribery, the Soviets made him sign an agreement that he would submit to their orders, whereupon his own party impeached him, forced him to resign from his job, and elected in his stead in June, 1947, the newcomer from Turkey.

"Anybody but him!" yelled Soviet Major General Alexander Kotikov, "anybody but that man Reuter." The Western commanders tactfully tried to elucidate the principles of democracy. "This is a basic principle of democracy as it stands in America. . . . If we give the Germans the right to select their candidates, we ought to accept their choice unless removal by cause is agreed unanimously," General Lucius D. Clay declared. The Soviets, not to be outdone by anybody in their fervent dedication to democracy, had an easy answer to that—Reuter was an anti-Communist and therefore an enemy of democracy, a fascist and a Nazi! That the Berliners had elected him showed that they themselves were not yet educated to democracy, and therefore should not have the right to elect their representatives at all. "His election," General Kotikov said to his colleagues, "should serve as a warning . . . of the undesirability of hasty abatement of Allied controls." Facing this veto, the Western representatives gave in.

Since Reuter, although legally elected by his people as their mayor, could not take office, his deputy, Frau Louise Schroeder, a kindly old Socialist, served in his stead. In December, 1948, new elections were held. But this time, the Soviet representatives vetoed them in advance. "The three Western military governors," General Clay, who was himself one of them, reported, "would not intervene because the constitution placed this matter in German hands." The Berliners went ahead with their elections, despite the opposition by the Soviets and the rather unfriendly attitude of the Western powers, which led to heated altercations between Reuter and the generals. When it was evident that the elections would take place and that they would lead to results unacceptable to the Soviets, the Communists—five days before Election Day—set up a "city government" of their own, manned only by faithful Communists, and headed by Fritz Ebert, Jr., a drunkard and a weakling who hardly understood what went on around him, with nothing to his credit but a famous name: his father had been the first President of the Weimar Republic and won notoriety among Communists and the respect of democrats for his dictum that "he hated revolution like sin." When the people of West Berlin voted for the new assembly, 86.3 per cent cast their votes for resistance to the Communists who now threatened to subdue the city by force. Ernst Reuter was again elected mayor and could at least take office. His city government was driven out of the Soviet-controlled sector and had to meet in the American-controlled sector of West Berlin, at first in an old and half-burned building where there were not even tables and chairs. From then on, the city was effectively split, with two different currencies, two different governments, two different mayors; only the telephone exchange still remained the same for both sectors—since both half-cities were too poor to install a new one; if a caller asked the operator for the office of the Lord Mayor, she would inquire from which street he was calling and then connect him with either the Eastern or the Western Lord Mayor.[1]

Two years later, in December, 1950, the West Berliners went

[1] In June, 1952, the Soviets finally cut off their telephone system from West Berlin; from then on telephone communications from one half-city to the other became impossible.

again to the polls, as their constitution demanded. The Soviets ordered them to boycott the elections, since every vote was to be counted as resistance against Communism, and eventually to be prosecuted as a crime when the Soviets took over West Berlin, as they would very soon. At the time, the Soviet victories in the Korean War were shocking the whole Western world; most of Europe trembled before the Soviet Power. But 90 per cent of the West Berlin electorate, with the Soviets literally in the front yard and ready to capture the defenseless rebels within an hour, challenged the totalitarian enemy and voted again for democracy.

Reuter's party received this time a plurality rather than the majority of the vote. The nationalist and anti-Western politics of the Socialist Party in Bonn, to which Reuter belonged and for which they had to vote if they wanted to vote for Reuter, made it difficult for most Berliners to choose between the party they disliked and the man running on its ticket, whom they adored. In addition, the economic difficulties of West Berlin and the incompetence of some members of Reuter's administration, made his party lose many votes. When it turned out that Reuter's party could not again form a majority government with him at its head, a coalition was organized for the sole purpose of enabling him to remain as Berlin's mayor—a truly democratic achievement (sharply contrasting with the West German conditions). Significantly, "negative" resistance to totalitarianism as imposed on the Berliners educated them to acting in the spirit of positive democracy. That they succeeded in their resistance was proof of their leader's living example.

Shortly after Reuter became mayor of West Berlin in 1948, he was visited by an American college professor on a tour through Europe. "You are in a terrible spot here," the professor said. "When the Russians decide to grab Berlin, it will be impossible for you to resist them." Reuter thought it over quietly for a minute or two, and said slowly: "But to resist them is the only thing possible for us." After another minute of thought, he added: "That's why the Russians won't grab this city."

Only a few weeks later, what the two men had been speculating

about actually happened; Reuter's short and quiet thought turned
into reality. The Soviets tried to grab Berlin. To conquer the last
free city behind the Iron Curtain, they used every weapon short
of war. On April 1, 1948, they stopped all supplies to West Berlin
from the surrounding Soviet territory and cut off all land communications to West Germany. The blockade was to leave the
beleaguered city without food and fuel until it was frozen, darkened, and starved into surrender. "We shall not tolerate West
Berlin's obstruction of our will," Moscow thundered. Reuter said
to the Berliners: "If you can hold out for four weeks, we shall
win. Communists always retreat when and where they encounter
a firm resistance."

How the city could be held, though, was a mystery to everybody. At the time General Clay was visited by Lieutenant General Albert Wedemeyer, then chief of the Planning and Opera-
tions Division of the U. S. General Staff. As Commander of the
American forces in China during the war, he solved their supply
problems mainly by air transports over the famous "Burma Road"
from India. Remembering this, and discussing the paramount
Berlin question, he asked Clay: "Couldn't you organize an air
lift from West Germany to West Berlin?" If the most vitally
needed supplies could be flown in, he suggested, it would give
time to bargain with the Soviets. "You've got an idea there," Clay
said. "Two months ago the Air Force brought thirty flights into
Berlin on a special request. If they could do that much in thirteen
hours, we could double the order, ask Washington for more
planes, and perhaps hold out."[2]

In the next fifteen months, nearly 300,000 round-trips to Berlin were made. The mileage equalled 3,960 times that around
the earth at the equator, or more than 200 trips to the moon. The
combined Allied Air Lift Task carried 2,324,257 tons of supplies
to West Berlin. The incoming cargoes averaged 67 per cent coal,
24 per cent food, and 9 per cent raw materials, medicine, and
newsprint. If this was a miracle, it could not have happened with-

[2] Lowell Bennett, *Berlin Bastion,* Frankfurt am Main, 1951.

out the previous proof that the people of Berlin wanted the miracle to happen and were willing to do everything to make it take place.

Fifteen months later the Soviets called off the blockade. After suffering this great defeat, they continued a war of nerves, which, though it seemed only a series of self-plagiarisms in the headline-tired eyes of the outside world, never ceased to challenge the harassed West Berliners. In July, 1950, they cut off the East Berlin power stations which supplied electricity to West Berlin. By this time, however, the West Berlin city government could reveal that with Marshall Plan funds it had built a new power station of its own for use just in such an emergency, and the new Soviet attempt at blackmail was frustrated at its inception. In 1951 and again in 1952, the Soviets held back the freight cars coming to Berlin, the barges supplying the city on the waterways; as in medieval times, they issued a statement that they controlled the highways, and consequently leveled a head tax on every vehicle moving to and from Berlin on the autobahn. In April, 1952, two Soviet airplanes shot at an unarmed French passenger plane which approached Berlin from West Germany over the air corridor. Several weeks later, the Soviets forbade to the Western military police patrol access to the autobahn.

Almost every week throughout 1951 and 1952 some new act of the Soviets—or at least the threat of such an act, sometimes merely the planted rumor about such an act to be taken soon—disturbed the peace of West Berlin. Trucks were on occasion held up on the autobahn for twenty-four hours. Was this the beginning of a new blockade? West Berliners were kidnapped by East German bandits. Was this the beginning of the rule of force over the resisting people? The border between West Berlin and Soviet Germany was changed during the night by the People's Police, adding a few yards to Soviet territory. Was this the beginning of an invasion?

Berliners found no peace in this permanent war of nerves. The economic situation of their half-city remained precarious. The psychological situation deteriorated. With the spectacular victory in the battle of the blockade slowly receding into historic memory, with the outside world far away from what seemed the "small events" of the Berlin front, the West Berliners felt again alone. The Soviets, who had failed in their frontal attack against Berlin's freedom, now tried patiently to unnerve it to defeat.

Although the Soviets never used direct force, they often threatened to use it against West Berlin, hoping that the threat would break the will to resist. On Whitsunday, 1950, half a million Communist youths were deployed to East Berlin. "We shall take Berlin this time," Gerhart Eisler boasted; the West Berliners declared they would fight any invasion, and General Maxwell Taylor, then commanding the small U. S. garrison, backed them up. "We shall not tolerate this provocation," the Soviets shouted; at the last minute the invasion was called off. Whenever the Soviets drew a new weapon from their arsenal of fear, Reuter quietly told his people: "If we can hold the dam against the flood of slavery here, we shall prove that it can be staved off everywhere. By showing that resistance succeeds, we make the Soviets retreat until people everywhere shall again be without fear."

That Reuter himself did not fear the Soviet power he demonstrated in a very simple—and dangerous—way nearly every month when he took a trip to Bonn in Western Germany. Rather than board a plane as he easily could, he traveled on the autobahn, where the Soviets could arrest him and easily spirit him away, as they had done with other Germans. Yet for this very reason he preferred not to dodge the danger. "It's our right to travel on that road," he explained. "If from fear we forfeit the smallest of our rights, we would forsake everything." His West Berliners followed him in his fearless leadership. The overwhelming majority of Berliners never for a moment wavered in their will to stay out of the Soviet sphere.

The Communist propaganda-line—often communicated in diluted form from non-Communist or nominally anti-Communist intellectuals of the Western world—that Western freedoms meant little to people without bread, was proven false by the West Berliners, many of whom were unemployed, destitute, living in economic misery. They knew that the alternative between bread and freedom was fraudulent, since the Soviets did not offer bread, while even pauperism was more easily bearable for those who lived in the freedom of the West than for those who were ruled by the fear of the East. Fear of the Soviet jails or the loss of life was more compelling even than food to those who fell under Communist rule.

From their own experiences, the Berliners had learned the truth about life under totalitarianism, and how it compared with non-totalitarian life, although many of its least attractive features appeared in West Berlin. As the border line ran through their own city, they had the daily opportunity to study East and West. They saw "over there," on the Eastern side of the street, People's Police pouncing in open daylight upon a passer-by, drawing him for some unknown reason from his bike, beating him up on the way to headquarters, from which his cries could soon be heard, half an hour later carrying to the waiting police wagon a bag dimly revealing the outline of a human body. Most West Berlin families had at least one relative who, for some reason or other, had disappeared in the Eastern zone.

To the doctors on the outskirts of West Berlin near the Eastern border there came a continuous stream of strange patients—sick people who were secretly smuggled to them across the border to get the medicines available to them only in the West. Dying children were transported, at great risk to their parents, in search of sulfa drugs, penicillin, and other drugs that might save their lives and did not exist in the East.

Looking across the street, West Berliners saw empty shop-windows and East Berliners queueing in front of a store to get some desperately needed item like soap or foodstuffs available for one day; more often, East Berliners came secretly to West Berlin to buy their dried herrings, their candy bars, a pair of gloves, or a muffler for the winter.

The Catholic and the Lutheran churches of West Berlin were open to, and attended by, the people, while in East Berlin, churches were dynamited by the Communist wreckers. In West Berlin, eight newspapers were published every day, giving all points of view from conservative to socialist, enlivened by lively entertainment sections; in East Berlin, there were only the deadly dull, uniform party newspapers of the Communists.

In its isolation, West Berlin came to live like a village. As the Berliners liked to joke, the same sixty people were seen everywhere—at theatre openings, official receptions, university lectures, or funerals. Yet it was a truly cosmopolitan village where the latest and the best books, plays, movies, pictures from all over the world were shown to a population which felt it almost its patriotic duty to see, discuss, enjoy them. In contrast to the uneasy relations between occupation troops and the West German people, and to the hate-ridden relations between occupation troops and the East German people, in West Berlin a sincere friendship between both flourished; the GI and the West Berliner felt as comrades-in-arms and allies jointly defending the beleaguered city, jointly braving the same dangers, jointly drafted for the same destiny. On every level of the population from top to bottom, the *Amis* and the Berliners became friends who forgot their former status as occupants and occupied.

To visitors leisurely strolling on the Kurfürstendamm or another West Berlin boulevard, sitting at a sidewalk café, dining in a restaurant, it was easy to forget for a happy hour that this was a beleaguered city which rightfully was called "freedom's capital" or "the bastion of the Western world"—until you met a chance acquaintance who had just escaped from the East, and who told you how his sister "over there" had disappeared.

There was gaiety, and life on the Western side. Across the rusty barricades, there was darkness and fear. The great globe itself, divided by the Iron Curtain into a lighter and a dark side, was sharply focused in the microcosm of Berlin. At least, the city split up by the "Curtain" was focusing Germany, herself split up by that "Curtain." To many Germans, this Curtain seemed little else but a short-lived entrenchment behind the front-lines of the cold war. In the eyes of many Germans, though, it appeared as a national punishment, imposed upon a defeated Germany rather than a global challenge. Since no other nation was, like Germany, divided by the Iron Curtain into two hostile halves, the political origin of a "world half free and half slave" was lost in the national question of a Germany half free and half slave or, as even more Germans felt, simply of a Germany whose eastern inhabitants were not permitted by the victors to talk, visit, trade and live with the western inhabitants. The image of "Germany's bleeding frontier" was more widely accepted among Germans than that of the Iron Curtain; since the line of division was drawn when the zones of occupation were set up by the victors, many felt that the Curtain was an anti-German maneuver of which all the Allies were guilty, and it was seen as a result of defeat rather than of totalitarian Communism. When in 1950 a radio commentator in Munich suggested—as a kind of German equivalent to world-wide "containment"—that the Soviet-ruled parts of Germany be cut off from West Germany "like a cancerous growth," he was answered by a spontaneous and general public outcry of protest, and had to retract; this was the only time that such a suggestion was publicly voiced in Germany.

How to remove this Curtain was a matter of dispute; yet there was no Berliner, no German west of the Curtain, nor east of it, who did not wish for its removal.

Rigid as the Curtain was between the two Berlins—as well as the two Germanies—there were leaks in it through which a persistent trickle of men and ideas was able to pass back and forth. Most of the Germans who crossed into the Eastern zone did so against their will. They were victims of *menschenraub,* "people robbing," as the West Germans called it. More than 800 people were spirited away from West Berlin after 1947 in this fashion. The outside world rarely heard of these mysterious kidnappings. But when, in June, 1952, Dr. Walter Linse, an anti-Communist lawyer, was dragged into a passing car while walking home and sped to the near-by Eastern border (where the gate had already been lifted to speed his abduction), Berliners were so shaken that they made the world take notice.

These abductions proved that the mighty arm of the Soviets extended far across their official lines into the West, where people were still free and, alas, unprotected. They gave warning that nobody, including these "free" Westerners, was beyond the arm of the Soviet police.

The organized underground resistance in the Soviet zone, which had its headquarters, supply base, rallying point, signal center, and advance combat post in West Berlin, was continually threatened by the abduction of its leaders and members. From 1948 on, an intricate and at first spontaneous network of organizations had sprung up in West Berlin encouraging and directing those East Germans who opposed the dictatorship under which they lived. The Soviets tried to discredit these opponents by show-trials that accused them of murder, arson, espionage. In spite of this, the participation of the East Germans in 1952 gained rather than lost active participation in the resistance of the West to Moscow's domination.

If Berlin was the sluice-gate through which the men and ideas of the anti-Communist resistance flowed into and out of East Germany, it was even more the bigger hole through which fugitives from East Germany escaped into the free West. In 1949 there were 70,000 refugees who escaped from East Germany to West Berlin; in 1950, 60,000; in 1951, 131,000. In the summer of 1952 the number suddenly multiplied to a thousand refugees a day. For a city unequipped to handle its own poverty and unemployment, this mass migration presented a major catastrophe.

This abnormal influx of refugees to West Berlin in 1952 was occasioned by a sudden move on the part of the Soviets to make the border between East and West airtight. Fields, forest, orchards, farmhouses, and barns in the margin area were set afire or torn down. West Berlin was the only readily available haven to these stricken people.

On the other hand, West Berlin was more than ever cut off from the East. Letters, telephone connections, newspapers ceased to go forward even at a limited and often underground rate from West to East. West Berliners could no longer visit their little vegetable gardens in the Eastern zone, or the cemeteries where their dead were buried.

The West Berliners, led by their mayor, learned that they could resist the fear of totalitarian evil only if everyone resisted, ceased being "non-political," and participated in the choices and responsibilities guiding the community of their city, sometimes at their own cost and risk. They set this pattern when they refused individually to register in the Soviet rationing office when the blockade was imposed, although there was no guarantee of the desire, and little hope of the ability, of the Allies to feed and hold West Berlin. Thus they created the situation which made it morally impossible for the West to abandon them. For the first time, Germans were not the objects of military administration or civilian *Obrigkeiten*, but citizens whose courage prepared the way for Allied plans and planes.

Under the pressure of the East, backed by the power of the West, Berlin by its own will became the first German democracy in action, a hope for the West, a threat to the East.

XII

Welfare State and Workers' State

WHILE totalitarian socialism was forced upon Eastern Germany, there developed by trial, error, and experiment in Western Germany a new social and economic order that was neither totalitarian nor socialist. Both systems were established under equally unfavorable conditions, on the same foundation of ruins, among people with similar history, habits, and hopes. This made Germany the first laboratory in which the comparative merits of two social orders could be gauged—in a "controlled test," as scientists call it when comparable conditions are created for an experiment to permit valid conclusions. The two worlds of Germany supplied an adequate testing ground for the question which had been discussed for more than a century—whether economic "freedom" or "planning" was more beneficial to more people, in particular to the working class.

It is not easy to classify the order that emerged in West Germany. Neither a truly free nor a planned economy, officially and rather ambiguously termed a "social market economy," it was more like the "welfare state" of American definition. It attempted to preserve the free market place for production and distribution of goods and services, while at the same time it controlled the distribution of income and wealth, chiefly by means of taxation. But in reality, West Germany was less of a welfare state than a relief state.

The free market was re-established in June, 1948, in a West Germany disorganized and disintegrated, resembling somewhat the economic ways prevalent under Nazism. The chaos of the Nazi "planned economy," whose dictatorial controls, autocratic interferences, blueprints, red-tape, and rationing had reached their heights during the war, had strangled all normal commerce. After Germany's surrender, with currency and production totally disrupted, many controls of the wartime economy were retained, which only made the chaos worse. Three years after the end of the war, the so-called Currency Reform put an end to this chaos. With an act of great courage and daring, the government devaluated all money holdings by a ratio of ten to one and established a new, firm, and single unit of exchange. By abolishing all rationing and the whole system of bureaucratic state control over economic life, the new money—the Deutsche Mark, or DM— became again the only valid unit of exchange. "The German currency is so sound now," many people bitterly joked at the time, "that few Germans can afford it."

The operation which established quite literally overnight a normal peacetime currency and thereby the basis of a normal peacetime economy, was costly, even cruel to many West Germans. It expropriated nine tenths of the property and income of those who lived on their savings, annuities, or pensions—altogether some 20 per cent of the West German population—and it enriched those businessmen and black-market speculators who had invested their earnings in goods, hidden them away for better times, and could sell them now again at normal prices and profits.

Almost immediately after the currency reform, the recovery that some—notably foreign—observers chose to call a "miracle" developed. This miracle consisted primarily in the fact that a very hard-working people, given a sound currency, the tools to produce, and help from abroad, could in free competition overcome chaos. Industrial production in 1951 was 40 per cent higher than in 1936, the last year considered normal before the economy of the Nazi warfare state expanded and became dominant. The balance of exports over imports improved over that of the prewar years, with a figure in 1951 of approximately $300,000,000 a month. This meant a shrinkage in volume from the prewar times, with a larger share of production going to the domestic market, but a reduction of the foreign trade deficits. By the end of 1952, Germany had run up a huge credit in the European Payments Union.

Gauged by the figures of production, competitive capitalistic industry showed that it was able to overcome the state of decay into which it had fallen and to tie together the loose ends of the economy until it could begin again to provide the greatest number of people with the greatest amount of material satisfaction possible. The job was more than one of pioneering. The destruction had to be removed before the construction could begin. And while the capitalist order seemed quite adequate to do the job of reconstruction, the ground for it had to be prepared by the job of removal, which, by its very nature, it was not in a position to undertake, although it could provide the means necessary to do the job.

Gauged by the material well-being of its citizens, the miracle of German recovery appeared rather as a mirage above the ruins —although the mirage had a good chance of becoming the reality of the future. To keep going, the free economy itself was based on relief from abroad. Neither the currency reform nor the re-establishment of competitive industry could have succeeded had not Marshall Plan funds begun to flow into Germany at the same time. From 1948 to 1952 West Germany received almost $5 billion from the United States government in various ways and forms. This amounted to as much as about one tenth of West Germany's income in the same period, and provided every family every year with more than an average worker's additional wages of one month. (Marshall quota per family; 393 marks a year; average worker's wages, 250 marks a month.) Supplying the capital with which to import food and raw materials, the

Marshall Plan contributed greatly to putting the ruined economy on its feet again.[1]

The process by which the wheels of the economy were freed from controls and from the rubble of the ruins until they could produce meant inevitable hardships for the people. In addition to the near-expropriation of one fifth of the nation, the buying power of the West Germans suffered seriously from the discrepancy between income and prices. The price level boomed upward after restrictions were removed. While the average worker earned 1.20 to 1.30 marks[2] per hour in a forty-five to forty-eight hour week—with skilled workers making 1.40 to 1.50 marks— this was only slightly above the prewar level and did not suffice to buy necessities like meat (the price of a pound had risen from 90 pfennigs in 1938 to 2 marks in 1948 and 3.50 in 1952), or butter (the price rose from 1.80 marks a pound in 1938 to 2.56 in 1950, and 3.17 in 1951), not to mention such highly-taxed luxuries as a package of cigarettes (at 2 marks) or a pound of coffee (at 16 marks).

Yet despite the deficiency of buying power, general consumption improved. The average West German consumed 38 kilograms of meat in 1951—15 per cent below the prewar average for the whole of Germany. The average milk consumption was 116 kilograms per person in 1951, 4 per cent higher than in 1950 but 11 per cent less than the prewar average. The average daily calories intake of 2,800 was 110 calories higher than the 1950 figure, but 160 calories lower than the prewar average. The average fat consumption was 97 grams in 1951, 20 per cent more than in 1950, but still some 15 per cent below the prewar average. In short, supplies were still deficient. (A widespread myth to the contrary, they were far below those of the United Kingdom, as the statistics of the United Nations Economic Com-

---

[1] There were other, additional sources of financial aid from the United States to West Germany, such as expenditures of the occupation forces, the "offshore purchasing procurement" of the army, and donations.

[2] The mark in Germany in 1952 was worth approximately twenty-five cents in U.S. currency.

mission for Europe in 1952 revealed.) There was still widespread poverty, but misery was overcome and the trend, as everybody felt, progressed continually toward improvement.

Rather than from ideologies and programs, the growth of the welfare state in West Germany stemmed from the postwar emergency. Had the authorities not taken care of large groups of the people who were destitute, unable to work, unable to emigrate, these people would simply have starved. Their situation—whether they were victims of wartime bombings, of mass expulsions from the East and Southeast, or of the currency reform—was caused by catastrophes beyond their control. It was clearly the duty of society to help them and to decrease the worst features of an inequality which society itself had brought about, and which—unless corrected—would perpetually endanger, and probably destroy, society.

In 1952, West Germany was providing public aid to one out of every four of its population. Thirteen million persons were receiving support or assistance from Bonn as war victims, pensioners, refugees, or unemployed. Fifty-two per cent of all tax revenues and 22 per cent of the national income was spent for the welfare of the needy, in addition to an almost equivalent amount spent by the local governments. Pensions paid to the families of the 3,500,000 war dead and the 2,000,000 war-maimed, and the pension given to the old and the ill among the 9,000,000 postwar refugees (whose numbers were soon increased by the arrival of several thousand new refugees from the East every week), as well as the public housing program—all this made West Germany in many respects more a relief state than a welfare state. Public relief for the ruined rather than public welfare for the insecure was its underlying principle.

After years of preparation and discussion, a staggering share-the-burden plan, almost a share-the-wealth plan, was realized in May, 1952. The so-called *Lastenausgleichsgesetz,* or Law of Balancing the Burdens, seized billions of marks either in bank accounts, real estate, or other capital assets from those whose

houses and business properties were intact, in order to provide
for those who had lost all their possessions as a result of the war
—the refugees from the East, the victims of wartime bombings,
and to some degree the people expropriated by the currency reform. Starting with 1952, all private estates valued at over 5,000
reichsmarks (approximately $1200) before the currency reform
must for the next thirty years pay a special tax to be used for the
twenty million dispossessed victims of the war and postwar
period. Providing annual cash payments to those dispossessed at
a rate of 2,050,000,000 marks (or approximately $488,000,000)
from the new property tax, almost one out of two inhabitants
of West Germany would be aided through and by the *Obrigkeit,*
which, in order to remove the social ruins and to lay a foundation
for social reconstruction, was forced to an interference in private
property far surpassing any aims of a welfare state.

In the first years of West Germany's economic recovery, organized labor abstained—with minor local and regional exceptions—from strikes for higher wages and better hours by which
they might temporarily have succeeded in getting a bigger slice
from the small cake. To some degree this was because poverty
extended to the union treasuries, where the accumulated reserves
were still too low because of the war to sustain strike struggles.
But in the main, the unions preferred not in any way to hinder
the first stages of economic recovery with its upward trend, from
which in the long run they would profit. Rather they pressed
their claims to more permanent power for themselves in the
councils of economic leadership, which would later enable them
permanently and peacefully to have a larger share of the social
product and a higher status in society.

The spokesman and center of the working class was the German Federation of Trade Unions *(Deutscher Gewerkschafts-
bund)*, established when occupation authorities ordered there
should be a single federation of all trade unions in order to prevent a return to the traditional three federations of different

political and social allegiances that had existed until Hitler dissolved them and founded his totalitarian Labor Front. Organizing five and a half million workers, its leadership concentrated its efforts on a basic reform of the West German social structure, in which it claimed a new, powerful role. The lever by which it hoped to achieve this general social reform was the union demand for the *Mitbestimmungsrecht,* the right of co-determination.

In 1951, after the unions threatened to call a general strike unless this right was granted them, a law was voted establishing it in the main basic industries—in the large corporations producing coal, steel, and iron. By the law of co-determination, labor was privileged to a half share in running big business. According to the law, the board of directors of every corporation in the three industries should consist of five representatives of management and five representatives of labor; both co-opted jointly an eleventh, non-partisan co-director. Of the five labor representatives in the industrial directorate, three were to be appointed directly by the union leadership while the other two were to be approved by the union.

This setup provided the union leaders with such wide power that the fear was understandable they might use it for centralized systematic economic dictatorship leading to a planned economy —the planning to be done by the union top command giving its orders to all the labor representatives in the directorates. This would be facilitated by the fact that management representatives were rather split, especially as the laws against cartel and similar agreements imposed by occupation authorities were stringent. But with both groups equally strong on the board, much would depend on the eleventh neutral director; as several authors and critics said, *"Mitbestimmungsrecht ist Drittbestimmungsrecht"* —the third force on the board might actually determine the outcome of arguments.

The idea of co-determination was initiated by a group of young intellectuals active in the West German trade union movement and backed by the Socialist Party, by the "left wing" of the CDU, representing mainly Christian unionists from the industrial areas of the Rhine and Ruhr, and by numerous Church elements. A national Catholic Congress in 1949 spoke of the "natural right of co-determination," which in its view did not conflict with the natural right of private property which most Catholics upheld. Chancellor Adenauer himself came out in favor of the law, which potentially could explode the entire traditional framework of German economic society.

Since the new order of co-determination increased labor's social power rather than its material profits, it was more of a social than an economic revolution. It left the basis of property and profits untouched (in contrast, for instance, to the experiments of Great Britain's Labor Government), although the power of economic determination would in the long run provide labor with a great influence on profits, if not an indirect share in private property. In the first place, however, the experiment aimed at giving the West German workers social equality as a class. Unlike American workers, German workers as individuals traditionally had little chance to rise by individual achievement from their lowly status to a higher status in a society in which a man was a worker because his father had been a worker. In an effort to overcome the class frustration from which German labor suffered, the co-determination law aimed at the social values of class equality and partnership. Co-determination that would bring to the workers in social matters the same participation, sovereignty, and independence, which, in the political community, "co-determination" gives all citizens, aimed at the extension of democratic concepts to a sphere to which they were alien.

The absence of such a political community and of a democracy which would have given the workers equality, partnership, and "co-determination" as citizens led to the substitution of economic and social "co-determination." Since the workers felt that their economic equality and social status could not be achieved within

the framework of collective bargaining, they had to induce the
state to decree for them equality by law. By thus acquiring collective power, labor won a victorious class peace, or, at least, class
armistice, from the *Obrigkeiten*.

That it was to be a law which made labor share in the managerial activities and responsibilities and that this legal share
would give social equality to the workers indicated their insecurity within society, as well as their misconception of genuine
equality and responsibility—a misconception they shared with
the majority of their fellow-citizens. Their invasion of the domain of management seemed a little like the invasion of the male
domain by the early feminists, who, eager to attain equality with
men, began dressing like men and demanding men's jobs in
a mistaken concept of equality that subsequently backfired against
feminism in general and its more reasonable goals. For the
equality of women's rights and women's status could not be
achieved by blind denials of the intrinsic difference between the
two sexes, each of which has its own particular responsibilities
and activities. In the same vein, the workers—or rather,, their
bureaucratic and sometimes power-hungry representatives, and
their hired experts, economists, and accountants to whom they
frequently had to resort in the early days of co-determination—
were likely to interfere with the natural division of responsibilities by taking over responsibility based on property that was not
theirs. Instead of the successful rise of individual workers to
property and management, and of the successful integration of
all workers as citizens into their political and social community,
they tried to usurp the economic functions of another group,
thereby strengthening the power of the trade union leaders
within the state as well as the power of the union leaders over
the workers.

While co-determination gave to labor powers equal to those
of management under the great umbrella of the state, the state
also tried to protect the workers from the consequences of free
economy and managerial determination by a vast system of

obligatory social insurance to make them secure against the
dangers of unemployment, old age, sickness, and accidents. First
introduced by Bismarck as a defense measure against socialist
and revolutionary propaganda among the workers, widely elaborated by the Weimar Republic, social security became one of the
bases of the Bonn Republic.

While the "deproletarization" of the working class in America
came about by rise of the workers to a social and economic status
that placed them in the middle classes, the "deproletarization"
of the West German workers began in the opposite direction
when the middle classes lost their higher status and fell to that of
the workers or below, to that of relief recipients. Represented by
their unions, the self-confidence and power of labor increased
largely because the self-confidence and power of the middle and
upper classes decreased so considerably after the end of the war.
This was evidenced in the fight over co-determination, when the
management association would not hire propagandists at a salary
as high as that of a high union official to fight the bill they feared
and hated. When labor was aware of the loss of strength suffered by its former class enemy, it considered it more profitable
to press a negotiated peace upon him rather than indulge in open,
costly warfare.

Socialism of the Marxist, revolutionary kind had always been
alien to the majority of the German workers, appearances to the
contrary; the very name of their "Social Democratic Party" indicated the German liberal origins rather than Marxian anti-
democratic ideas. Throughout pre-Hitler history, the "Socialist"
rank and file opposed and rejected the revolutionary fervor
of their theorists and fanatics. After 1945, they ceased paying
even lip-service to it. In their overwhelming majority they preferred to class warfare a Welfare State which would give them
equal standing and security with the bourgeois middle classes
and the peasants.

The West German Welfare State continued where the old
authoritarian state of the army and the civil servants had left

off. In the eyes of most workers, it remained for the state to give and guarantee economic justice and legal equality to all its citizens. Now that the workers were as numerous, as powerful, and as conservative as the old middle classes, they joined the state-conserving classes, *Staatserhaltende Klassen.*

With the demand for "economic democracy," a slogan of German unionists since the last years of the Weimar Republic, German labor wanted political democracy implemented, and authenticated by the participation of the workers in the economic as well as in the political leadership of the nation. The spokesmen of the workers claimed that the whole people must determine the economic fate of the nation as well as its political fate, lest political democracy be merely a window-dressing behind which the minority of property-holders in big business and industry ruled and decided. This conception of economic democracy, reflecting the weakness of German political democracy, fulfilled nevertheless a genuine hankering of the German working classes for new forms of social justice, and a search for "democratic" forms different from those of England and America.

To come closer to their goal, the union leaders struggled for an extension of the right of co-determination from the three basic industries in which it prevailed in 1952 to all public utilities, chemical industries, and railroads. In addition, they demanded national, regional, and local works councils *(Betriebsräte)* such as existed already in the individual plants; elected by the employees of a shop, these councils had the right to consult with management and to veto certain of its decisions. The *Betriebsräte* date back to 1920 when they were created by the moderate Socialists to offset the Communist-advocated factory soviets; but they never succeeded in acquiring genuine influence. The Nazis in their Third Reich used them as totalitarian instruments of control. After the Second World War, the workers wanted them re-established. In the more comprehensive nationwide form, they could indeed grow to a powerful body wielding its influence outside parliament, political parties, and governmental mechanisms, and West German union leaders did have, in fact, from 1949 just such a goal. Social and economic problems, they maintained, should be taken away from the "purely political" parliament (as if there were such a thing!) and fought out in the nationwide social parliament. An *ersatz* idea for the already poorly functioning democracy, the chances of the success of this idea did not seem too bright. But the West German workers were more responsive to these plans than to profit-sharing and similar schemes proposed by younger employers, for instance, by the textile industrialist Gert Spindler with his Spindler Plan. They were trying to stake their new place in an old society; their new positive ties to the state laid the ground for the possible regeneration of that society. Behind all the wrestling and experimenting, a new social equilibrium was sought in freedom.

At about the same time West Germany voted its co-determination law, a new and equally revolutionary law was adopted in the Red Reich of East Germany, when it introduced in 1951 the collective shop contracts *(Betriebskollektivverträge)*. This new social institution—tentatively developed before in other parts of the Soviet empire—deprived the East German worker of the last vestiges of equality and social partnership, robbed him of his personal rights in the planned economy, and to all practical purposes expropriated him by abolishing his collective rights and social powers.

In the new socialist order, the traditional works councils were dissolved and substituted by "Shop Trade Union Centers" *(Betriebsgewerkschaftsleitungen)* under direct orders of the Communist Party itself. The next step was the abolition of the instruments of collective bargaining and collective contracts for which labor had striven so long throughout the world. Wages and hours were now fixed in every single factory by its Communist party-appointed managers and its likewise Communist party-appointed union leaders. Neither group, however, could fix the level of wages and hours, since it was predetermined by the "plan order" handed down to the factory from the supreme planning commission. The factory had to fulfill these "plan figures," and to enable it to do so, the output and compensation of the workers were figured out at the lowest marginal rates. In practical terms, the workers were paid as much according to the collective shop contract as their factory could pay them after producing the plan-requested output and making the planned profit. The basis of the wage scale was set by the record working performance of one worker. All workers were encouraged to speed up their performance like Adolf Hennecke, the miner who in imitation of Alexei Stakhanov, the Soviet Russian miner from the Donetz Basin, raised his output from 14 to 102 tons. Overtime was abolished. While the "Hennecke" of every shop set the wage basis, the wage ceilings were fixed for all companies by the wages paid in the least profitable marginal company in the least profitable marginal branch of a given industry. When, for instance, in the East Berlin building industry, "wages prevailed which were not supportable in comparison with other branches of industry," as the Soviet German press stated, they were simply lowered to the level of these other industries. In the text of the collective shop contract written by the government, the manager of every factory—a Communist party faithful—filled in the "supportable norms and wages," after consultation with the party faithfuls of the shop union committee. Industry-wide contracts or collective bargaining, on which the economic power of organized labor is based, "are a thing of the capitalist past," it was announced by the Soviet spokesmen in 1951, and this view remained the order of the day.

The classical methods of capitalist exploitation were rediscovered by the rulers of the Red Reich, given new names, and enforced upon the workers in the name of socialist reconstruction. "There is," they proudly reported (*Rundschau am Montag,* East Berlin, November 19, 1951), "under way a great movement of weavers to work simultaneously at several looms." The same great new movement, previously forced upon the weavers under "capitalism," had led to proletarian revolts that still stand high in the heroic history of the workers' movement. Now the new science of Soviet industrial psychology would study, the Communists explained, "which special intellectual capacities do these weavers have to do this work best? How can systematic education contribute to the development of their special abilities? How can we give jobs to weavers who can work at most looms in the shortest time for the largest output?" But a few decades ago, the same studies undertaken by industrial psychologists, efficiency experts, and human engineers in the service of capitalism had provoked the most violent protests of the Socialists and Communists.

Soviet German workers were punished if they did not fulfill their quota: "He who produces a machine part which turns out to be unusable has no right to buy for himself something he could use. The workers have to save every inch, every minute, every penny of the people's property, or they are saboteurs of reconstruction, and must be punished," President Pieck declared.

To compensate the workers for this system of speed-up and exploitation unknown in any capitalist country of the Western industrial world in our time, though well described by Karl Marx a century ago in the twenty-fourth chapter of *Das Kapital,* the Communist propaganda hammered on the fact that the workers—as the privileged class of their state—must be proud of being subject to the sacrifices of speed-up and exploitation. It is a worker's privilege, the Communists proudly proclaimed, that he "can fulfill in the current year the plan figures of his shop."

Communism attempted to turn its workers—like the citizens in general—into Soviet men who carried out orders with active enthusiasm, and forsook with joyful exertion their rights to personal independence, dignified working conditions, and decent wages. Yet East German workers were in constant underground opposition to the new order; rebellions flared up. In 1952, the workers of the uranium mines of Freiberg, Saalfeld, and Hag-

enau rioted for twenty-four hours, wrecked the police headquarters, and stoned the Prime Minister of Thuringia. The riots
were brought to a standstill only by the application of martial
law enforced by MVD troops. The most widespread revolt occurred when the new collective contract was to be accepted by
the workers of the Leuna Works, the largest chemical plant of the
Red Reich. Four thousand young workers assembled before the di-
rectorial offices, made speeches against the "dictators over the proletariat," and finally smashed its windows with sticks and stones.
The People's Police dispersed the rebels with machine guns; several dozen workers were killed; the leaders of the factory branch
of the Communist Free German Youth—Erhard Voigt, Willy
Krutsch, Herbert Sorger, Horst Assig, Konrad Halliger, and
Margarete Liske—were prosecuted for "toleration and support
of enemy propaganda," and sentenced to twenty and twenty-five
years at hard labor by the Magdeburg court. In small plants,
similar revolts took place in protest against the new dictatorship
over the proletariat.

The majority of East German workers resorted to less violent, less conspicuous forms of resistance, which the Communist
leaders had continuously to recognize by publicly attacking them.
Using every weapon available to them—from "passive resistance," deliberate laziness at, and absenteeism from, the job, to
"faulty and insufficient working discipline" and "too many
working hours lost"—the workers resisted the workers' state
in which they felt as much oppressed and as resentful as the
other "less privileged" classes. Although the right to strike was
guaranteed by the Soviet German constitution, the strikes of
the Red Reich were merely perverted political instruments of the
dictators, against the liberties of the people. "By a warning
strike," the Soviet German News Agency reported, for instance,
on November 25, 1951, "the workers of the Hanover tool factory
of Rosenkranz, Dreyer, and Dropp enforced the firing of a
woman worker who defended the desecration of the monument
for the victims of fascism by calling it a boyish prank." When

the party functionaries demanded that she join in the officially described vehement protest against a few school boys who may have thrown a paint pot at a Communist monument, her quiet remarks were considered treasonable and sufficed for the Communist union leaders to rob her of employment after the "strike."

The decrease in buying power of the East German average worker's wage from the years 1936 to 1951 was estimated at 40 to 50 per cent. In the first place, there was such a shortage of goods that prices of consumers' goods skyrocketed and the goods remained unavailable to the people. In a planned shortage, as requested by Lenin and executed by Soviet economic policies, consumers' goods were reduced to a secondary and discouraged branch of planned Soviet production. According to Soviet theory, contented workers who enjoy necessities as well as a few luxuries of life as they do in the West easily turn into petit bourgeois and class enemies, and are lost as raw material of Soviet men. Furthermore, the production of the Soviet economy was set to turn out war materials and build up a war economy rather than goods needed by civilian workers. Finally, the Soviet German sector of the Soviet economy, like other satellite sectors, had to gear its production primarily to the Soviet Russian market for unpaid exports without benefit to German workers.

What remained for their personal consumption was so scarce that they could almost never buy the full amount of goods to which they were entitled by rationing. Except for potatoes and fish, workers were able to buy no more than once a month the meat, bread, and milk to which they were entitled once a week according to their ration cards. Milk consumption per head in East Germany in 1951 was only 52 kilograms, as compared to 116 kilograms in Western Germany, or 238 kilograms in Switzerland, or 253 kilograms in Norway; fat consumed in 1951 was 42 grams a day, as compared to 97 grams in West Germany, 126 in Britain, or 133 in Norway. Other consumers' goods like clothing and furniture were equally scarce. Only at the state-run, state-owned H. O. *(Handels-Organisation)* shops which existed in every town, many goods were plentifully available without ration cards, but at black-market prices prohibitive for workers. In the ration shops, they were offered only *Schundproduktion,* or rubbish.

The letters-to-the-editor columns of the East German press in the early 1950's were full of complaints against the goods and the service given to the workers. To publish these critical letters seemed to the rulers a safe way of releasing pent-up resentment by making it appear that the government and party did not know or approve of these faults of the economy, that merely minor officials were responsible for them, and that they occurred in isolated instances rather than generally. Since the Soviet Germans read only their local papers, they remained ignorant of the countrywide extent of these complaints about shortages and shortcomings.

In the East Berlin newspaper, *BZ am Abend,* in October, 1951, for instance, a reader complained that she had bought at the H. O. shop a shirt which caused wounds and burns on her body; on closer analysis, she discovered that it contained little chips of wood. But during the next days, a number of readers answered her complaint. "Why not do as I did," one girl wrote, "and take a few evenings off to remove, piece by piece, those tiny splinters? It was hard work, but worth my while, for since I finished it, I have worn the shirt always with great enjoyment." Another woman wrote: "Wouldn't it be a good idea to sell these shirts by the yard, with a warning that they can be used for curtains, pillow cases, and similar purposes?" Two men joined the discussion—one hinting that American saboteurs resorted to such tricks as spoiling shirts in order to keep the suffering Soviet girls from doing their full quota of work; since American intelligence agents were evidently working in the shirt factories, the secret police should investigate the matter. A second man suggested that "the Minister of Light Industry ought to take energetic steps to correct the situation and punish the guilty ones." But next day the letter of another girl brought the solution. "I too bought such a new shirt, which was itching and hurting terribly. But when by mistake I once happened to wear it inside out, it did not hurt me at all. As a matter of fact, it felt so good that it made me improve my performance on the job. This goes to show that people shouldn't criticize before they have tried to improve a given situation."

There were also continuous public complaints against the service in the state-run shops, against the shortage of shops, against "lack of proletarian marketing culture," which was a euphemism for cheating. A woman wrote to her paper that she bought twin beds which, when delivered several months later, turned out to be two different-sized, unfinished sofas. "The twin beds were not available anymore, and the comrade should be happy that we are producing sofas," she was reprimanded by the shop manager, who suffered from lack of proletarian marketing culture.

Twenty-five per cent of the Soviet German industrial production in 1951 was devoted to consumers' goods, while of the much larger West German production 60 per cent served to satisfy the needs of the people. At least 50 per cent of East German industrial production was ear-marked for foreign use—under the title of reparations as well as exports. According to an estimate of Professor Gleitze, president of the German Statistical Administration in the Soviet Zone, the Red Reich between 1945 and 1950 supplied a minimum of 11.3 billion dollars in reparations and occupation costs to Soviet Russia and her satellites—more than twice the value of what West Germany received in that time from the United States in the form of Marshall Plan and other funds.

On May 5, 1950, Stalin declared that the German satellite would have to pay merely 900,000,000 East marks per year for the next fifteen years to the Soviet Union. But actually in 1951 six billion East marks had to be paid. Most of it was delivered in the form of industrial products—43 per cent of the optical and precision instruments output, 42 per cent of the steel production, 25.5 per cent of the pharmaceutical production. In addition, the Soviet zone had lost five times more than the Western zones of the available machinery for industrial production, by Allied postwar dismantling.

Some of the channels through which the products of East German work were shipped abroad were cleverly camouflaged from the East Germans themselves. While all the industrial factories of East Germany were expropriated, only 70 per cent became "people's own," or *volkseigene Betriebe*. The more important ones were organized as Soviet corporations, or *Sowjet-Aktiengesellschaften* (SAG), more recently called State Corporations; as official property of Soviet Russia, they did not have to pay taxes at all, while the East German government subsidized them from the profits which the "people's own" corporations were ordered to make; in 1951 the SAGs had to deliver a "net profit" of 1,218,000,000 East marks to the Soviet Union according to the Five Year Plan; one third of this amount, 415,000,000 East marks, stemmed from governmental subsidies—or the taxpayers.

The workers employed in these foreign plants—18.9 per cent of the total employees of Soviet Germany—were specifically exempt from the laws and provisions prevailing for the other East German workers. The rules of Russian slave labor camps alone prevailed, enforced by the Soviet Russian Ministry of Defense, the Ministry of the Interior with 5,000 MVD troops, and the Soviet Russian Communist Party in charge of these plants. The Wismuth-AG, which mined the uranium for Soviet atom bomb production, with 300,000 forced and slave workers, was the most important of these plants. Thus German workers had to work either directly or indirectly for the foreign rulers, without rights or chances to improve their conditions.

About the only privilege given to workers in the East German workers' state was their preferred status in the community where a "proletarian background" was considered an advantage over a "bourgeois background" when entrance tests and exit purges in schools, the party, the mass organizations were held. Yet since this privileged status entailed also new, special duties and dangers, and since status as such was consistently threatened by the totalitarian mechanism of fear, it did not compensate the workers for their loss in material and social well-being. In the workers' state of East Germany, labor had no chance to struggle for its status, to improve its conditions, to experiment and, if need be, fight for its rights as it had in the welfare state of West Germany, whose basically capitalist method of production supplied them with the goods they needed at prices they could afford. The workers could struggle for a just society in the Western welfare state; they were oppressed in the Soviet workers' state.

XIII

America in German Eyes

IN THE summer of 1950, potato crops throughout Europe—
especially in East and West Germany—were threatened by
an invasion of the so-called potato bugs or Colorado beetles,
an insect which a century ago came from America to Europe
and has been a pest ever since. The bugs were successfully fought
off in West Germany, but inflicted severe damage to the East
German crops. The Soviet German Propaganda Ministry explained that this misfortune took place because American planes
dropped millions of potato bugs over East German farmland
"with the aim of inflicting damage on the food supplies of
the German people." "The primary aim of the American warmongers who flew the bugs into Eastern Germany," the Soviet-
controlled Radio Berlin added, "was preparation for their bac-
teriological warfare; in addition, the bombing accuracy of the
American planes for atomic warfare was tested by dropping the
beetles. American *Kriegsminister* Johnson [Louis Johnson, then
U. S. Secretary of Defense] and other Wall Street millionaires
who are chief stockholders of I. G. Farben, the great chemical
combine, expect by dropping the beetles to sell their insecticide
to Germany for their own profit."

Most people in East Germany laughed at the story, especially
when they learned from RIAS, West Berlin's radio station, that
East Germany had not been able to defend herself against the
beetles for a political reason: the experienced East German insect
fighters—Drs. Zimmermann, Sauer, and Scheering—had been

fired as non-Communists by their masters, and the chemicals and instruments necessary to fight the pest had been shipped from East Germany to Soviet Poland as reparation goods. Helpless on account of the self-inflicted lack of men and materials, East German authorities shifted the blame to the Americans.

The potato-bug incident, which inaugurated the Hate-America campaign that the Soviets waged ceaselessly in East Germany from 1950 on, contained already the major themes of this campaign. In the official East German view, "America" came to stand for evil. The children in kindergarten, the highbrows who read *Die USA in Wort und Bild,* a pocket-sized cultural magazine devoted exclusively to the defamation of America, the movie, radio, and theater audiences, the semi-illiterate peasants—everybody in the Red Reich had it constantly dinned in his ears that the great threat to mankind was America. "Democratic patriotism consists, first of all and above all, in hatred of the enemy," Fred Oelsner, member of the East German Communist Politbureau proclaimed in 1951, "and the enemy is America."

If many Americans spoke of "the Germans" when they meant the Nazis, and sometimes spoke of "the Russians" when they meant the Communists, the Communists themselves hardly ever spoke of "the Americans"—although to identify the Americans with their government and their institutions would come closer to the truth than it would with the Germans or the Russians; the Communists referred rather to "Wall Street," the money-mad barbarians of monopoly capitalism and dollar dictatorship supposed to dominate America. According to their book of revolutionary recipes they expected by this "to deepen the gap between government and people" and to give their own people the hope that America was on the brink of revolution, that it could not resist the Soviet power, that, on the contrary, it would soon join it.

In daily reports from America, the Communist press of the Red Reich confirmed with verse and chapter that the oppressed American people were violently opposing its government and its policies. Abundant proof was supplied by quoting from "the great American press"—to be exact, from publications such as *The Daily Worker, The Compass, The National Guardian,* or *The Nation*—by messages from such "great Americans" as Paul Robeson and Howard Fast, whose giant portraits decorated the streets of East Germany, or by personal appearances of lesser-known Americans, such as one Hope Faye, a girl widely advertised in the Soviet sphere as one of America's most famous singers, who toured the Red Reich; her pictures appeared on all Communist front pages, which presented her addressing mass meetings. In many of these messages from America, the East German people were told: "We live in a country where the working class, the racial minorities, the artists and all free people are persecuted in the most horrible way. While America's concentration camps are filled, and the FBI goes on lynching sprees every night, progressive Americans look for their liberation to the Soviet Union and its glorious ally, the German Democratic Republic."

That Germany was a ruined country was, according to Soviet propaganda, exclusively the responsibility and the guilt of the Americans. As bloodthirsty barbarians, the Americans alone had destroyed the German cities with sulphur bombs and other terror weapons. The Soviets tried to make the Germans forget that they themselves had done exactly the same to Germany and had even boasted of it, as proof of their valor in a war which they claimed to have won singlehanded. They now denounced their former Allies for their warfare against their former enemies. The East German city of Dresden, which was punished by one of the most cruel air raids, became in Soviet propaganda the great symbol of the Americans' inhumanity to Germans.

The American occupation of West Germany, the Soviet propagandists claimed, was but the preparation for a new, even more horrible war of destruction against Germany. According to Soviet myth, Americans had built explosive chambers under the Lorelei Rock; this is a sort of national monument on the shore of the Rhine River where, according to a folk myth, the blonde siren sits luring sailors to disaster. Americans prepared to dynamite it like the rest of Germany, and to destroy the country with their bombs and bacteria.

Venereal diseases had been brought from America and spread throughout Germany by the American occupation. Furthermore, the occupying Americans were continually raping German women, murdering German men, looting and vandalizing German property, prostituting German children, corrupting—with Coca-Cola and hot jazz, *Ami* cigarets and gangster movies—German youth, remilitarizing German young men, burning villages. In short, the American occupation was a reign of terror. Rich, bloodthirsty, and barbarian, decadent in culture and primitive in thought—the image of America in Soviet German eyes was a collection of old European prejudices blown up to pathological proportions and calculated to create hate hysteria in the cold war.

But most East Germans reacted to this propaganda by secretly longing for all the things American against which the Soviets warned them. Crowding the cinemas in which American pictures were shown, enjoying Coca-Cola which became the symbol of pro-American rebellion as did the boogie-woogie East German youngsters danced at secret gatherings, wearing flashy clothes supposed to be American-inspired, such as *"Ringelsöckchen"* (brightly-colored striped socks denounced by the Communists as an American fashion), the overwhelming majority of people in the Red Reich answered the Soviet denunciations of America with demonstrations for America. How Soviet propaganda against this country backfired was shown when Josephine Baker, the Negro artiste, complained that she had been refused service in New York City's Stork Club, the meeting place of café society. The incident, headlined in the Eastern press as proof that racial prejudice was rampant in America, was received by most East Germans with a shrug of disbelief. The Communist hate-America campaign which usually overshot its mark so widely, found deaf ears even when, as in this case, it reported a story that was believed by many in America. Every Soviet charge against America became in the eyes of the people a ridiculous "potato bug."

There was a good reason for this failure of the hate-America campaign. The Soviet rulers prated to the East Germans continually of the freedom, progress, and happiness of life under the Soviets. Since the East Germans knew that this talk was all a lie, they almost automatically assumed that the converse Soviet propaganda line—concerning tyranny, reaction, and unhappiness in the United States—was equally a lie. They sensed that the Soviet picture of America was merely an inverted picture of the Soviet reality they knew—its oppression, starvation, physical and cultural barbarism. And since they hoped for liberation from Soviet rule, and the Soviet rulers assured them America planned war against the Soviets, they came to put their hopes in liberation by America as a country superior in everything to the Soviet Union. In the end, the Soviet-developed hate-America stereotypes led East Germans to accept the contrasting love-America stereotypes; their firm and sometimes touching pro-American sentiments were inspired by the Soviets rather than by America itself.

If the effect which the incessant pattern of anti-American propaganda had on the East Germans was so far from Soviet expectations that it actually ran counter to them, its impact on the people of the West probably exceeded the Communists' hopes.

In the first place, the hate-America campaign, the denunciation of Chancellor Adenauer's government as "a puppet of Wall Street and American monopoly capitalism," the blaming of the loss of German unity on "American disrupters and their West German lackeys," became a significant factor in West German politics. It acted as a form of ideological blackmail, spurring some West German politicians to strike nationalist poses and to assert belligerently their independence from the West in general, and from America in particular. That the East Germans who talked most vociferously about national unity and independence were themselves spineless lackeys of the Soviet dictatorship everyone knew. But so effective has the technique of the Big Lie become in our day that even those who knew it for a lie felt constrained to act as if it could be refuted only by first accepting it as the truth. Except for Konrad Adenauer and Ernst Reuter, who, with the great courage of genuine statesmen, firmly resisted giving in to the Communist line and joining the anti-American chorus, few German politicians overcame the temptation of showing occasional outbursts or continuous animosity against America and the American.

West German opinion of America became ambivalent, insecure, complex, full of misgivings and often contradictory. Based on the varying impressions of a whole century when one layer of stereotypes was laid over the other, a series of new observations was added by the closest, day-by-day contact of the last seven years when Americans met Germans in the quickly-changing roles of enemies, victors, rulers, educators, secret allies and open allies—and, in addition, as individuals in uniform. Composed of contrasting experiences, German opinions of America in the early 1950's became, to some extent, a rationalization, if not an alibi, of the German attitude toward America which Germans advocated. If America appeared as a country whose main values, interests, and purposes were similar to those of Germany, it was right for Germans to follow America in the Western Community. But if America was as alien to Germany as Soviet Russia, and close to the latter in its nature, it was wiser for Germany to remain neutral.

In the end, those Germans who—for quite different reasons—tended to be neutral justified their attitude by developing an image of America as displeasing as that of Soviet Russia. Their attitude of distrust and dislike toward America was strengthened by the arguments supplied by the Soviet Hate-America campaign.

For more than a century, America had been in German eyes a country far away and fabulous. Lacking the direct relationships and experiences, antagonisms and sympathies, that brought England and France historically close to America, Germany imagined America as the land of noble savages and wide wilderness, a country without history and without despots. The "letters from America" which German emigrants wrote home in the nineteenth century and which were passed from hand to hand and reprinted in the newspapers of their home towns confirmed the benevolent picture of "a young country of freedom." Exactly because America enjoyed the freedom that Germany lacked, it became more fabulous and far away than ever. On occasion, a German poet wrote an ode in praise of the distant country, but when the poet Nikolaus Lenau emigrated to America to be a free man on free soil, he soon returned in melancholy disappointment; freedom, he found, among the pioneers was shockingly different from the dream.

Toward the end of the century, America changed in German eyes into "the country of unlimited possibilities" and "the country of unlimited contradictions," as the two most popular slogans put it. Still a fabulous land, where people got rich quickly, America was often looked upon with some condescension, a picture far removed from the American stereotype of the oppressed European coming to its shores in search of freedom and a better life. Germans (as other West Europeans) rather saw these emigrants as adventurers, runaways, and ne'er-do-wells: the officer who had to quit the service for some dishonorable act, the boy who had got with child the family cook, the employee in a merchant's office who had embezzled a petty sum escaped to America, "the Promised Land of failures."[1] The very fact of emigration seemed somewhat suspicious to the Germans, who have a favorite proverb: "Stay at home and make an honest living." It was "the German urchin in America"—the title of a runaway's autobiography which was popular in Germany and shaped the image of America from the turn of the century to our day—who later returned as "the rich uncle from America." These Americans were viewed with a mixture of respect (for their money) and disrespect (for their

[1] The literary prototype in West Europe of the new American was Moll Flanders, the heroine of Daniel Defoe's great novel. After a life of vice and crime in Europe, she settled down in America, where she became a rich and respected lady.

past). As late as 1948 a "Primer on America for German Adults" explained ponderously that "the emigrant is for him [the American] not to be pitied or to be scorned [as he is for Germans], but to be revered."[2] Many Germans looked down from their solid superiority on those shady emigrants who got rich quick in America. Their boasts soon helped to form the second stereotype of "materialistic America," where mammon was idolized and multi-millionaires ruled supreme over a people of millionaires, millionaires-to-be, and derelicts.

The third stereotype which received almost general currency among Germans was that Americans were convinced the United States was "God's own country." In Germany this slogan became as current a foreign word when America was discussed as, in recent times, Herrenrasse (the Master Race) had become current in American usage for Germany. Germans used to be as angry at the hypocritical and chauvinistic slogan of American self-regard as Americans were at the German one. Ironically, both slogans became more popular abroad than at home where they had been coined. This German stereotype of a hypocritical and chauvinistic America was nourished by the disappointment over President Wilson, whose program of peace was betrayed at the Versailles Conference—something the Germans never quite forgot.

In Germany's Red Decade of the 1920's, when—as in America in the 1930's and early 1940's—much of the intellectual and cultural life of the country was controlled by Communists and their fellow-traveling camp followers and dupes, the stereotype of America was further and deliberately made to appear unattractive. America, the bastion of capitalism, had then as now to supply the dark contrast to the glowing Great Experiment of the Soviet Union. From most reports on America published at the time there again emerged the stereotype of an America dominated by the dollar, sadly lacking in civilization, backward in terms of culture, social progress and human decency. This picture was

[2] Margret Boveri, *Amerikafibel für erwachsene Deutsche,* Freiburg Br., 1948.

portrayed yet again by the Nazis, whose propaganda depicted the plutocratic, racially contaminated, brutal and greedy American. Only a small minority of cosmopolitan intellectuals, out of secret opposition to the Nazis, developed a new cult of America as the country of youthful strength.

After 1945, the hordes of tourists, visiting relatives, students and professors who had personally represented America in Germany in the previous decades were followed by the American occupation army and the Military Government for Germany, thus giving birth to new images of America in German eyes. The new German images reflected the contradictions, uncertainties, vagaries, and follies of American policies or misinterpreted American purposes; these policies appeared in German eyes as indications of the true nature of America, which seemed to lack the democratic justice, civic responsibility, peacefully flourishing culture, and human understanding of which it liked to boast. To some degree, the images also reflected German feelings of inferiority, insecurity, resentment, and guilt, which were projected onto the powerful victor.

America's dark record in the first German postwar years, which was never fully publicized in this country, was a personal and unforgettable experience to millions of Germans. The Americans had come, in the words of their commander-in-chief, "as conquerors, not as liberators," and they acted indeed like tough conquerors rather than democratic liberators. These were the years when "fraternization," or, to be more exact, the simplest expression of human politeness, kindness, and decency toward the defeated, was unlawful for an American soldier; when a few Americans—well-fed, often luxuriously well-housed—announced that in their billets Germans, DPs, and dogs were not admitted, and secretly bought precious family heirlooms from half-starved, homeless Germans for a carton of American cigarettes or a pound of American coffee; when an American general in charge of information control forbade the playing of music over a German radio station "to bring home to the Germans

that there is no reason for them to enjoy life"; when the Germans
—among them people whose parents had been executed by
Hitler's hangmen for participation in the plot to kill him, Germans who themselves had suffered for years the agony of Nazi
concentration camps because they resisted Hitler, Germans who
had been three years old when Hitler came to power and fifteen
years old when he fell—were told by occupation officials that to
them all Germans were alike, and they had to bear the punishment for the crimes committed by Nazism.

In these dark years, American judges sat side by side with
Soviet judges to try German crimes against inhumanity. A few
American investigators and prosecutors beat up, threatened,
maimed Germans in order to extract confessions. To be tough
with the Germans appeared a mark of virility to many Americans,
and their toughness sometimes included, as the Germans observed, an infamous imitation of the infamous Nazi methods.
German industries were dismantled by American experts "in
order to keep the Germans from ever again producing for war";
patents were taken from their German owners, assets abroad expropriated from individuals and corporations. "The Americans
are just as bad as the Nazis were," some Germans whispered
among themselves in these first postwar years.

Although this analogy was more often wrong than right, even
in individual instances, and all wrong as a generalization, quite a
few Germans retained material wounds, and many of them moral
wounds from the acts of the tough American conquerors, who,
they were told, were democratically expressing the will of the
American people. Guilty, or helplessly ashamed of what the
Nazis had done in their name, the Germans felt that this new
stereotype of "the Americans who demonstrated so valiantly that
they weren't better than the Nazis" contributed a good deal to
relieve them of their bad conscience.

Their resentment was not to vanish with its cause. In 1951,
when relations between the occupation and the occupied had become civilized, one of Germany's best-selling books was *The*

Questionnaire (Der Fragebogen), the cynical autobiography of Ernst von Salomon, a. former terrorist gleefully indulging in vitriolic and spite-ridden denunciations of the American occupation. The first openly anti-American book to be published, something a great many Germans had evidently waited for, it described in a hundred pages the author's one-year internment in an American camp where a crowd of GI's beat him up once, and an American lieutenant stole his wrist watch. (The author's participation in the murder of Walter Rathenau, Foreign Minister of the Weimar Republic in 1923, was merely mentioned in passing as a "boyish prank.") That the Americans were as brutal and greedy as the Nazis, though more hypocritical and more naïve—the running theme of this best-seller—appeared again and again in letters-to-the-editor and private talks, usually in a transparent though wholly invalid attempt to justify the Nazi crimes by equating them with the tough methods the occupying army used after the war, and with cases of genuine "excesses" in which individual—and not at all typical—military and civilian members of the occupation expressed their personal feelings of hate and revenge in disgraceful acts.

From 1947 to 1949 the tough American policy of conquest was softened by a wavering, confused, half-hearted policy of cooperation. In this new policy the Americans who before had unashamedly played the role of conquistador now turned into an uneasy and implausible mixture of conquistador and social worker. While they ruled Germany by force of arms, they set out to educate her to democracy by force of argument. After first being "conquerors, not liberators," they now pretended to be conquerors as well as liberators. A pseudo-hermaphroditic figure, the Military Government suffered in peacetime from its double nature, the military one ruling by orders and requests, and the democratic governmental one expressing the will of the constituents. The Military Government, in addition to being a purely military army organization, was the very opposite of democratic government, since first it combined the executive, legislative, and judiciary functions without division of powers, and later kept the supreme right to veto these functions when performed by the Germans.

The Germans saw in all this a reaffirmation of their old stereotype of America's hypocrisy. The Americans pretended to rule Germany democratically and exhorted the Germans to be American-like—democrats and pacifists—while at the same time they actually ruled Germany in the admittedly undemocratic ways of Military Government. It was the idea and the conception of Military Government which stuck, and when in 1949 its name as well as its functions were changed into the rather inoffensive and tactfully restrained High Commission for Germany, practically nobody in Germany acknowledged the change; in German usage as well as German thinking, it was still the "Military Government." In the German mind American hypocrisy was superimposed on, and merged with, American toughness; Americans —in contrast to the Nazis as well as the Soviets—hid their acts of power and violence behind moral and democratic masks and pretenses.

In the period of High Commission rule beginning in 1949 the politics of conquest were quietly shelved.[3] On the whole, the High Commission presided with benevolence and often generosity over a Germany which, as everybody knew, was soon to be given back her sovereignty. For the Americans there remained little but to encourage the democratization of that country. As America needed its active good will, the conquerors suddenly became missionaries.

This change, pleasant and profitable as it was for the Germans, did little to improve their stereotype of America. On the contrary, new unfavorable sidelights were added, and old negative stereo-

---

[3] Though not without an occasional and isolated revival, such as in 1951 in the Kemritz case, which offered the Germans an opportunity for violent protest revealing some of their pent-up resentments. (See my article, "The Kemritz Case," in *Commonweal*, October 26, 1951.) A number of other conflicts, mainly on issues of economic policy, between High Commission members and Germans had similar effects.

types strengthened. What it seemed to show was that Americans were superficial and fickle; most of the principles which two years ago they had enthusiastically advocated, and many of the principles which they had requested the Germans to accept seemed forgotten overnight and replaced by opposite principles. If, as late as 1947, the Americans had not permitted the Germans to publish anti-Communist books translated from the American, now they themselves encouraged their publication and distribution among Germans. If, in 1945, to get an American license to edit a newspaper Berliners had to prove they were friendly to Communism, if in Frankfurt and other cities the Americans appointed Communist editors on the staffs of their papers, in 1948 they fired the same Communists and demanded proof of anti-Communism from their licensees. It was the same in the ministries, in the unions, everywhere. Since the Americans failed openly to admit and to explain their own total reversal, the Germans concluded that "you can never know what the Americans are up to next—they change their ideas overnight." As they compared American occupation speeches of 1946, proclaiming that no German should ever bear arms again, with American occupation speeches of 1951, scolding the Germans who never wanted to bear arms again, it was difficult for them not to accept this stereotype.

Many Germans, it is true, recognized that this seeming American fickleness and instability originated less with the Americans than with the Soviets. But they also saw that almost every American change in attitudes and policies toward Germany came about only in reply and as a reaction to a Soviet move; in German eyes, as a matter of fact, American policy in Germany seemed dictated by Russia. In the first stage, America made every concession to the Soviets that the Soviets requested; after 1946 America began taking defensive countermeasures against the Soviets and their aggressions; after 1948 America made concessions to the Germans in order to "contain" the Soviets. In other words, the Americans never seemed to have an independent political purpose of their own, and no insight into what they should do in Germany. To many Germans, Americans appeared as a people sadly lost on the international scene, unable to perform their part in foreign politics, perhaps because they lacked the necessary power and the political understanding. At any rate, America seemed to regard and treat the Germans as passive objects which, like figures on a chessboard, it pushed in this or that direction, in a helpless defensive against the aggressive, power-hungry, politically shrewd Soviets, while it propagandized its ever-changing political practices by preaching to the Germans on never-changing eternal principles.

The American program to educate, or re-educate, Germany, which became one of the basic targets of occupation policy, did very little to remove these misconceptions or to create a more proper image of America in German eyes.

By a misunderstanding based on deeper differences between the two cultures, the Germans resented the very idea of "education" and "re-education," which in their eyes had an offensive background of arrogance. In contrast to America, where "education" means many things, to Germans the term smacks of the three R's —the elementary schooling given to children, colonial peoples, and illiterates, with the use of the rod. That political education— *politische Bildung*—was needed in Germany, many Germans agreed; but in its literal translation as *Erziehung,* which became accepted in Germany, the American program of "education" seemed an arrogant American attempt to treat the Germans as illiterate children and to teach them with authoritarian sternness.

The idea of education to democracy, or "re-education," was, as the Germans correctly sensed, a "typically American idea." The Nazis, for instance, would not "re-educate" the countries which they conquered; Russia's great cities were to be destroyed, according to Hitler's plan, and to be replaced by fortified garrisons where racially selected German Nazis would rule and repopulate the country. The Russians, kept by a strict "non-fraternization ban" from any contacts with the occupying Germans, would be denied all education, and most of the food they produced would be shipped to Germany. Instead of medical care, they were only to get generous supplies of free contraceptives.[4] Weakening them by ignorance, disease, and sterility, and starving them to death, the Nazi conquerors would not have to re-educate the inferior Slavonic race.

Based on the democratic faith which believes in the improvability of the individual by education and information, the Americans resorted in their German "Education Program" to the methods they had used successfully at home to change "backward foreigners" into democratic citizens when—with evening classes and adult schools—they had "Americanized" the immigrants. Hadn't these foreigners been taught to adjust themselves to the superior American ways? And hadn't their young generation, which grew up in the slums, been kept from delinquency by playgrounds, the encouragement of boy scoutism and "Y's," the Americanization in schools? The "Education Program" for Germany seemed to view the country as a nationwide slum. By presenting the German adults with evening classes and free lectures, establishing baseball teams and playgrounds for the German youth, this backward people would be kept from crime and elevated to the level of democratic citizenship.

Social workers set out to deluge Germany with a torrent of lectures, articles, books, movies, evening classes, speeches indulging in, and explaining, the miraculously good, efficient, and beautiful thing called American democracy. To Germans, it soon seemed that Americans were suffering from an obsession to talk, talk, talk about democracy, and never let a sentence pass without having used once at least that magic word. Living in a country which was not democratic, in which there was little opportunity for the citizens to act as democrats, and where the very representatives of democracy ruled in an autocratic way, many Germans came to see democracy as a verbal fetish of the Americans. The

[4] Cf. Henry Picker, *Hitlers Tischgespräche, Geordnet, eingeleitet und veröffentlicht von Gerhard Ritter*, Bonn, 1951.

jocular expression *Demokratur*[5] was popularly used to describe the split personality of American government in Germany. To some, the hypocritical nature of the Americans was again confirmed. To others, democracy painted in such glowing and wonderful colors by the American educators seemed something great and beautiful indeed—yet unobtainable for Germans; it must be the special conditions of America and the special character of Americans, they concluded, which made this political ideal work over there; but Germany was not made for it.

In addition to political education to democracy, a vast program of non-political offerings was presented by the occupation to create good will, understanding, love for America in Germany. In 27 Amerika-Haus centers and 120 reading rooms spread throughout the American occupation zone, the American government—through its officials, who had to double as impresarios, propagandists, and entertainment managers, in addition to their jobs as educators and social workers—gave the Germans a glimpse of life and culture in America. Whole regiments of itinerant lecturers enlightened German audiences on topics such as the national parks of America, new trends in the American novel; American singers, dancers, actors, American paintings, music, books, were showered upon them. Many Germans came to the Amerika-Haus simply because here they could find a warm room for an evening. It seemed to many Germans that Americans, as typical among the nouveau riche, threw away their money boastfully to show off their newly acquired "culture." That Americans were desperately eager to be admired, and that they wasted their money to buy admiration, seemed more conspicuous than the authentic great values of their civilization clumsily presented to people who were not prepared to discern them.

To most Europeans, and Germans in particular, the real greatness of American culture, the genuine achievement of American civilization, lay in the spirit and technique of its social structure.

[5] "Democratatorship"—an impossible word and an impossible system that sets out as "democracy" to change midway to dictatorship.

The art of living together in peace and mutual trust with a common moral purpose; the freedom in which equal citizens form their community, and the community in which the individual is neither atomized in private isolation nor submerged in a collective mass—this seemed America's greatest contribution to mankind. The architecture of American society appeared in the eyes of thoughtful Germans more admirable than the architecture of American skyscrapers and mansions; American freedom in everyday life seemed to them a greater work of art than, say, American ballets or symphonies. Yet, except for the few who had either experienced it in America itself or carefully studied it, this culture of daily life and living society could hardly be shown convincingly at a distance.

What the educators employed by the American Military Government lectured, exhibited, and demonstrated to the Germans of American life was not bad in itself. What was bad and what deprived it of all possible good results was that the program was undertaken by the government; as a matter of fact, this governmental background backfired against the program.

In the first place, Germans—after their past experience with Nazism and their present one with the Soviets, both most active in governmental enlightenment and thought control—were conditioned to "propaganda" emanating from governments—and all information circulated by governments was wearily regarded as "propaganda." The same facts they disbelieved when spoken by employees, experts, or other representatives of the American government, they were ready to believe when stated by independent individuals.

In the second place, America seemed ill-equipped for efficient governmental propaganda. The commonplace paradox that this country "is great at selling soft drinks and toothpaste while it fails in selling its ideas" might, in the light of the German experience, be explained by the fact that the former is sold in free competition and free enterprise while the latter was sold by a bureaucratic state machine. It was a contradiction in itself that

"the American way" of freedom, with its resistance to bureaucratic entanglements and state power, was advertised by the state
on a non-competitive, bureaucratic basis. Indeed, the fumbling
manner in which the education program represented America
with an eye on possible approval or disapproval of State Department bureaucrats, Senators, Congressmen, and other people in
power back home, proved that America could not be "sold"
abroad by propagandists with a civil service rating. The immense-
ly varied, infinitely many-faced American reality was necessarily
distorted when governmental propagandists selected this or that
feature, this or that facet of America and seemingly provided it
with an official stamp of approval, shifting the emphasis to one
part of a combination whose harmonious wholeness alone is
really America.

While the government-employed salesmen tried to convince
the Germans of the political and cultural superiority of America,
a very different picture emerged from American plays, films,
literature, and art, often consisting—in the best American tradition—of self-criticism, usually social self-criticism. Transplanted
from Broadway and Fifth Avenue to Berlin, Hamburg, Munich,
they appeared as accurate and typical descriptions of the American scene rather than one writer's or artist's personal protest, and
seemed to confirm all the stereotypes of anti-American propaganda. Successful American plays—from "All My Sons" and
"Death of a Salesman" to "Born Yesterday" and "A Streetcar
Named Desire"—seemed to mirror a dehumanized country whose
people were ridden by anxieties and would one day crack up
under its economic and psychological strains. It was the same
with American books that became best-sellers in Germany—
James Jones' *From Here to Eternity,* for instance, or Norman
Mailer's *Barbary Shore* (a novel of social protest little noted in
America). Social criticism, especially American self-criticism,
did not prove a good export product; foreign audiences, not
familiar with its true context, were likely to receive it as snap-
shots of reality. It was like eavesdropping on a family quar-

rel and assuming it to be the normal, everyday life of the family.

This was especially true as the voices of America beamed to foreign countries belonged most frequently to members of the American "intelligentsia" who were apt to be obsessed by their desire to criticize their own country, a function as useful at home as it is misunderstood abroad. Their own somewhat abnormal position in American society made them less valid spokesmen of America than the farmers, workers, manufacturers, teachers, and doctors whose feelings about America were rarely heard abroad. America's bitterest critics often came to represent America in foreign countries.

This tainted, distorted, highly unpleasant image frightened and repelled many Germans, since they believed that America wanted to remodel the whole world, including Germany, in its own image, with "God's own country" as the blueprint according to which all other countries of the globe, especially Germany, were to be shaped. Erroneous as this impression was on the whole, it contained a kernel of actual truth. For there were American experts in many fields, backed by the American Military Government, who came to Germany to advise the Germans that from now on they should forget all their traditions and customs and do things the American way; only if they did things as Americans did them could their country be transformed into a democracy.

In virtually every field the Germans were advised to change their ways and imitate American examples. German newspapers should be written, edited, and made up like an American newspaper; German youngsters should play baseball rather than soccer; German students should address their instructors by their first names rather than by the stuffy title of *Herr Professor.*

Some of this—often ignorant, sometimes foolish—advice came from the self-centered specialists who held their pet ideas as the key to world reform; to them the occupation was a field day. Others came from narrow-minded experts unable to see deeper relations between their particular subject and society. Finally, many advocates of reform belonged to the International of provincials, who are certain that everything is better the way they know it at home; unfortunately, they had authority and prestige when they told off to the natives. What many Germans concluded from this was that Americans—superior to Europeans in some fields, but not in others—wanted to remake Europe as an exact replica of the United States, first by force and then by persuasion. And the Germans resented these attempts. Eventually many Americans tended to resent on their side these natural and almost necessary resentments, which they mistook for prejudiced hostility against America and for a sign of German recalcitration to be a democracy.

If there were added also many friendlier colors and more pleasant features to the picture of America in West German eyes, they came in the main from personal contacts Germans had with America or with Americans. In 1949, the U. S. Department of State, supported by many private American organizations, began an Exchange Program; carefully selected Germans from all walks of life were invited to visit America for a number of months. The guests selected were chiefly Germans who felt already friendly towards America and democracy. The large majority of these visitors returned with intensive pro-American convictions based on their impressions, experiences, and friendships in this country. "Americans at home are certainly better than Americans on occupation duty," a Bavarian government minister said to me after his return from such a tour of the States, and this was the conclusion of most travelers, who remained often unaware of the fact that most people abroad seem less attractive than they do at home, be they tourists, convention guests, or occupation personnel, be they German, British, or American.

However, a number of Americans in civilian or military branches of the occupation genuinely contributed to a more balanced, better image of America in the eyes of the West Germans, especially when they were able to speak the German language and were not completely alien to the ways of German life—in the first rank, Ellen McCloy, wife of the U. S. High Commissioner for Germany, a warmhearted, simple, energetic woman, and George Naumann Shuster, the U. S. Land Commissioner for Bavaria, on leave as president of New York's Hunter College and a gentlemanly scholar deeply devoted to democracy; Melvin J. Lasky, a New York magazine writer who edited in Berlin the U.S. sponsored monthly, *Der Monat*, successful in bringing international thought and life close to the Germans, and German thought and life close to the international audience; Hans Wallenberg, publisher and editor of the U.S. sponsored daily newspaper, *Die Neue Zeitung,* which called itself on its masthead "an American newspaper for Germany," and which combined the better features of American and German journalism and succeeded in presenting American purpose and culture to its German readers. In the labor, industrial, and religious activities, in the youth, education, information, and public affairs divisions of the Military Government and High Commission, quite a few other practical idealists established by professional and private intercourse with Germans a more sympathetic, more accurate picture of the country they represented.

Chance contacts with, and observation of, a number of GI's had similar effects. Generally called "der *Ami,*" an abbreviation of *Amerikaner* (and not, as an American correspondent reported, the French word for "friend,") the foreign young men in American uniforms were conspicuous in West German life and, quite naturally, regarded by the Germans as representative products of America's people and culture. The first German words they usually picked up were *Dankeschön,* "Thank you very much." When they ran after an elderly gentleman's hat blown off by the wind and handed it back to him with a friendly *Dankeschön,* as I once saw in Munich, or when they stopped their jeep on a mountainous road where a little German crowd had assembled over a peasant woman's broken bicycle, and wordlessly repaired it to drive off again with a grin and a "S'long," the Germans found that the *Ami,* or rather, the Americans, were not so bad at all, but kindly and nice young men. That most did not behave as overbearing victors impressed many Germans as much and as favorably as that there was little class consciousness in the army, that they were generous, and that they were often poorer than Americans were supposed to be. Especially the latter fact, revealed when a GI in a train would tell his German acquaintance about the troubles of his "folks back home" and their hopes, impressed people who tended to resent the newly rich millionaries.

Negro GI's were especially well liked by the Germans. Many Germans used to say that they preferred them to white Americans, because "they are more warmhearted," and there were fewer rowdies among them than among the white soldiers. The story was widely told that a jeepful of Negro *Amis* once followed a German girl late at night to protect her against "the white folks prowling the streets."

Prejudiced people, of course, tend to see what they expect to see. For the many West Germans with a grudge against the Americans, it was rather easy to see many *Amis* whose behavior bore out their anti-American image of America. The *Amis* who misbehaved were only a small minority of the whole occupation army; but then, they were considerably more conspicuous than the better-mannered and more typical majority. As a matter of fact, occupation rules made the minority of "bad eggs" more visible to the German view. The "bad eggs," for instance, traveled in civilian German trains, where they had to pay the fare out of their own pockets, but could drink freely, which often led them to annoy the German fellow passengers, whereas the sober majority traveled in the military trains on which no liquor was allowed, but where they also did not meet any Germans. The same minority of "bad eggs" loitered every evening on the main streets of the German cities and garrison towns, molested passing women with a few indecent German words they had picked up, or in more concrete ways, visited shady saloons and night clubs and started brawls, while the majority consisted of rather shy young men who rarely ventured out of their service clubs, barracks, snack bars; bashful toward the German girls, they wished they were back home again. German statistics reveal that after 1949 there was a rise in riots between GI's and Germans, many of which were actually started by Americans. In several smaller cities, so many incidents occurred that visitors were warned "It's not safe to be on the streets after ten in the evening, on account of the *Amis*"; and for a self-respecting girl to walk unescorted in the main thoroughfares of Frankfurt, Munich, or Nürnberg was at least likely to be very unpleasant.

To sum up all the contradicting traits composing the image, America emerged in West German eyes as more civilized and less crude, more wealthy and less aggressive than Soviet Russia, but very similar to Soviet Russia in many respects—actually closer in its nature to Soviet Russia than to Germany. Like Soviet Russia, America was tremendously proud of its culture and tried hard to convince the Germans of its value. Like Soviet Russia, America wanted to be feared as well as loved by the Germans. Like Russia, America was a backward "young country," and its people "naïve" and "primitive." Like Russia, America saw itself as the great example for others, and wanted to force its own social order, habits, civilization, on Germany. Like Russia, America was unpredictable. In short, America was like Soviet Russia, only less so. Less backward, less cruel, less primitive, less forceful in imposing its culture, America in German eyes seemed less dangerous than Soviet Russia. With its laws, its military police, that arrested and punished the misbehaving American soldiers rather than the victimized Germans as the Russians did, with civilized men and women in its ranks, with the impact of its occupation over the years getting less and less oppressive while the Soviet impact was becoming more and more oppressive, America seemed the lesser evil. Most West Germans admitted this; comparing *Amis* and *Ivans,* the American and the Soviet occupation soldiers, the United States and the Soviet Union, they insisted that the latter was "altogether worse" than the former. Yet this qualified and half-hearted admission only pointed to the desirability of the third alternative—to steer clear of both, and to keep aloof from friendly understanding or co-operation with both big foreign powers. "The Americans are Russians with creased pants," some Germans liked to say.

In 1952, the Allensbach Institute for Demoscopy asked a cross section of the German people (including refugees from East Germany) about their experiences with the American occupation since 1945. Of this cross section, 36 per cent had seen little of the U.S. troops; 15 per cent had pleasant experiences; 32 per cent had unpleasant experiences; and 17 per cent, very unpleasant experiences. While the British rated somewhat better and the French considrably worse in the same test, all three evoked incomparably better memories than the Soviet occupation. Only 5 per cent had seen little of them or had pleasant experiences, while 24 per cent had unpleasant—and 71 per cent very unpleasant—experiences!

"Which of the four occupation powers do you prefer?" the Bielefeld Institute of German Public Opinion asked a representative sample of West Germans in the fall of 1951. While 12 per cent refused to give an answer, 1 per cent expressed preference for the Russians; 1 per cent for the French; 8 per cent for the British; and 33 per cent for the Americans. Almost one out of two questioned, or 45 per cent, said they did not prefer one power to the other. The majority group saw no difference between the four foreign powers, but the second strongest group, one out of three, considered the Americans "relatively" preferable.

When in the early 1950's four characters appeared on German stages with different accents and different mannerisms, yet alike in their rather ridiculous foreign nature, representing the stereotyped four foreign occupation powers—in the satirical motion picture, "The Wives of Herr S.," or the play, "The Four Colonels," in the cabaret sketches and night-club ballets—the American was not basically different from his Russian antagonist. Most typical was a dance scene in the program of a low-life spot of Hamburg's waterfront, where a young girl, in the nude but for a coquettish nightcap, which introduced her to the audience as unmistakably German, was wooed first by a Russian, who alternately played the balalaika and threatened her with a whip; a mustachioed Frenchman, who cavorted with her gallantly; a wooden-faced Britisher, who did nothing at all to win her favors; and finally, by an American, chewing gum, his pockets bulging with cigarettes and bottles, humming a children's melody. But the nude girl turned graciously away from them all; while the four foreigners started pulling their guns and shooting at each other, a German boy appeared from the wings and danced happily, peacefully, away with the German girl.

To some degree, the reawakening of self-respect of a nation that had tried to emerge from ruins and rubble asserted itself when the Germans coldly turned their back on the foreign powers, which to them appeared all in the same distorted, unfavorable view. Like a high school boy who in his last year of school is yearning for freedom and dislikes all his teachers without reflecting that some were better than others, the Germans in their last years as a non-sovereign or semi-sovereign state came to dislike equally all their teachers with foreign accents. America, whose picture in German eyes differed widely from the way it saw itself and the way it wanted itself seen by others, did not succeed in making most Germans understand why it saw itself in such a different light. While most Germans did not want to see America as it was, and preferred to see it in dark, repulsive colors—to compensate for their own feelings of guilt by proving to themselves that "the others weren't better," to find a foreign target for their resentment of defeat, to rationalize their dislike of the powerful victors and the rich benefactor—America had also to blame itself for this failure. It had tried too hard to make itself beloved by the Germans, after it had tried very hard to make itself feared by them. Too rarely had America treated the Germans as equals and as fellow men.

In the summer of 1951, a man named Mr. Smith visited the principal of the girls' high school at Flensburg, a middle-sized North German town in the British zone. He was, he said, a public health officer working for the American High Commission, and he wanted to select the twelve healthiest girls over fourteen years of age, who were to be sent on a visit to the United States. He spoke very broken and faulty English, as the principal noted. Since the trip to America was to take place very soon, he set out immediately, examining, one by one, all the girls of the school. Each had to undress in order for him to examine her in an extremely thoroughgoing, though perhaps not quite expert, way. He repeated his survey in another girls' high school of the same town. Altogether, several hundred girls underwent his scrutiny. Only by chance was it discovered that Mr. Smith was a native and lifelong inhabitant of the town of Flensburg rather than an American, and that he was a sex pervert with a long prison record. Impressed by his airs of a bureaucrat connected with the *Obrigkeit,* none of the girls, their parents, or their principals had protested or even as much as asked for his credentials.

After the man was arrested, all concerned explained that they hadn't suspected "Mr. Smith" because everything he did was so typically American! "That's how the Americans are, I thought," said the high school principal, "charitable and rich, but with uncultured manners repulsive to our tastes; nevertheless, I thought a trip to the States would be worth it to the girls." His colleague added: "I realized that the man couldn't speak correct English, but then I knew that most Americans don't." One of the examined girls explained: "Well, everybody knows that Americans are sometimes crazy." "If they give you something, it is because they want to get something out of it for themselves; they are so materialistic," her friend said. Mr. Smith, who had never been in America, almost got away with his hoax because he fitted so well the new German stereotype of the American: rude and respectless of traditions, without social manners, but offering gifts which you want to accept; outlandish and childish, but powerful; charitable and friendly, yet perhaps for some ulterior, selfish interest. In a word, Americans were very strange strangers.

XIV

CONCLUSION

The Test of Tomorrow

A S IN a fragment of a shattered mirror, Germany reflects the world in which we live. Behind the blurred, distorted picture of ruins and chaos, the outline of our world can be discerned. Or rather, of the two worlds that have emerged since the war.

What we see in Germany is a greater drama than that of Germany alone, extending far beyond the particular situation of German politics or the fact of German recovery, which seem in comparison almost provincial. The two most powerful ideas of social organization in our time exist side by side in Germany; there they measure their strength and appeal, challenge each other and claim the future. Scientifically speaking, Germany is the laboratory in which—for the first and perhaps the only time in history —the democratic experiment and the totalitarian experiment are being tested under almost exactly equal conditions, with the world of tomorrow as the winner.

It seems rather ironic that Germany should be the scene of this contest between democracy and totalitarianism. For Germany, according to the victors, was to be a sort of model One World, ruled by a happy condominium of the four powers. Actually it became the bloodless battleground of two hostile worlds. It was the misfortune rather than the guilt of seventeen million Germans who happened to live in the country's eastern section that they became the raw material of the totalitarian experiment, just as it was the luck rather than the merit of forty-seven million other Germans that they were assigned to the democratic experiment. Their national traits were reasonably similar, they had gone through identical recent collective experiences, they spoke the same language and felt closely related to one another. If, after a short while, 99.71 per cent of the East Germans voted for their totalitarian government, while the majority of West Germans voted democratically for parties with a democratic program, in short if "the Germans" seemed to be totalitarians or democrats according to the arbitrary line the victors had drawn on their military map, it was but further evidence that the German character has little to do with the form of government the people have and seem to accept. Exactly for this reason, the German test, rather than being limited in its significance to the Germans themselves, has worldwide importance. It presents in sharp focus the comparative strength and weakness of the democratic and totalitarian societies in their global struggle.

Measured by the standard of the democratic ideal, the West German experiment has not been altogether successful. It began under the most inauspicious conditions possible: with ruins and poverty, many values—"civilian courage, sincerity, faith in convictions, charity and piety" (as the German writer, Erich Kästner, said in 1946)—destroyed by Nazism, demoralization and corruption rampant, the blundering, naïve, occasionally vindictive occupation rule, and the traditional *unpolitische* lethargy among the Germans themselves. Many of these unhappy conditions were not greatly improved after seven years of occupation. As previously, the German private citizen tried to live independent of society, for which he felt no responsibility and whose course he did not shape. Keeping aloof from the community, he retired to the total privacy of his individual world. He did not favor a new totalitarian ruler—neither Communist nor Nazi, nor the newest version combining both. However, his precious privacy rendered him virtually defenseless against the totalitarians whom he rejected.

The separation of the individual and the community, the conflict between the organization of modern mass society and the

20

preservation of personal freedom—these shortcomings in the West German experiment are but the oversized, underlined imperfections confronting every free society of our time. The free society, imperfect by its very definition and nature, is nevertheless, continuously open to, and striving for, reform, improvement, regeneration. The German experiment, most of all in its Berlin phase, has shown that even under the worst possible conditions a decisive though small minority can acquire the awareness of their responsibilities, and that they do act as free citizens if they are given a chance to act, and if they feel that theirs is a genuine community.

Pointing to the imperfections—the diseases and the discontent of the free society in the Western world—the totalitarian experiment sets out to free the individual from his isolation, to give a larger significance and dignity to the workers, to force man into being part of his society. The East German totalitarian experiment has demonstrated that it is successful in abolishing the faults of the free society and putting in its place the final failure of the collective society. The seeds of responsibility, the shoots of a community, the nuclei of free decision which can flourish in the Western society are rooted out like weeds in the totalitarian collective, by means of concentration camps and death sentences.

The basic conflict between the individual and society in our times is illustrated by the individualistic, atomized, lonely mass of West Germany, as well as by the lifeless mass of East Germany, where the "politicized" individual must strive to fit himself into the collective like a brick in the wall, and to cheer at the funeral of his own liberty. While West Germans tend to have the fearful feeling that they are strangers to their neighbors and deserted by God, East Germans must betray their neighbors and denounce God, if they hope to survive. If the imperfections of the democratic experiment lead many, especially the young, to hopelessness, selfishness, and cynicism, still every step foward in attaining its own standards is bound to decrease their number, while every progress of the totalitarian experiment toward its own goal is bound to multiply the hopeless, the selfish, and the cynical. The free society appeals to hope; the totalitarian society, to fear. Between the extremes of West Germany's individualistic mass of private men and East Germany's collectivist mass of passive men, the goal of a genuine democratic community is considerably nearer the West German way.

Whether measured in terms of material well-being, personal dignity, or spiritual regeneration, the totalitarian experiment of East Germany falls incomparably shorter of its avowed aims than does the democratic experiment of West Germany.

So unmistakable was the result of this test that, except for a few party agents, advocates of Communist revolution almost disappeared from West Germany after 1945. The totalitarians themselves were well aware of the disastrous showing their experiment had made in comparison with that of the West. This was one of the reasons why they tried so hard to annex West Berlin, the most conspicuous illustration of the two experiments. It was also the reason why they had to put up the Iron Curtain between "their" Germany and that of the West, thereby preventing a comparison of the two ideas in action. But the Iron Curtain was only a makeshift measure. It could not shut off altogether a glimpse into the other half of the world. Therefore, even if their ideology, their strategic blueprint, their revolutionary drive for conquest, had not made it imperative for them to win West Germany, they would have to keep trying to infiltrate, neutralize, dominate West Germany. As a free society, however faulty, in the democratic orbit, West Germany continues to be a dangerous contrast to Soviet Russia's East. To "contain" itself within its present borders, the Soviet system must destroy the West German experiment. The two worlds cannot co-exist except in deadly enmity, each awaiting the moment when one will defeat the other. At the same time when Soviet Russia was fighting its laboratory war against America in Korea, she was fighting a second laboratory war against America in Germany, although many Americans were not even aware of it.

Germany is our test. On the bloodless battleground which extends from West Germany to East Germany, America's strength in the world-wide contest with the Soviet power is being explored. The paradoxical fact is that, while Soviet Russia has failed in the totalitarian experiment of East Germany, it has nevertheless a good chance to win the contest finally over the democratic idea despite the latter's more successful results in the test. In this contest, America's own vital interest is at stake. If it loses Germany, it will—in addition to the perhaps decisive weakening of its defensive power by the loss of German raw materials, manpower, strategic space—lose the great battle of ideas. Either Germany shall in the future be an independent free country integrated with a free Western Europe, or America shall have to live as a beleaguered continent in an isolation enforced upon it by its enemy against its own will.

Only if West Germany lives and works as a democracy can it defend itself against totalitarianism from within and without, and be an outpost and ally of America. To help Germany grow into a democracy, America must show its faith in freedom and its faith in man—in this case, its faith in the German people as well as in the values, the moral strength, the great purpose of America.

Germany can certainly not be converted to "Americanism," nor will she become a satellite of America. She will probably have to walk on a long road, with detours and blind alleys, before she becomes the society of free citizens which we call democracy. Many differences between America and Germany do not stem from German faults or shortcomings; but neither do they bar a common perception of values, interests, and purposes. If the Germans are led to feel that their democracy was imposed on them by a foreign power, they shall perhaps never arrive at being a democracy. They want to be treated as an independent nation by America, and as equals in the sincere spirit of fellowship, even if the political structure of Germany does not measure up to the standards of American democracy. America will win in Germany only by an attitude of understanding and brotherhood.

It is another facet of the German test to measure the degree to which the two half-countries shall be fettered by the two great powers which dominate their orbit and which embody the ideas of democracy and totalitarianism. That Soviet Russia is destroying the last shred of the East German satellite's independence is obvious. Whether America lives up to its program of respecting the independence of other nations, or whether it will also practice actual, though more subtle, domination is a matter of grave concern to all those who watch with great fear for signs showing that the new American world leadership is to turn into a new imperialism. To win Germany as an ally, and to succeed in the German test, America must not interfere with the way in which the German proponents and friends of freedom conduct their affairs even if they seem to make mistakes; otherwise the West German democratic test is a failure.

Germany is our challenge. To repel the tyrants on their way to conquest, we cannot do without fellow-defenders of freedom. There are such men and women in Germany, and they deserve our friendship—without condescension or reservations. Their number will be greater, and they will be stronger, if West Germany herself can regain her health—as a political community, as an economic unit, as a new, decent, better society. While this recovery and this regeneration is a labor to be undertaken by the Germans themselves, it can be helped from the outside—as a matter of fact, it needs some help from the outside; we can give this help by offering our understanding, and our material support.

America must extend its helping hand to the victims of Soviet tyranny—the refugees streaming to the West and the people still suffering in the East. America's solidarity with the German believers in freedom must extend, first and most of all, to those East Germans who are resisting surrender to the totalitarian idea. Like the democratic minority of West Germany, these fighters share their basic values and purposes with America. Every day they risk their lives to weaken the totalitarian system, and to strengthen the democratic idea. They are America's best and bravest allies, although America has done little to show them friendship and closeness. Worried about "containment," trusting rather the number of guns than the spirit of the people who hold them, America has not yet promised that it will eventually liberate the suppressed. To back up such promises, made in good faith, by actions, would give proof of the vigor of the democratic idea in its contest with the enemy. By committing itself to—and engaging in—the weakening of the ruling totalitarians until they have to quit the scene, America would live up to this democratic idea which has made it great, which is the ground on which it stands, which is now being attacked by its mortal enemy, and which it must defend if it is to save its own greatness, its soul, its very existence. If America lives up to this democratic idea in the future as it has done in the past, it will have friends and allies in Germany—on both sides of the Iron Curtain, until that curtain vanishes with the totalitarian evil it hides and protects.

Germany is still ready to take the road America opens to her; what is not possible (although our diplomats seem to think it is, and act accordingly), is to bind a free Germany to the West without binding the West and ourselves to a free Germany.

Two worlds face each other in Germany. One is dyed in the blood-soaked, monotonous red color of revolution, terror, tyranny. The other is made up of many colors, as if reflecting a rainbow in which the new light of freedom is broken by the last drops of passing rain, while the uncertain, variegated hopes for tomorrow form its arc. The rainbow over the ruins of the West can be seen from the slave camps of the East. It seems to crush the evil red flags, and to span the horizon, and to promise freedom and peace to men of good will.

The End.

Acknowledgments

THE MATERIAL for this book was gathered in Germany in the last four years. In several chapters, I used excerpts from articles of mine which have been published by the *Reader's Digest, The New Leader, Commentary,* and *Commonweal.* To these magazines and their editors, I wish to extend my thanks.

I wish also to extend my thanks to the Foundation for Foreign Affairs for the grant which made it possible to gather material for this book.

New York City   NORBERT MUHLEN
December 1952

Index